DIANA SOUHAMI

MURDER
AT WROTHAM HILL

Quercus

First published in Great Britain in 2012 by Quercus

This paperback edition published in 2013 by

Quercus
55 Baker Street
Seventh Floor, South Block
London
W1U 8EW

Maps © William Donohue

A CIP catalogue record for this book is available
from the British Library

ISBN PB 978 0 85738 285 6
ISBN Ebook 978 0 85738 422 5

10 9 8 7 6 5 4 3 2 1

Text and plates designed and typeset by Ellipsis Digital Ltd

Printed and bound in Great Britain by Clays Ltd, St Ives plc

Diana Souhami is the author of *Selkirk's Island* (winner of the 2001 Whitbread Biography Award), *The Trials of Radclyffe Hall* (shortlisted for the James Tait Black Prize for Biography and ᴠ ner of the US Lambda Literary Award), the bestselling *Mrs* ʜ *ʒel and Her Daughter* (also winner of the Lambda Literary ⸴ ᵣd and a *New York Times* 'Notable Book of the Year'), *Coconut* ⸤ ᵓs, *Greta and Cecil*, *Natalie and Romaine*, *Gertrude and Alice* and ʜ *h Cavell* (winner of the EDP – Jarrold East Anglian Book of ᵗ Year award). She lives in London

ᴐsychological tour de force'   Terry Castle

ᴜhami's hypnotic narrative grips throughout. It is commonly ᴉd that murders tell us something about the societies in which ᴇy took place. But this post-war case does something else too. ᵗh killer and victim stood at an angle to society, and the ᵃangeness of their stories resonates deeply in another way, ᵃding one to meditate on ideas of malevolent fate and evil'

Sinclair McKay, *Daily Telegraph*

Murder At Wrotham Hill is more than a pacy whodunit. It is a ᴊnapshot of a historical moment, a time when there was as much concern with moral debates as there was worrying about whether there was enough sugar to last the week'

Kathryn Hughes, *Mail on Sunday*

12568782

'Souhami's closely researched casebook can be read superficially as a sad, sordid true crime story, but it is also evocative of the social attitudes of austerity Britain in the bleak aftermath of war. Souhami's dissection of the murder is completely engrossing in its insistence that fatality is about fallible human beings'

Iain Finlayson, *The Times*

'Persuades us that the death of one seemingly unimportant woman can be opened out into a profound scrutiny, not only of the past but of human conscience'

Jane Jakeman, *Independent*

'Souhami evokes these drab, joyless years with painful brilliance, so that one can almost feel the shabby poverty and smell the foggy, coal-dust-filled air. She plots the lives of the murderer and his victim with chilling precision'

Juliet Gardiner, *Spectator*

'It's [a] willingness to open up the expected format that makes *Murder at Wrotham Hill* so compelling about its time and the attitudes of those living in it, rather than simply a voyeuristic account of a misfortune of bad timing that caused two miserable and pointless deaths'   Jenny Diski, *London Review of Books*

To my mother
Freda Marie Souhami 1911–2006

dead is dead yes dead is really dead yes to be dead is to be really dead yes to be dead is to be really dead

Gertrude Stein

An eye for an eye makes the whole world blind

Mahatma Gandhi

CONTENTS

1

THE CRIME

A woman's shoe, flat and dark blue, lay on the grass verge two feet from the kerb halfway up Wrotham* Hill in Kent. The hill was steep, the weather cold and showery. At noon on Thursday 31 October 1946 Joe Hammond, a driver for the London Paper Mills on his way from Aylesford to Dartford taking six tons of baled paper from one mill to another, saw the shoe. He double declutched his lorry into first gear. The shoe, like the corpse of a dog, suggested a casualty of traffic. Hammond wondered if there were other signs of trouble. He stopped his lorry. The shoe looked new. If he found the other they might do for his wife Nada. She and Joe had married five years previously and now had two children, Julia four and Kenneth sixteen months.

The shoe was for the right foot, blue, flat, a mix of leather and suede, new, size 6, the maker's name Oral embossed in gold italics inside with the style number: A12146. Oral was a good make. They had a large factory in Rushden in Northamptonshire, the country's main shoe-manufacturing town. There were over a hundred boot and shoe factories up there. Nada took a 6. A pair of Oral shoes might cost £2 10s and use up five clothing coupons. Rationing was tighter than ever since the war's end. A chance find was not to be passed by.

* Pronounced root'em

3

The grass looked trampled, the hedgerow disturbed. Hammond parted the brambles. He saw a woman's legs. The toes of her right foot stuck out through a torn stocking, her left leg was bent, on its foot was the other shoe. Her face was half covered by the top of her coat, her coat and dress rucked up, her right fist clenched. Damp leaves had fluttered down on her from autumn trees. The stillness of this crumpled discarded corpse riveted into his memory with other detail of the moment: the susurrus of tyres on the wet road, the smell of wet foliage, his own alarm and exhalation of breath. This was murder, that he knew.

He took his lorry up the hill to the nearby village of Kingsdown,* to a phone box near the Portobello Inn. He told the operator at the local exchange what he had seen. She put him through to the Maidstone police station. An officer asked him to spell his name, give the number of the phone, the location of the body. 'Wait by the phone box,' was his instruction. 'Someone will come.' Hammond phoned his works manager and told him what had happened, then sat on a bench by the kiosk, holding the shoe.

Joe Hammond

No policeman came, the rain drizzled down, this was not how Joe Hammond had planned his day. He lived in Dartford and had hoped to be home early. Now he had a corpse in his head and explaining to do.

---

* The village was also known as West Kingsdown, to differentiate it from Kingsdown in east Kent. The name West Kingsdown became official on 16 August 1948

He was thirty-seven, tallish, sturdy, broad-shouldered and with wavy brown hair. He was a Londoner, born and brought up in Stepney. His father had worked as a ship labourer at the Limehouse docks, loading and unloading cargo. In his prime Joe played outside right for Queen's Park Rangers and his picture was in the papers for the goals he scored: seven in twenty-one matches between 1933 and 1936. Now he was a family man with a living to earn and football was only a spectator sport.

He waited. He did not sit in his lorry in case the phone rang in the telephone kiosk. The war had been over for eighteen months. King George had told them the years of darkness and danger were ended and urged them to 'make the world such a world as you desire for your children'. There was supposed to be an end to fear at the siren's wail, the lust for killing.

Half an hour passed. Hammond again phoned the Maidstone police. He said he could not sit by the phone box all day in the cold and rain, he had a delivery to make, he needed to leave. He was given directions to the home of PC King, the Kingsdown policeman, instructed to go there, give him the shoe and make a written statement of what he had seen.

Mrs King told him her husband was out on his bicycle somewhere in the village, she did not know where. She expected him back for his lunch. Joe Hammond drank her tea. Mrs King thought the dead woman might be local. Three months previously, five miles away in woodland near the village of Fawkham Green, a man walking his dog found the body of eleven-year-old Sheila Martin. She had been raped, then strangled with her own hairband. Chief Inspector Fabian of Scotland Yard and Detective Superintendent Smeed of the Kent CID worked together on that case. They were unsuccessful. The Kingsdown villagers believed a local boy murdered the Martin girl. Several said they saw her at a motorcycle race at Brands Hatch with a boy in long grey flannel trousers and a tan jacket. But lots of the boys dressed like that. It was the fashion.

Fabian questioned all the boys, but if anyone had seen something suspicious or noticed unusual behaviour, he was keeping it to himself. The 'golden hours' when the crime was fresh passed. Fabian checked such evidence as there was – fingerprints, hair, semen – with the Criminal Record Office. Nothing came up. He was a thorough man, a true professional, a tactician and good on clues. But he needed interlocking bits of the jigsaw: a scarf with the maker's label, a receipt, something to start piecing a picture, something to follow. The case eluded him. He had a profile but no evidence. The killer was a stranger, the motive sexual, the trail led nowhere. A murderer was out there somewhere and perhaps had struck again.

PC King came home for his lunch, took a statement from Joe Hammond and wrapped the shoe in cellophane. Serious crime was not his domain. Now peace had come to Kingsdown crime had shifted from infringement of blackout regulations and suspicion of draft dodging to cheating on the black market and selling potatoes at below the recommended price. There was the recent case when the car carrying the Maharajah of Jaipur to Leeds Castle crashed on the London Road by the Portobello Inn ... But a body in the bushes at Wrotham Hill was for officers superior to him.

Sergeant Pettitt

Neither Joe Hammond nor PC King knew it, but Sergeant Thomas Pettitt from Maidstone headquarters had reached the crime scene on his motorcycle within ten minutes of the emergency call. The days of isolated local policing ended in Kent in April 1943, when all the county's forces merged into a single police authority: the Kent County Constabulary. Now there was a chain of law enforcement. But there was little money for technology and communicating with villages remained slow. It was not like London's Scotland Yard with their information room and Flying Squad equipped with a fleet of radio cars with transmitters in the boot and loudspeakers, controls and microphones on the dashboard.

Sergeant Pettitt inspected the corpse. He touched nothing and tried not to disturb branches or brambles. First the victim must be certified dead. From a nearby police phone box he called his senior officers and Dr Norman Hay-Bolton, who lived at West House, a Georgian mansion in the main street of Wrotham. Dr Hay-Bolton served as GP for the surrounding villages. Once a week he held morning surgery at Kingsdown, then another in Farningham in the afternoon.

Thomas Pettitt was a Maidstone man, the son of a plumber, and he knew the area well. The summit of Wrotham Hill was a favoured beauty spot for trippers and picnickers. All sorts of strangers visited. The hill was renowned for its views high over the Kent Weald and Downs. Gypsies had set up camp there not long back with their caravans but the residents of Wrotham complained and the gypsies were soon moved on. Behind the hedgerows where the corpse lay, a tortuous path

7

called Labour-in-Vain Road wound up to the summit. A ravine adjacent to the lane was known as Devil's Kitchen.

Labour-in-Vain Road, Devil's Kitchen, a corpse in the bushes and a wet and windy October day. They were dark portents in this tranquil rural setting.

Sergeant Pettitt stood guard and waited for his superior officers and the doctor. The village of Wrotham lay in the valley at the foot of the chalk hills. It featured in the Domesday Book, William the Conqueror's land survey of England. Then, it was owned by the Archbishop of Canterbury and had a church, three mills, acres of meadow and dense woodland where hundreds of pigs rooted for beechnuts. Their owners paid taxes to the archbishop for grazing rights for these pigs.

Dr Norman Hay-Bolton arrived at the crime scene at 1.30pm. The woman had no pulse. He certified her dead. He saw she was middle-aged. There were marks of strangling, but he did not disturb her clothing or investigate further for fear of destroying police evidence or compromising the post-mortem.

The Crime Scene

Police gathered. This, it seemed certain, was a capital crime, an event of national concern. A manhunt must ensue. Inspector Wood from the West Malling police station cordoned off the hedgerow and road adjacent to where the body lay and sent Sergeant Pettitt to PC King's house in Kingsdown to collect the shoe Joe Hammond had found on the verge.

Detective Superintendent Frank Smeed of the Kent Criminal Investigation Division arrived at three in the afternoon with

Detective Inspector Jenner. Jenner noted the position of the body, a hairnet caught in the brambles, a skein of blue wool with hair grips and hair in it lying among twigs and leaves, shreds of lisle stocking. Detective Inspector Henry England from Maidstone photographed the body, the bushes, the hill, the shards and shreds of what might be evidence and the road newly widened, asphalted and painted with broken white lines for three traffic lanes. Back in his darkroom he made prints from the negatives and marked the precise position of the corpse on an Ordnance Survey map.

Smeed summoned the Home Office pathologist, Dr Keith Simpson, then, mindful of the murder of the Martin girl, phoned Chief Inspector Fabian, who agreed to head this case too. He and Smeed arranged to meet at West Malling police station that evening. Fabian reserved rooms for himself and his assistant, Detective Sergeant Harry Rawlings, at The Bull, Wrotham, a fifteenth-century inn with oak-beamed ceilings, log fires and substantial breakfasts.

At 6.15pm Dr Cedric Keith Simpson, the Home Office pathologist, arrived at the crime scene. Before doing an autopsy he first needed to examine the body in situ. He worked by the headlights of police cars. He recorded the temperature of the corpse and its exact position. He collected loose bits of hair and earth for analysis and checked that Henry England's photographs were adequate. He noted the woman was fully clothed, including a winter coat, but without a hat or gloves or her right shoe. She lay on her back on the ground, screened by a bramble bush. Her head faced east, her arms lay by her side, the left one bent inwards slightly at the elbow. There was no disarrangement of her clothing to suggest sexual assault.

Her coat was torn and there were deep scratches on her right leg.

Simpson thought she had been killed elsewhere and her body hauled, dragged then dumped in these bushes. The tears and scratches looked as if made by the barbed wire that fenced the hedgerow. He and Smeed agreed she might have lain undetected for much longer had it not been for Joe Hammond's curiosity about the shoe lying on the verge. The A20 was for traffic, not pedestrians, and Labour-in-Vain Road was the other side of a steep overgrown bank. Simpson confirmed the woman had been strangled and asked for her body to be taken to Borough Green mortuary three miles away so he could carry out an autopsy. Speed was important and he would work into the night.

Dr Simpson

Strangulation, Keith Simpson told his readers in his soon to be published textbook of forensic medicine, was 'one of the most fascinating chapters in forensic medicine. For it is impossible to strangle oneself: as you lose consciousness your hands relax their grip. The same thing happens if you tie a ligature round your neck.'

'Vagueness and theory have no place in forensic medicine,' he wrote. The precision of incontrovertible empirical evidence was his concern. His attention to detail was absolute, his focus unswerving. No man could have written more exuberantly about strangling, hanging, wounding, abortion and corrosive poisons. He illustrated his textbook copiously with photographs of crushed skulls, pistol and stab wounds, decomposed corpses and semen stains on trouser buttons. He expressed not a shiver of recoil at the cruelty and grotesque deeds of the perpetrators of violent crime.

Born in 1907, Cedric Keith Simpson was thirty-nine at the time of this murder at Wrotham Hill. He became a doctor because his father was one – an old-fashioned GP who bought a practice in Brighton and drove round with a deaf chauffeur in a black Buick to see patients in their homes.

Keith Simpson trained at Guy's Hospital in London and became a senior lecturer in pathology when he was twenty-five. He married a nurse, Mary Buchanan, and they lived in Tring in the Hertfordshire countryside with their son and two daughters.

At first at Guy's in the 1930s he did most of the post mortems, including those on unnatural deaths reported to the Southwark coroner, Douglas Cowburn. Medico-legal crime cases went to Simpson's senior, the forensic pathologist Bernard Spilsbury. But then Cowburn and Spilsbury had a falling out about the fee for an autopsy on conjoined twins. Cowburn paid Spilsbury a single fee for his work. Spilsbury argued there were two bodies and he had examined both. A feud ensued and in 1934 Cowburn asked the superintendent of Guy's, Sir Herbert Eason, to allow him to use Simpson as his chosen pathologist instead of Spilsbury. A title was created especially for him: supervisor of medico-legal post-mortems.

Forty Years of Murder, as Simpson called his autobiography, followed. His reputation grew and by the time of the Wrotham Hill case he combined his Home Office and university work with writing and a Harley Street practice.

'It is curious,' he wrote, 'that many people, even some doctors, dislike looking at a dead body.'

A well-known London surgeon can hardly bear to go to the mortuary. Even when he can be persuaded to enter the post-mortem room he stands well off, handkerchief over nose and mouth, muttering incomprehensibly and indeed seldom seeing what he has come to see.

No such shrinking afflicted Simpson. There was not an orifice, secretion or mangled remain from which he recoiled. Few doctors, he averred, could enjoy a more exciting life than his: 'such a challenge to be constantly on the qui vive or should it be the qui meure?'

He said that in the courts he met 'colourful slices of vivid life' – all kinds of doctors, detectives, policemen, prostitutes, barmen, old lags, 'distinguished lawyers and drug-addicted layabouts'.

It's so different from looking into ears or throats muttering 'Say Ah' or 'Now breathe in', handling distasteful skin diseases or trying to persuade hysterical women they haven't got cancer. The smell? No worse than the unwashed. Harrowing? There is, as H.E. Bates wrote, 'a beauty of the dead'. And wasn't it John Wesley who wrote:

> Ah, lovely appearance of Death
> What sight upon earth is so fair?
> Not all the gay pageants that breathe
> Can with a dead body compare.

His patients, he said, never complained, and if their symptoms proved perplexing he could always put them back in the fridge and return to them later. And though his job involved tipping out at all hours, standing around with dead bodies in ditches, fields, sheds and filthy rooms, and though he had to dance to the tune of judges and lawyers, he considered the rewards great. It was, as he put it, all 'so different from catching the 8.15 to the office in the City every day; or from looking down throats and examining smelly feet.'

He was a man with a moral imperative to do his job well. To this murder at Wrotham Hill he brought more than a decade of accumulated experience. There was no taking sides, no evasion, no dwelling on the concepts of good and evil. His sole intention was to present his medical observations and deductions to the police and the courts. It was for them to follow the process of the law. If he had opinions on justice, mercy, punishment and the psychological forces that compelled people into wrongdoing, he did not voice them

The Autopsy

The mortuary at Borough Green was a small makeshift building with a corrugated-iron roof, beside the fire station. In 1943 both buildings had been hit by an anti-aircraft shell in a blast that short-circuited the air-raid alarm which then sounded for hours.

The dead woman's eyes were blue-grey, her top teeth protruded, she had a small healed scar under her left nostril. There was no identification on her, no labels on her clothes, no bag, purse or keys. The intent of the killer was unclear. Her clothes

13

were drab and suggested she was poor: a pink woollen vest, dark blue rayon frock, blue and beige jumper, a home-made coat. A net, now torn from her head, had kept her hair in place. She had working hands, the knuckles gnarled. By examining her bones and cartilage Simpson gauged her age as about fifty. She was unmarried. There was no impression on her finger from a wedding ring that might have been stolen for its gold. She was a virgin, or not, in his words, deflorate. Her hymen had not been ruptured by any penetration, masturbatory or medical. There was no bruising, scratching or tearing of the vulva or hymen, no seminal fluid.

She had been strangled with an untied ligature. There was no mark from a knot. Simpson surmised that a folded cloth had been held tight at an unusually high level on her neck. The impressions of the folds had left four distinct lines across the front of her neck and also at the sides, particularly on the right. These marks faded toward the back of her neck. They showed she had been strangled from behind and from the left. There was no weave or pattern from the ligature. Simpson therefore surmised the cloth had been plain. The high level of the marks meant the woman had collapsed or been forced forward on to her knees. She did not appear to have struggled. There were no bruises that suggested an attempt to restrain her, no skin under her nails to suggest she scratched her assailant in self-defence.

Actions leave traces: footprints, the shedding of hair or spit, the disturbance of grass. He read the precise clues that might reconstruct this wrongdoing. He estimated the time of her murder at between 7 and 9am that day. A clothed corpse, he wrote, cools at about 2½ degrees for the first six hours. Over twelve hours the cooling averages out to 1½ – 2 degrees.

It had been a strong strangling. But he calculated it might only have taken fifteen or twenty seconds. There was little evidence of asphyxia: 'Reserves of oxygen are slender. Struggling or convulsions may quickly use them up. Vagal inhibitory mechanism supervenes and its effects are superimposed on those of asphyxia or even anticipates them.' Fear, he suggested, had stopped her heart. Time was of forensic importance. A grip of fifteen to twenty seconds that caused death was very different from persistent pressure for four to five minutes. With such speedy killing circumstantial evidence was required to establish intention.

Simpson had taught his students how unintentional strangulation could be. He had observed deaths caused by a scarf, a rope, a piece of bedding, a strap or stocking – twisted once or twice round the neck, drawn tight, held or tied – in the time it took to pour a cup of tea. It was so easy: a surge of anger, a loss of control and a life extinguished. At inquests he had given evidence of erotic masochistic experiments in binding and hanging that ended in death. 'A tie slips and tightens on the neck and the vagal reflex follows.'

One of his corpses, a woman of sixty-three, had died the moment her husband put his hands on her neck and threatened to strangle her. In court the man told of his years of nursing her, how he shopped, cooked, did the housework, and received nothing from her but nagging. His patience broke on the day when he trod on a corn on her toe as he got her out of bed and she called him a clumsy blundering fool. Simpson's autopsy showed no signs of strangulation. Evidence for the prosecution could not override the defence contention that death was sudden and unintended. Murder was commuted to manslaughter.

Simpson knew that women gripped by the neck in a pin-ning hold in a struggle to resist rape often died unexpectedly. He had heard the defendant plead, 'I put my hands round her throat and she suddenly went limp,' or 'I tried to bring her round but she was dead.' It was fragile and brief, the time it took to stop a heart, to lose a life. On an evening in March 1943, in what became known as the Tube shelter disaster, 173 men, women and children died at Bethnal Green Underground station. Simpson was their pathologist. The air-raid siren sounded prior to a bombing raid. The station was serving as a shelter. Pedestrians and local residents rushed into it. A woman and her child slipped at the bottom of the steps. Those behind could not stop. Bodies piled up. In his autopsies Simpson found that for many of the victims death from asphyxia had occurred within thirty seconds of their being crushed, though they had no wounds.

With strangulation the intention was usually to kill, facilitate rape or stifle cries for help. And the law was absolute: if evidence was acquired of intended felony, like rape or robbery, then no matter how unintended and speedy the death, it was murder.

The body on the slab before him at Borough Green mortuary on the night of 31 October 1946 unambiguously revealed signs of violence: strangulation marks, a fractured neck, a surface graze on the left cheek, a swollen left eyelid. The victim was sit-ting when strangled, then she slipped to her knees. Her closed right fist Simpson termed 'cadaveric spasm'. It occurred at the moment of death as a reaction to violence.

He knew from the lividity, the deep stains on her buttocks, that she was seated upright for some time after she died. 'When circulation stops,' he wrote in his report, 'blood settles into the lowest available vessels. Red corpuscles settle first and form within an hour a livid colour. Clotting fixes the stain.' The surface on which she had been seated was hard. It was not rough ground, not an upholstered car. Her rigid corpse was dragged into those roadside bushes on that cold, dark, wet autumn morning. Barbed wire, twigs and brambles then grazed her already dead skin. Injuries caused after death, Simpson informed his students, all have one thing in common – they lack a vital reaction. 'Abrasions harden like parchment without local flushing.'

He checked her clothes for hair, blood, semen, saliva, opened her body with a routine incision from chin to pubis. He worked methodically and took notes as he went. He examined her for signs of disease. She was for the most part healthy but had fibroid tumours in her womb. Bleeding from these had troubled her, so she had contrived a pad out of towelling and fastened it with a body belt. He wondered if medical records of these fibroids existed. He was mindful of one of his recent successes, the Dobkin Baptist Church cellar murder. On 17 July 1942 the dismembered, partly burned remains of a body were found by demolition workers under a cellar floor at the rear of a bombed Baptist church in Vauxhall in London. Simpson reconstructed these pieces into a woman 5 feet 1 inch tall, with greying dark-brown hair, aged forty to fifty and with a fibroid tumour of the womb. Police enquiries revealed that Mrs Dobkin, the estranged wife of the fire warden at the Baptist church, disappeared without explanation on Good Friday, 11 April 1941. A search of medical records showed she refused surgical treatment at two London hospitals for a fibroid tumour of the womb.

Mr Dobkin was arrested. For eighteen years his wife had been pursuing him for arrears of maintenance.

Dr Simpson completed his dissection of the Wrotham Hill victim, then crudely stitched the body with large cross stitches. There was no healing now of the incision he had made, no cosmetic requirement for a neat scar. Inspector England went to the mortuary and took more photographs of the head and neck of the corpse. Simpson wrote up his report – the marks of violence, the cause of death – and late into the night handed his findings to Fabian at The Bull, Wrotham. In summary he told him the murder had definitely taken place elsewhere, the body had been dumped in the hedgerow, there were no indications of sexual assault and the woman was seated upright on an unupholstered surface for some considerable time after she died.

Fabian of the Yard

Fabian's first task was to identify the murdered woman. By teleprinter he sent out a description from the Yard's information room to police stations and the press: a woman's body had been found in shrubbery at Wrotham Hill on the A20 road at noon on 31 October 1946. The suspected time of murder was between 5 and 8am that morning. There was no identification on her. She was aged about fifty. She had mid-brown hair, blue-grey eyes, a small scar under her left nostril and slightly protruding front teeth. She was wearing navy blue leather and suede shoes, a grey-blue coat with an orange lining, a dark blue frock, a blue and beige knitted jumper.

'The murder of Sheila Martin must be taken into consideration while investigations are being made,' Fabian wrote. 'It is not beyond the bounds of possibility, but I don't say it is so, that this murder is tied up with the murder of Sheila Martin.'

Fabian and Dr Simpson knew each other well. Both exuded confidence and authority. Fabian was forty-five and had been a policeman more than half his life. He was tall, brilliantined his hair, wore a bowler hat, pocket handkerchief and army tie. He was born Robert Honey Fabian in January 1901. The Honey came from his maternal grandmother, Susanna Pinwill Honey. His parents were hard-working, lower middle class, respectable and struggled to better themselves. He was brought up in a small four-roomed flat in Lewisham in south-east London and shared a bedroom with his year-older brother Andrew. His paternal grandfather had been raised in an orphanage and his father, a Devon man, worked as an engineer's fitter and hoped for his sons to become engineers with all the rewards and privileges of a well-paid white-collar job.

Robert Fabian trained as an engineering draughtsman but disliked the sedentary life. Inspired by his father's friend Inspector Frederick Rolphe, in 1921 he applied to join the Lewisham police force. He fulfilled the necessary requirements: he was over twenty and under twenty-seven, five foot ten, weighed ten stone four, had 20/20 vision and was of British birth and pure British descent. He began at Vine Street police station behind the Piccadilly Hotel in London as a police constable, patrolling the area at the regulation rate of 2½ miles an hour.

He championed the bobby on the beat, was sceptical of new-fangled technology and dependence on radio-controlled patrol cars and prided himself on his familiarity with, and understanding of, the criminal class. He appeared personal and affable, as if he knew their mindset, problems and motivation. To extract confession he first won confidence and trust. He was the governor giving them his time – tea by the fire, cigarettes, a hot meal if desired. He had a way of ingratiating himself so the arraigned did not see conversation with him as a gamble for captivity or escape. He enjoyed the theatre of crime: the disguises and deceptions of a thief – front teeth blacked, false moustaches, the teasing game of extracting confession. He knew shicing meant welshing, a pimple and blotch was a Scotch and a pig's ear a beer. He loved his criminals the way a farmer might love the livestock housed on his farm but then, relishing a roast, be unfazed by their journey to the abattoir. For the moral betterment of adolescent boys Fabian advocated more playing fields, 'healthy alternatives to the street corner', the censoring of gangster films and reintroduction of the birch.

He married Winifred Letitia Stockwell in 1925 and their only child, Peter, was born a year later. As children he and Winnie, as he called her, had lived a few streets away from each other. She was a practical woman, a home builder. She made her own hats. On one were two nesting doves.

Fabian was a conformist with censorious views about homosexuals and perverts. He called homosexuality 'an offence against decency' and thought it right that it was punishable by heavy imprisonment. 'As a law-breaking act it is parallel with robbery with violence,' he wrote. 'You may walk the streets of London for months and never see an actual instance of robbery with violence. But there is not one night in London when – if you go to the right places – you will fail to see an example of persons soliciting to commit the offence of homosexuality.' He became a good friend of the hangman Albert Pierrepoint, said gunmen always had grey eyes, and liked playing snooker and betting on the horses. For both work and pleasure he went to boxing and wrestling matches, ju-jitsu classes and places where crooks might gather: public houses, racecourses, transport cafés.

He described himself as having a 'scavenging mind' and after two years as a constable applied to join the CID. Attention to detail, speed of action and breadth of enquiry singled him out as an exceptional detective. He knew that seemingly futile checks might lead to a vital clue and that unlikely avenues were sometimes the revealing ones. Any information or observation, he learned, might be useful – the smattering of a foreign language, odd facts about company law. He became tuned to the inflection of a lie, the contracted pupils in a drug-taker's eyes, the demeanour of the recidivist crook.

He soon became well known in the dives of Soho. He described prostitutes as innately wicked and morally derelict, but was on good terms with Battling Annie and Purple Lily, who carried out their business in West End apartments, lived respectably in the suburbs, worked hard and had business acumen. He was sorrowful about young people addicted to morphine, heroin or cocaine and scathing about pimps and drug peddlers. 'Despicable men,' he called them.

In 1929 he worked for eighteen months in the Criminal Record Office, where files were held on almost every known crook in Europe. There was an intricate cross-reference system: if a man was a burglar, had a club foot, a cleft palate, a scarred brow and crumbled his bread into pellets, such facts were noted and cross-filed along with names, aliases, age, height. Fabian studied the particulars of a hundred thousand convictions and copied details of cases into his private notebook. The work intrigued him and he had tireless enthusiasm for it. He perceived detection as an art and a science, and looked for patterns of offending, and defining features in different categories of crime. A good detective, in his view, needed both inspiration and the zeal for methodology of a chemist or physicist. Innocent until proven guilty was the determining rule: the imperative was empirical proof. Hunch and suspicion were useful but had to give way to the precision of evidence.

Though conscious of rank, as he rose in the force he affected humility and said a successful detective was only the coordinating element in a team that included pathologist, chemist, photographer, patrol car driver and reliable witness. He enjoyed the idea of the detective as hero and cases that created publicity for their drama, like Rudolph Franklyn who robbed an Oxford Street jewellery shop in daylight in September 1932. Fabian's small-time criminal friends, the street seller of duff watches and George the match seller who drank wine mixed with methylated spirits, gave him the tip-off that led to arrest. 'Franklyn received three years penal servitude and 20 strokes of the birch.'

In 1940 Fabian was awarded the King's Medal for Gallantry for defusing seven gelignite bombs planted in brown paper parcels by the Irish Republican Army in Piccadilly Circus. He was flattered when a group of crooks whom he knew invited him to a bar to present him with a bronze medal on a blue silk ribbon. It was inscribed: To Inspector Bob Fabian, For Bravery, 24-6-39. From The Boys. They told him they had been 'on the dilly' that night and thought he saved their lives.

At the time of the Wrotham Hill murder Fabian, Winnie and their bulldog called Buller were living in Surrey. He enjoyed his growing reputation as a celebrity sleuth and gave gardening as his favourite hobby.

'IN' or 'OUT'

Mrs Petrzywalski, known locally as Mrs Peters (her maiden name was Marshall and she was born in Clapham), was seventy-nine and lived in Houston, a bungalow in Hever Avenue on what was known as the Hever Estate, in the village of Kingsdown, five miles from the murder scene. She was matronly in appearance, round faced, and always wore a hat and gloves when out.

On the morning of Friday 1 November 1946 she got up at seven. It was cold and her bungalow felt damp. She lit the paraffin stove and went down the front garden path to collect her *Daily Telegraph* from the box in the fence and to check if there was a note tucked there from her daughter Dagmar with a laconic reassurance written on it: IN. Dagmar lived in an adjacent hut. She was a solitary woman who liked her independence. Only rarely did Mrs Petrzywalski go inside her daughter's hut, but they had an agreement that when Dagmar was out or in she would leave a note to say just that. There was no need to say where she had gone or why. Just the note. Just so her mother should know.

Mrs Petrzywalski's husband Jules François had died seven months previously. They had lived in the village for fifteen years. He was buried in the serene graveyard of St Edmund's church, Kingsdown, and etched on his tomb was 'Jules F.R. Petrzywalski died 8 March 1946 aged 80'. Just family went to his funeral.

Dagmar had walked to the church with her mother. Mrs Petrzy-walski's son Ralph was there with his wife Elena. So was her grandson Jules and his wife Phyllis though they were scarcely speaking to each other.

Looking after her husband had been hard for Mrs Petrzy-walski and not only because of the war and the shortages, rationing, blackouts and air raids. He had needed constant care. Toward the end he became incomprehensible. His death had left her feeling afraid and purposeless, though he had been a rather unsatisfactory husband. And her son George, her eldest most dependable son, had died in 1944 from a heart attack on Charing Cross station. He was only fifty-five. Jules, his son, was a prisoner of war at the time, somewhere unknown in Russia. Through all those difficulties Dagmar had been her rock, even though she was not quite the daughter she had wanted and was undoubtedly odd and so much a law to herself.

By the gate there was only yesterday's note in red ink OUT and no sign of life from her daughter's hut. Mrs Petrzywalski supposed Dagmar had stayed overnight in Woking with Ralph and Elena. That was not usual. It was usual for her to go there and back the same day, but maybe the trains were bad or she had stayed to help with the new puppy she had bought that week and taken with her to give to them.

Mrs Petrzywalski read the paper with her morning tea. Reading the news, you wouldn't believe the war was over: British soldiers blown up in Haifa; the British Embassy bombed in Rome; Jews fleeing Poland because of hatred against them ... And October had been the wettest month of the year. But Winston Churchill was presented with the Freedom of the City of Birmingham – a scroll in a silver casket – in honour of his leadership during the war, and the Radio Corporation of America had demonstrated the first-ever colour television. This, their spokesman said, was 'one of the greatest steps in the whole of radio science'.

And then there it was. Late news. Stop press. A paragraph about a murder. No signs of a struggle. No identification on her. A woman aged about forty to fifty, wearing a dark blue coat with an orange lining, dead behind a hedge at Wrotham Hill in Kent on the London to Maidstone road. Strangled. A lorry driver found her, alerted when he saw a blue shoe lying on the grass verge.

The woman was Dagmar, that her mother knew. She read the paragraph over with incredulity and alarm. The coat with the orange lining: that was Dagmar's coat. Dagmar made it herself; they bought the orange satin together in Maidstone market, it wasn't on the ration. Mrs Petrzywalski had thought it a bit bright with the dark blue but Dagmar liked it. She did not know who to tell. She did not have a phone: it cost £1 a quarter just for the rental and anyway her son Ralph hadn't got one yet. There were 4 million phones in the country now, but they were for people with more money than she had. She left her tea and walked to the box at the corner of Hever Avenue to phone the police.

Dagmar Petrzywalski

At 9am Detective Sergeant Martin from Dartford police station told Superintendent Smeed of information received from a woman who had read an account of the murder in the *Daily*

Telegraph and thought the description was of her daughter who had not returned home the previous evening.

A police car collected Mrs Petrzywalski and took her to West Malling police station. Fabian and Smeed coaxed information from her and tried to console her. Her distress was acute. She was shaking and kept saying she didn't know what she would do. They showed her the coat with the orange lining, a blue shoe, a blue and beige hand-knitted jumper, a dark blue sleeveless frock. She wept. Yes, those were her daughter's clothes.

They offered her tea which she refused and asked her if she needed to see a doctor, but she said she was all right. She told them her name was Mame Ann Petrzywalski, but people often called her Mrs Peters because it was easier for them. She lived at Houston, Hever Avenue and was a widow. Her husband had died that March after a long illness. Dagmar Petrzywalski was her only daughter, she wasn't sure when she was born, she thought it was 1897. Anyway it was 25 October, that much she knew. Dagmar was single and lived alone in a hut on the plot of land adjacent to hers. She couldn't think of anyone who would want to hurt her. No one would want to hurt her. No one in the world.

The first she knew of her being missing was when she went to collect her morning paper and there was only the note from the morning before with OUT written on it. Dagmar had undoubtedly left home early the previous day. She was going to Woking to visit her brother Ralph and her sister-in-law Elena. She often made that journey. She'd leave before dawn, then hitch a lift on a lorry because it was too early for the buses. She never accepted a lift in a private car. She didn't think it safe. She'd have had with her a yellow string bag Elena crocheted for her as a birthday present and a little brown attaché case that she, Mame, had given her. She always took her sandwiches for the journey in that. The handle was broken and she'd fixed it with string. She'd have the Yale key to her hut with her of course, and her brown purse. And she always took a present of some sort for Elena: eggs from her chickens, or part of her butter or cheese ration.

She also had with her a little black and tan smooth-coated puppy. Three days ago, on Tuesday 29 October, she and Mame had gone together to Maidstone market. Mame bought the dog for herself, she paid 15 shillings for it, but on the Wednesday morning gave it to Dagmar because she couldn't manage it. It was too much trouble. It yapped a lot. It kept her awake all night. She didn't think Dagmar would keep it. She might have been intending to give it to Ralph and Elena.

Fabian asked her if Dagmar bought anything else at the market. Mame said she bought several bits and pieces: she paid a shilling for a man's white woollen vest with a darn on the shoulder and said she might be able to make something out of it. The last time Mame had seen her daughter was on the Wednesday afternoon at about three. She had called for tea at Mame's bungalow. Most days Dagmar called in for tea. She left after about an hour because she wanted to feed the chickens before it got too dark.

Fabian had coaxed enough detail out of Mame Petrzywalski to start investigating. It was of less immediate interest to him that Dagmar had worked in London for twenty-five years as a telephone operator for the Post Office or that five years ago she had taken early retirement because, as Mame put it, she wasn't a strong girl, she suffered with her insides and physically could not do much. He also learned from Mame that Dagmar called

27

her hut The Vic, had had it built five years ago after the London house she was in got bombed in the Blitz and that she lived in rented rooms in Swanley while it was being built.

Did You See Anything Suspicious?

Fabian ordered a check on all lorry drivers who used the A20 road at Wrotham Hill early in the morning of 31 October. He wanted to find that yellow string bag, the brown attaché case, the purse, the puppy. They had called the puppy Hedy, Mrs Petrzywalski told him, after the actress Hedy Lamarr. She and Dagmar had been up to see Hedy Lamarr in *The Strange Woman* at the London Pavilion, but they hadn't had the dog long enough for it to know its name.

Fabian wondered why, if Dagmar was heading for Woking, her body should have turned up on the Maidstone side of Kingsdown, five miles down the road in the opposite direction to the route she would have taken.

Within an hour he sent police stations an update on his previous bulletin, with instruction for action:

The body is that of a woman who lived alone some miles from Wrotham and was in the habit of hitchhiking in lorries. The body is now believed to have been concealed before 07.00 hours on Thursday 31 October 1946. Urgent enquiries are requested to trace and interview all transport drivers who travelled between London and Maidstone between 5 and 8 am on 31 October 1946.

The same alert went into Scotland Yard's newspaper the *Police Gazette*. Issued daily except for Sundays and bank holidays, it published photos and descriptions of wanted people and stolen goods.

At 3pm Detective Superintendent Smeed circulated a further message:

It appears probable that the deceased left her home at about 06.00 hours on the 31st October 1946 to go to London and she had with her a black smooth coated puppy dog. The puppy is missing. Also apparently missing is a home-made crocheted handbag, yellow, with single loop handle and zip fastener.

Traffic from all parts of the country used the A20, not just milk lorries and lorries for the London vegetable and flower markets. Detectives and uniformed constables nationwide were told to go into every one of 10,000 garages, haulage contractors, farms, delivery, vehicle hire and commercial firms and ask to see their journey books. Next morning, Saturday, before sunrise, Flying Squad officers waited at the London markets to question drivers. Early-morning lorries using the London to Maidstone road were flagged down by police and their drivers questioned by torchlight: 'Were you on this road between five and eleven Thursday morning?' 'Did you see anything suspicious?' 'Did you see any vehicle pulled up near this spot?' 'Did you see anyone near the roadside?' 'Did you see any clothing on the road?' 'Did you see a yellow handbag?' Thirteen hundred lorry drivers were questioned. There were checks on transport cafés. Smeed sent policemen to scour the hedges along

Wrotham Hill for the yellow knitted bag, the attaché case, the purse, the dog, the keys.

Mindful of the unsolved Sheila Martin murder, CID officers were sent to question servicemen at the RAF station at West Malling, six miles from where Dagmar's body was found. Smeed and Jenner went to Woking to break the news to Mrs Petrzy-walski's son Ralph, take him to Borough Green mortuary formally to identify his sister, then bring him on to West Malling for questioning. Murder by strangers was rare. Usually it was someone known to the victim. Everyone was a suspect until the killer was caught, but particularly family members and friends.

Ralph Petrzywalski: Friday 1 November 1946

Dagmar's brother Ralph was a civil servant, a quiet-living man who did *The Times* crossword each day and kept a distance from his sister, whom he viewed as moody. He was forty-nine – a year older than she was. There had been a coolness between them since Dagmar's London lodgings were bombed in the Blitz in 1941. Traumatised, she came to stay with him and his family and wanted to make this a permanent arrangement while the war raged. It made her afraid to live alone in the centre of London when hundreds of people were killed or injured each night in air raids, but her job was there and she needed a home. Ralph had said no. He just had not wanted it and thought it would upset his married life. He said she must find lodgings elsewhere. After that rejection Dagmar had the hut built in Hever Avenue.

Neither he nor his wife were expecting a visit from her on

Thursday 31 October 1946. She seldom gave warning of a call. She just turned up, usually at a disconcertingly early hour. In Friday's paper they too read news of the murder and feared it was Dagmar. Ralph did not go to work and they were unsurprised by the arrival of a police car, mid-morning, at their house in Triggs Lane, Woking.

Ralph told Smeed and Jenner he last saw Dagmar two weeks previously on 18 October, a week before her forty-eighth birthday. It had been an unremarkable visit. She arrived, as ever unexpectedly, at two minutes to eight in the morning. He was about to leave for work. She told them she left Kingsdown at 5am, got a lift on a lorry to London, then bought a workman's train ticket to Woking. She always tried to be in time for those tickets, on sale up to 8am and half the usual price. Saving pennies mattered and she was careful with her money. She told Elena her mother did not know of her visit that day. She and Elena stayed in the house until noon. Elena gave her, as her birthday present, the bag she had crocheted in yellow string and in the afternoon they went shopping together, then Dagmar went home by train and bus.

Ralph was taken to identify the corpse. Mrs Petrzywalski had not felt able to look at her daughter's dead body and Fabian viewed this as an unsuitable task for a woman. Jenner drove Ralph to the mortuary at Borough Green. Ralph formally identified his sister in the presence of him and Smeed, then made and signed a statement: He was Ralph Petrzywalski, aged 49, a civil servant. The body was that of his sister Dagmar. She was born on 25 October 1898. She was a spinster. She had worked as a General Post Office telephonist for twenty-five years, then retired early because of ill health. She lived on her

GPO pension and modest capital. She was reserved and had no close friends. He had not seen her since 18 October when she had called at his house. He knew of no one who might want to harm her.

Smeed sent Ralph's fingerprints to Chief Inspector Birch at the fingerprint bureau at New Scotland Yard. Birch classified them and checked the files but found nothing to match them.

The Hever Estate: Friday 1 November 1946

Among the villagers on the Hever Estate at Kingsdown there was much talk of this murder. Kingsdown was thought to be a safe place to live. Selling bags of coal short, cheating with ration books, those were the bad things that happened.

There was fear the murderer would kill again. Hilda Taylor, who lived with her parents next door to Dagmar and Mame Petrzywalski, was sixteen and worked in London. It was November and the evenings were dark when she came home. She got the train to Farningham station, then a bus to the corner of Hever Avenue. When she got off the bus there were no street lights, it was an unmade road, there were trees and shrubs and few houses. In fear the murderer would leap at her from behind the bushes she kept to the middle of the track and ran with her heart pounding.

At the end of the long day after her daughter's death, Mame Petrzywalski was driven home in a police car. She told Ralph she would be all right. She sought no consolation from her neighbours and did not want to talk to anyone. Her husband and five of her six children were now dead. This was a blow too many. It was intolerable to think of what might have happened to Dagmar – what she had endured. The war was over, there was the promise of better times. Mrs Petrzywalski was nearly eighty and now there was no one to look after her. No one to have tea with or go with her to Maidstone market on Tuesdays, or bring her eggs or care for her if she was ill. She did not know how she would manage. The bungalow was so thinly built and hard to keep warm and there was always something that needed doing.

Dagmar had looked out for her, even if they were never close. She was difficult. There was that nervous breakdown before she left the telephone service, after the worst night of the Blitz when the house in Camden Town got bombed. And the way she went off tramping the countryside all alone or took the train somewhere and picnicked by herself. She'd never had a man friend. She seemed to have no interest in men. And she would not go to the doctor about her internal troubles.

There was shame to this murder and a squalor. Time after time she had warned Dagmar against thumbing lifts the way she did. The danger of it. 'But she would not listen to me,' Mame told the newspaper reporters who waited at her door. It was a humiliation to her and made her feel she had failed as a mother. And there was a murderer at large.

Police Enquiries: Friday 1 and Saturday 2 November 1946

Information came into the Yard from lorry drivers and transport depots. Details and alibis were checked and card-indexed and drivers eliminated. Joe Hammond was not the first to see Dagmar's shoe on the grass verge. William Crittenden, who lived in East Farleigh, a village by the river Medway not far from Maidstone, told the police he noticed it much earlier in the day, at about 7.15 on the morning of Thursday 31 October. He too was driving his lorry to London. But he did not stop. It was just an incident in the stream of information that lies dormant unless memory is challenged. He saw it but did not think about it again until next day when he read of the murder.

Cyril Norman from Maidstone, who drove a lorry for Fremlin Brewery, told the police that as he went up Wrotham Hill on the morning of the murder at about 5.30am he saw a grey saloon car parked on the verge at the spot where Dagmar's body was found. A body, he said, could easily have been pulled from this car into the hedgerow without anyone seeing. Several other lorry drivers spoke of seeing a small van parked yards from the murder spot at about 6am and of a man going into the bushes near by.

Henry Alfred Bennett and Henry Norris Bennett, father and son, farmers both, who owned Hartlake Farm in Golden Green, near Tonbridge, spoke of being hailed by a woman at Farningham Gosse, one and a half miles from Hever Avenue, at approximately 5.10am, while driving their lorry to London. There were haystacks in the field to their right. The woman was standing on the left. Henry Norris said he thought of stopping but on principle never gave lifts to strangers. Her clothes scarcely showed up in the shadows of morning but she had something light-coloured round her neck. He thought she was between thirty-five and forty. His father said that two or three minutes later a loaded lorry drove past, going the other way, uphill, and that the driver of that vehicle must also have seen the woman.

Sixty miles away, in the pretty village of Little Abington in Cambridgeshire, in the kitchen of her cosy thatched cottage, Daisy Sinclair read the *Daily Mirror*'s account of the crime out loud to her husband Sidney. It was headed 'Blue shoe on road reveals a murder'.

A lorry driver saw the shoe on the main London Maidstone road halfway down Wrotham Hill in Kent. No handbag or documents which would help in her identification were found near. She had been strangled by having something pulled tight round her neck. A police statement last night said the woman was probably killed at about 8 o'clock yesterday morning. Superintendent Smeed, Kent CID said, 'We believe her body was taken from where she was murdered.'

'I was on that road yesterday,' Sid told Daisy.
'You don't need to tell the police that,' Daisy said.

'The Hut Woman'

Detective Inspector England went to the Hever Estate to photograph the inside and outside of Dagmar's hut, The Vic. The whole structure was not much larger than a garden shed. There was a butt for collecting rainwater, an improvised outside toilet, no tap water or electricity.

Detective Sergeant Rawlings searched among Dagmar's frugal possessions. He found letters from Mullen Coster, a lorry driver, referring to a possible meeting with her in London on

31 October, the day she was murdered. Rawlings tracked Coster down. His alibi was watertight, his concern genuine. Twice previously he had stopped for her; on both occasions she tried to make him accept the equivalent of the bus fare. Yes, they corresponded, she was a sweet woman, good company, old enough to be his mother. He told her if he was travelling her route he was always happy to give her a lift.

Police officers guarded the hut and questioned the villagers. None had been inside The Vic or seen anyone go in there. They said Dagmar, or Miss Peters as many called her, was reserved but polite. They viewed her as a recluse, had heard of a breakdown that caused her to leave her job as a 'hello girl' at the telephone exchange and thought her an unlikely person to be hitchhiking at all, let alone so early in the morning and in the dark. But she liked to go off for the day for long walks alone. They confirmed she never accepted a lift in a private car. Mr Hill, a builder, spoke of how she refused to get in his car, no matter how bad the weather, though he always offered when he passed her on the road and she must have known she'd be as safe as houses with him.

Hilda Taylor told them of the times in 1942 and 1943 when she was twelve and Dagmar packed cheese sandwiches for a picnic and took her to London for a day out. They caught a bus to Victoria. There was one an hour. They walked to Buckingham Palace, Westminster Abbey and the Tower of London. Once they went to look at the bomb damage where Dagmar had lived in Camden Town. The whole area was flattened. They didn't talk much but it was companionable. Hilda had liked the cheese sandwiches best. She never had cheese at home. Her father had her 2oz ration. Her mother made plenty of cream cheese –

soured milk strained through a cloth and left to drip all night – but the hard sort, the rationed sort, went to father. He worked up in town as a cabinetmaker and a jack of all trades. He had built their bungalow and it was better constructed than Mame Petrzywalski's.

Dagmar's neighbours thought her pleasant but eccentric. She was kind and courteous but this habit of walking alone and thumbing lifts from lorries in the dark hours of the morning was odd. She seemed closed in on herself and looked prim with her owlish glasses and protruding teeth. And then there was her name. Villagers called her Miss Peters, men raised their hats to her, but her real name was something quite unpronounce-able and unspellable with sses and zeds in it. Something for-eign, Polish or Russian perhaps, or even Jewish. Certainly not very Kent – where the familiar names were Smith, Taylor, Jones, Davies and Knight.

And village life revolved around the church. That was where social things went on in Kingsdown: harvest festival, choir prac tice, bring-and-buy sales. Dagmar and her mother took no part in such events. They seemed to put up a barrier, act like out-siders, set apart, as if maybe at heart they thought themselves better than others, their voices posher, their concerns different. As if having no money was a temporary thing. Old Mrs Peters never went out of her bungalow unadorned by a hat and gloves, did not chat with her neighbours, whom she appeared to deem socially inferior, and seldom went inside her peculiar daughter's makeshift home.

Newspaper reporters swarmed into Kingsdown then wrote of 'the hut woman', her eccentricities, impoverishment and reclusive ways. They described The Vic as 'small as a suburban toolshed'. The *Daily Mail* claimed the police had found her diary and it revealed the name of her murderer, 'a mysterious Mr X'. Each evening for the past two years, its readers were told, Dagmar had sat in her little wooden shack and in detail recorded the day's events. Her final entry on 31 October, the day of her murder, was of vital importance to the CID.

Little Abington: Saturday 2 November 1946

Saturday 2 November was another cold, overcast day. At 25 Little Abington Daisy Sinclair read Sid the update on the murder from the *Daily Mirror*. It was the lead story. She thought he would be interested as he had been on the same road that day. The dead woman had a funny name. Dagmar, then something beginning with P. She lived alone in a hut in the garden of her mother's bungalow in Kingsdown, read books and hardly spoke to anyone. In the paper it said she died in Devil's Kitchen, a one-time gypsy camping ground, and that a stocking or something like that had been wound round her neck.

'Then her body was carried in a vehicle along the high road and thrown behind a hedge,' Daisy read aloud. 'It was not yet dawn and the killer could not see the blue shoe that had fallen off on to the grass verge.'

Daisy was half relieved to read that Scotland Yard's Inspector Fabian had been called in to investigate whether it was the work of the same murderer as strangled the schoolgirl Sheila Martin on 11 June. She'd almost begun to think Sid knew something about all this. He'd been behaving so oddly these past couple of days, his hands shaking more than ever, his nerves playing up, not sleeping, and smoking half the night. And he kept saying he couldn't go on with his driving job.

'The mystery is why was she killed?' Daisy read.

She had no money. She was not young, nor beautiful. Outrage was not attempted. She was found in her home-made clothes – a fact that explains the absence of tailor's tags – and was identified by a scar on her upper lip and her prominent teeth. The scar was caused by a bite from her pet dog. She had the dog destroyed. It was the end of her only friend. Roaming was her only pastime.

Did she meet the man who killed Sheila Martin? Did she discover – she liked to hitchhike – that a driver along that highway was a sex maniac? Was she killed before she could tell the police what she knew?

Jules Peters

The police looked for a personal motive, a family psychodrama of jealousy, greed or revenge. They wanted a picture of Dagmar's life at the time of her murder, the men in it, her finances, her friends. After eliminating her brother Ralph as a suspect, Detective Sergeant Baker called later that day to interview her nephew Jules – son of her eldest brother George who had died two years previously on Charing Cross station. Like his uncle Ralph, Jules was disturbed by the interview and its implication of his involvement. The Petrzywalskis were reserved, disliked attention and were not given to displays of emotion. Jules answered truthfully but with a desire to disassociate himself from his eccentric aunt.

He was paranoid about his foreign-sounding name. The British, he knew, took a cautious view of foreignness. He wanted to be known only as Peters and intended to make this official by deed poll. As a child he was brought up to be anti-semitic and he feared Petrzywalski would be construed as Jewish. There was a family rumour that Dagmar's grandfather, Johann Sigmund Petrzywalski, pâtissier to the Rothschilds and the royal family, was himself a Jew. In fact the family was Catholic with no Jews in its tree.

Fear of Jewishness in Britain grew with Hitler's persecution of Jews and resolve to make Germany *Judenfrei*. It found expression in quotas at schools, exclusion from society memberships, typecasting in drama. Jews seeking refuge in Britain grew in number after events in Germany like *Kristallnacht* on 9 November 1938. That night, synagogues throughout Germany and Austria were burned and Jewish-owned shops and homes smashed. Police and firefighters stood aside, taking action only to prevent the spread of fire and violence to the property of non-Jews. The streets were strewn with shattered glass. Jews were beaten, raped, arrested and murdered, and 30,000 were deported.

The British government feared the mass arrival of Jewish refugees so the Aliens Restriction Committee ruled that only those with capital or qualification should be allowed in, temporarily, until they moved on to a more permanent place. Jews, they feared, might flood the labour market. Tribunals set up in 1939 – 120 of them, chaired by barristers and county court judges – sounded out and graded 'aliens'. A was high security risk, B was for doubtful cases and C was no security risk. Out of 73,000 German and Austrian nationals questioned, most were

Jewish and in flight for their lives. Scrutiny at these tribunals depended on the opinion and interpretation of the examiners. Refugees viewed as subversives were sent off to camps on the Isle of Man or shipped to Australia or Canada. And the popular press fuelled prejudice. An infringement of a blackout regulation by an immigrant played into a generalisation. German Jews tried to keep a low profile: not reading German newspapers in public, not speaking German in the street.

Jules Peters gave his sworn statement to Detective Sergeant Baker: He was a lance corporal with the Royal Fusiliers, had lived at his Ruislip address, 38 Seaton Gardens, for about nine years and had not seen his aunt since her father's funeral on 18 March when she had 'seemed her normal self'. On the morning of Thursday 31 October he was with his army unit at Cirencester. He was present at roll-call. Next day, Friday, he left the camp at four in the afternoon on 48-hour leave, travelled to Paddington with Private Jim Berkeley of his unit, then caught a Metropolitan line train to Ruislip Manor and went to his home. He knew nothing of the murder until he read about it in the papers on Saturday. Because of what he read he went with his wife that afternoon to visit his grandmother. They caught the 3.23 train from Harrow, had tea with her, tried to console her, and offered to help with all that needed to be done.

He told Baker that 'as far back as he could remember' his aunt was 'rather moody' and suffered from headaches and 'nerves', she liked to walk alone in the country, he couldn't remember her ever having a male friend. 'I wouldn't describe her as a "man hater" but she didn't have much room for men.'

He too said his aunt made unexpected calls to his house at early hours: 'on more than one occasion she came by a milk lorry'. He told Baker this was to save time not money. The road near Hever Avenue was used by milk lorries. It was her habit to walk in the direction of London and put her arm up to stop any passing lorry, never a private car. 'I know this habit has been going on for years and some of the regular drivers must know my aunt by sight.' Jules, like Dagmar's mother, brother and sister-in-law, spoke of her high moral character, modesty and honesty. She had, he said to Baker, a most generous nature and had mentioned paying the lorry drivers the equivalent of the bus fare.

A lorry driver, a Mr Wells, who on two occasions had given Dagmar a lift, corroborated this account. She was, Wells confirmed to Baker, a respectable maiden lady, clean and tidy, careful, well brought up and disciplined. A good woman who offered him money for her fare.

Police questioning and the morbid fate of his aunt compounded Jules Petrzywalski's paranoia and depression. His marriage had failed. His wife Phyllis wanted a divorce. They had married in 1936 when he was twenty-two. He was conscripted into the army when war was declared and fought in Italy at the Battle of Monte Cassino, one of the largest and bloodiest land battles of the Second World War. It spanned six months in 1944 and left 55,000 Allied soldiers dead.

The Allies fighting their way from southern Europe towards Rome needed to break the German stronghold of what was called the Gustav Line. Its pinnacle was the Benedictine monastery high on Monte Cassino. From within that vantage point German soldiers defended miles of surrounding land.

After months of failed efforts, in May a last and terrible offensive was made against Monte Cassino with troops from Britain,

America, India, France, Poland, Morocco and Palestine. It lasted seven days. On 18 May the monastery was in Allied hands. Eight thousand men had been killed. An eye witness who saw survivors wrote:

It was more than the stubble of beard that told the story. It was the blank staring eyes. The men were so tired that it was a living death. They had come from such a depth of weariness that I wondered if they would quite be able to make the return to the lives and thoughts they had known.

Among those taken prisoner was Lieutenant Corporal Jules Peters of the Royal Fusiliers. He was prisoner of war number 138305, sent to the Stalag 344 camp at Lamsdorf in Poland. He was never to speak to anyone of what happened to him in this camp, or of the fighting at Monte Cassino, or of his subsequent journey back to what he thought was his home in Seaton Gardens, Ruislip. He was never quite able to make the return to the life and thoughts he had known.

At Lamsdorf, prisoners of war worked in the coal mines or built roads. In under a year more than 500 died. In the final months of the war when the Soviet army advanced on Poland, the Nazis evacuated 30,000 Allied prisoners from Lamsdorf and other camps to prevent their liberation. What followed was variously called The Long March, The Black March, The Lamsdorf Death March or just The March.

Prisoners were evacuated on 22 January 1945, then force-marched in groups of 250 men toward Luckenwalde, 30 kilometres south of Berlin. January and February 1945 were the coldest of months. Blizzards took temperatures to -25°celsius.

The men had endured confinement, ill-treatment and starvation. Their clothing was ill-suited to even normal winter conditions. Depending on the weather and terrain, they marched between 12 and 48 kilometres a day. They scavenged for food, sucked snow, crossed rivers frozen by ice, slept outside on frozen ground, had blisters that froze on their feet. If they tried to take crops or water they were beaten, if they tried to escape they were shot. They died from starvation, exhaustion, hypothermia, typhus, dysentery. Some villagers gave food, others threw stones.

The prisoners thought they were to be used as hostages in a peace deal and would be executed if that peace deal failed, or that they were being force-marched to their deaths, or were being taken to Belsen to be exterminated in revenge for the bombing of Dresden and Berlin.

As columns of them reached the western side of Germany they were met by the advancing British and American armies. For Jules Peters this meant liberation. On 4 May 1945, RAF Bomber Command began implementing Operation Exodus. The first prisoners of war were flown home. In all, the RAF made 2,900 flights carrying 72,000 prisoners of war out of Germany.

The Long March was commanded by General Gottlob Berger, chief of staff for the Waffen-SS. At the Nuremberg Trials in 1947 he claimed his orders came directly from Hitler. He said he was merely doing his job. He said he resisted shooting many prisoners and opposed a Luftwaffe plan to set up prisoner-of-war camps in the centre of large German cities to act as human shields against Allied bombing raids. He said there was not enough barbed wire to make this feasible. His initial twenty-five-year sentence was later commuted to ten.

Jules Peters' mental and physical health were shattered. He imagined going home meant a return to his wife and previous life. But his wife Phyllis had started an affair with a friend of his whom she now wanted to marry. It was a frequent scenario. Serving soldiers were young and had not been married long. Wives tolerated separation for a while. But their husbands had gone and return was not guaranteed. Life was uncertain. They drifted into affairs. To pick up with another man seemed more like consolation and pragmatism than infidelity. Three hundred thousand illegitimate births were registered during the war. Abortion was illegal and drinking castor oil or gin in a hot bath was an uncertain way of terminating an unwanted pregnancy.

Dagmar hurried to see her nephew when she heard of his return at the beginning of May 1945. She arrived unannounced at seven in the morning. She had thumbed a lift on a lorry for it was too early for trains. That was the first of many unexpected early-morning visits. From the end of Hever Avenue she thumbed any passing lorry. Sometimes she got a lift on one bound for Covent Garden, sometimes it was a milk lorry; usually she was dropped at Elephant and Castle station.

Some days later on the warm Tuesday of Victory Day, 8 May, they went together to Trafalgar Square. People waved flags and streamers, jumped in the fountains and climbed lamp posts. 'The evil-doers now lie prostrate before us,' Winston Churchill's voice crackled through loudspeakers. Eleven times the royal family came out on the balcony of Buckingham Palace to wave at the crowd, who shouted and cheered and sang 'Land of Hope and Glory'. Humphrey Lyttelton played 'Roll Out the Barrel' on his trumpet. A long, long line of people danced the conga.

It was all 'Hokey Cokey', 'Knees up Mother Brown' and 'There'll Always Be an England'. Store cupboards were emptied for the parties: shrimp-paste sandwiches, Scotch eggs, chocolate delight, jam tarts, jellies, pink blancmange. When dark came, all the monuments of London were floodlit. There were fireworks and the burning of effigies of Hitler.

For Jules Peters victory was qualified. He stayed on in the army for he had no civilian life. While he was in the prison camp his father George had died. George, too, had returned from the First World War to find his wife had deserted him for another man.

Dagmar's murder was one more disintegration of family. But for the wider world the murder of an eccentric middle-aged spinster was of passing interest. No news mattered for long. The war was over, thoughts were of the future and managing the peace. There was a shortage of coal and Christmas was coming. In anticipation, a million turkeys were being imported from South America and Australia and 11 million bananas from the British Cameroons. During the war there had only been dried bananas and this was the first import of fresh ones since 1939.

On the day of Jules's questioning by Detective Sergeant Baker, survivors of a Dakota air crash spent five nights on a mountain in the Alps before rescue came. In Leicester Square the King, Queen and Princesses Elizabeth and Margaret attended the first Royal Film Performance at the Empire Theatre of Michael Powell's film *A Matter of Life and Death* and at the Central Criminal Court Lady Elizabeth Mary Gladys White pleaded guilty to three charges of stealing from her mother, the Dowager Marchioness Townshend, articles to the value of

£56. The Recorder said Lady Elizabeth had allowed herself to abandon all moral considerations and become a deplorable dipsomaniac and a shame to her own sex. 'Until your dying day I imagine you will devote to your mother the gratitude which she deserves and show it in an amended form of life,' he said.

2

THE VICTIM

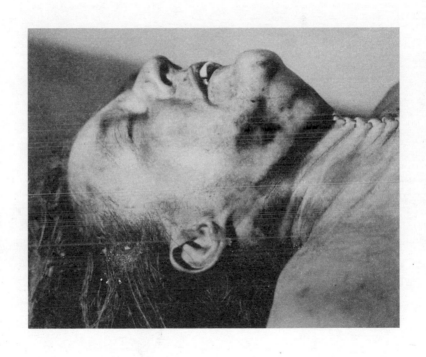

The last outing Dagmar and her mother made together was on Tuesday 29 October 1946. Tuesday was market day at the nearby town of Maidstone and, like most villagers, they went each week, looking for a bargain or something off the ration.

They left home after breakfast, walked up Hever Avenue to the bus stop by the Portobello Inn and caught the 478 to Wrotham, then the 21 to Maidstone. Dagmar borrowed a pound from her mother. Her GPO pension which she cashed at Kingsdown Post Office, did not come through until the last Friday of the month. There were three days to go and she had run out of money.

It was her idea to get a puppy for her mother. She said it would be company and protection now Mame was alone in the bungalow, her husband dead. Dagmar said she would take it for walks and prepare its food and it could stay with Mame in the day and at nights.

They chose a Jack Russell terrier, black and tan, smooth haired, about twelve weeks old. They joked about her being a *femme fatale* and it was Dagmar's idea to call her Hedy. The puppy had been treated for worms and fleas, or so the seller told them.

On other market stalls Dagmar rummaged for bits of

off-ration material to make clothes. Clothes were more of a problem than when rationing started in 1941. There seemed no end to the years of austerity. She and her mother each had 42 clothes coupons a year. But a coat used 18, a blouse 5, a night-dress 6, a scarf 2. It was easy to use up a year's supply and not have enough to wear for all weathers.

Like most people Dagmar patched and darned, unravelled and remade. On her Singer sewing machine in The Vic she turned a blanket into a coat, a curtain into a dress. On a stall that Tuesday she found the man's white woollen vest with a darn on the shoulder and paid a shilling for it. She would 'make up something with it for herself', she said to Mame. She thought she'd unravel it, then reknit it into a scarf. Throughout the war a welter of government leaflets encouraged and informed such thrifty, waste-free lifestyle. *Make Do and Mend* cost threepence and had chapters titled 'Unpick and Knit Again', 'Decorative Patches' and 'Where's That Moth?'

Dagmar and Mame had their identity cards and ration books with them – buff-coloured RB1s, issued from Kingsdown vil-lage hall. They were registered at Hever's General Store for their weekly allowance of 4oz of bacon, a shilling's worth of meat, 2oz of tea and 6oz of sugar. They used their coupons within the assigned week or forfeited them. Meat prices had gone up that year and now it was one can of Spam or corned beef a month. Whale meat was on sale, as much as you wanted, but tasted fishy and unfamiliar. The soap ration had been reduced in June: 4oz a week of hard soap for cleaning or 3oz of toilet soap.

Before the war half the meat eaten and 90 per cent of fat and flour was imported. War meant a switch to home production. Even bread was on the ration since July. And flour. There was a world shortage of cereals. 'Bread units', the new coupons were called. Mame looked for bread in Maidstone; there was more choice and it was not obligatory to use the coupons only in their registered shop.

Fifty thousand civil servants worked for the Ministry of Food, administering the government's rationing scheme, controlling prices and allocating subsidies: there were 19 divisional food offices, 1,500 food control committees, area head offices, local food and registration offices.

Mame and Dagmar owned next to nothing but were inured to being told by the government they should make do with less: 'Give us your aluminium. We want it, and we want it now.' Lord Beaverbrook exhorted housewives at the start of the war:

New and old, of every type and description and all of it. We will turn your pots and pans into Spitfires and Hurricanes, Blenheims and Wellingtons. I ask, therefore, that every one who has pots and pans, kettles, vacuum cleaners, hat-pegs, coat-hangers, shoe-trees, bathroom fittings and household ornaments, cigarette boxes or any other articles made wholly or in part of aluminium should hand them over at once to the local headquarters of the Women's Voluntary Service.

It was the converse of turning swords into ploughshares though when it came to it old kettles and hat-pegs proved not fit for purpose in the manufacture of bomber aircraft.

Though reports of Dagmar's murder described her hut, The Vic, as a shed, it was not much more basic than other shacks and bungalows on the Hever Estate. A few householders had piped water installed, but for each house the water company needed to sink 150 feet of pipe at a cost of £6 1s 6d. Not many residents opted for it. Boreholes, wells, butts and tanks served all right, the rain filtered through charcoal.

Keeping warm was a battle. Dagmar's Valor paraffin stove doubled as both heater and cooker. A Ministry of Food leaflet told her how to cook her dinner in a single saucepan: jam pudding and meat roll in used cocoa tins simmering in the same saucepan of water. She kept perishable food cool between slabs of stone outside her hut, used an oil lamp for light and went to bed early to save on fuel. In winter it was dark by five.

Women! the government exhorted 'Farmers can't grow all your vegetables':

> You must grow your own. Farmers are growing more of the other essential crops, potatoes, corn for your bread, and food for the cows. It's up to you to provide the vegetables that are vital to your children's health – especially in winter. Grow all you can. If you don't they may go short. Turn your garden over to vegetables. If you haven't a garden ask your local council for an allotment. DO IT NOW.

By the war's end some 10 per cent of food came from allotments. Railway sidings, school playing fields and golf courses were turned into vegetable patches. A quarter of the country's supply of fresh eggs came from garden hens and there were 6,900 pig clubs throughout the country for pork, bacon and ham.

Around The Vic and Houston was a quarter of an acre of land. Dagmar grew more than enough produce for her mother and herself. She fed the chickens, staked the beans and stored her gardening tools in a lean-to shed. On her impromptu visits to her London relatives she always took a few home-grown things. Milk was not rationed and even when it snowed old Mr Chapman used to fill jugs at all the houses. He put two churns on a sledge and pulled that round.

The Ministry of Food gave advice on healthy eating:

Get fit not fat on your war diet!

Make full use of the fruit and vegetables in season.

Cut out 'extras'. Cut out waste. Don't eat more than you need.

A hundred leaflets offered recipes and diet tips: how to make jam, save the fat from bacon, scoop out the marrow from bones and feed kitchen scraps to hens. 'No country in the world grows better vegetables than we do,' the Ministry wrote, 'and no country in the world cooks them worse. Keep the skins on, save the greens water for stew, steam cabbage for no more than ten minutes.' 'Hedgerow Harvest' told citizens what to do with blackberries, rosehips, elderberries and crab apples. There were others about turning the topsoil, planting seed, and growing peas, beans and tomatoes.

To power a wireless Dagmar had bought in Maidstone she kept two car batteries which she got charged at the garage. Every morning at 8.15, all through the war and after, there was a five-minute talk on the Home Service about thrift and food: Freddie Grisewood and Ambrose Heath advised on good potato dishes, and vegetables for victory. Elizabeth Craig explained how to puff up your Yorkshire pudding for your toad-in-the-hole.

Florence Greenberg and Mrs Arthur Webb told the nation's women how to cook a meatless Sunday dinner, make marmalade with carrots, and bread and butter pudding without butter, contrive hash from leftovers, pickle eggs, mix the fat ration with powdered milk or semolina to make it go further, use sugar beet as a sweetener, turn potatoes into flour and wash clothes without soap. Listeners were advised to ask for half a pound of broken biscuits for a fraction of the cost, or a quarter of a pound of mushroom stalks to liven up a stew.

Elsie and Doris Waters acted the parts of Gert and Daisy, two cheerful cockneys who told listeners what to do with their leftovers and how to stuff their murkey – mutton mocked up as turkey, of which there was none for Christmas until this peacetime year of 1946.

But all such exhortations did not redefine the British appetite. Dinner in the collective mind remained peeled potatoes, well-cooked greens and a bit of meat with gravy. A sandwich was cheese or jam between slices of white bread. Whale meat and Spam were no more part of the national menu than spaghetti carbonara and chocolate ants. Dinner was what dinner had always been and neither coaxing from the Kitchen Front nor all the coupons in the book would convince people otherwise.

Though 65,000 of the country's civilians died in air raids during the war, the State viewed itself as protective. The radio doctor, Charles Hill, broadcast daily on such matters as shingles and dandruff and whether vitamin C was good for boils. To avoid chilblains listeners should have regular exercise and a cold bath every day to improve circulation.

There was a paradox to frugality and rationing. The health of the poor was improved by having more food than before the war, the health of the rich was improved by having less. Few people were overweight. Vitamins were added to margarine, and schoolchildren had a third of a pint of free milk each day and an allowance of concentrated orange juice and cod liver oil.

In the khaki election of July 1945, the first general election since 1935, Winston Churchill's war government was defeated. Under the campaign slogan 'let us face the future' there was a landslide victory for the Labour Party led by Clement Attlee:

> The nation wants . . . good food in plenty, useful work for all, and comfortable, labour-saving homes that take full advantage of the resources of modern science and productive industry. It wants a high and rising standard of living, security for all against a rainy day, an educational system that will give every boy and girl a chance to develop the best that is in them.

Labour promised full employment, a tax-funded National Health Service, a welfare state. In the inter-war years, their manifesto said, the 'hard-faced men' had controlled the government, banks, mines, big industries, the press, the cinema. Economic power was concentrated in the hands of too few men, who acted in the interest of their own private monopolies and felt no responsibility to the nation. Labour advocated public ownership of the Bank of England and a diminishing of the power of the House of Lords, and promised to put the community first and sectional interests of private business second.

William Beveridge inspired this socialist dream. Born in Bengal, the son of a judge, he became a lawyer and enlightened social reformer. He listed the five 'giant evils' in society as squalor, ignorance, want, idleness and disease. He proposed that all people of working age pay a weekly contribution in national insurance. In return, benefits would be paid to them if they were sick, unemployed, retired or widowed. He defined a minimum standard of living 'below which no one should be allowed to fall'.

Here, in 1945, was the vision of a good society, the hope of the phoenix from the ashes. But hope was tempered by caution. People had seen the fragility of modern civilisation, how depraved and immoral at a turn it could be. And the war had cost the country a quarter of its wealth. Overseas investments had gone to pay for it. And talk of social equality was anathema to the entrenched upper echelons of society: the rich, the landowners, the 'hard-faced men' who viewed themselves as the nation's rightful elite. They were unused to opposition and tetchy in it. Churchill said none of what Labour promised could be afforded and that Attlee would have to 'fall back on some kind of Gestapo' to implement his policies.

The day after Dagmar's murder, on 1 November 1946, the Conservative Association at Ashford, twelve miles away from Kingsdown, hosted a talk by their constituency member of parliament Harold Macmillan on 'Socialist dogma and the grim nightmare of the Socialist State'.

For Dagmar a comfortable labour-saving home, a high standard of living and security against a rainy day were a far-off prospect. She was cut off, strange and emotionally inarticulate. Her life was hard, isolated and quite without privilege, and yet there was a sufficiency to it: harvesting the vegetables she had grown, collecting eggs her chickens laid, lighting the oil lamp, doing what suited her. The Vic was her independence. Layers of the clothes she made kept her warm. She dressed to go to bed. By the light of the oil lamp she read the books she rented for a few pence from the general store: *Romance on Ice* and *The Thorny Rose* by Margaret Malcolm, *Frail Amazon* by Juliet Armstrong, *House of Glass* by Sara Seale, *My Heart's Your Home* by Olive Standley, *Will You Go With Me?* by Frances Braybrooke, *Westward to My Love* by Jan Tempest.

And though there was wariness and much that went unspoken between her and her aged mother, she dutifully supported her in such ways as she could. At teatime over at Houston each afternoon she put the kettle on, washed the cups, gave her mother eggs from the chickens, fruit from the trees, a few carrots and potatoes. She filled the paraffin stove, brought in water from the outside tank, lit the fire under the outside copper for the washing. And when off on her excursions she always left that note tucked in the fence, saying OUT or IN. Just so her mother would not worry or feel alone. Just so she'd know her daughter was safe.

Thumbing a lift was an aspect of the thriftiness the government incessantly urged. If there was a spare seat in a lorry why not take it? The journeys she made – the early hours of morning, setting off, the road ahead – gave her a sense of adventure and made her feel free. From time to time she visited the 'hello girls', the women with whom she had worked for years at the telephone exchange – Pam and Gay and Nellie. She was not close to them and did not stay over. She liked to get back to her own place to sleep. The only way she could manage it in a day was by leaving very early. She packed her things the evening before. Sometimes a driver took the fourpence she always offered, which was the cost of the fare on the bus. Usually they refused.

On the Wednesday morning after they had been to the market together, she went over to see how her mother was getting on with Hedy the puppy. Mame said it had yapped and whined all night and kept her awake. It wouldn't settle. She asked her daughter to take the dog. They talked about whether Dagmar could manage it, her hut being so small. She wanted to keep it, but feared her chickens would disappear, or that it would kill them. She said she'd take it up to Ralph and Elena in Woking next day. She was sure they'd want it. Elena had talked about getting a dog. Their house in Triggs Lane was large, there was a walled garden, a woodland opposite. Dagmar had not planned to go up to town, but she had 15 shillings left in silver from the pound her mother loaned her. That would be enough for her workman's ticket to Woking, a bit of Christmas shopping with Elena and her bus fare home.

In the afternoon she called on her mother again, her usual teatime visit. She left shortly before four, saying she wanted to feed the chickens before it got dark.

Fabian's Brainwave

It continued to vex Fabian that the victim's body was found five miles down the road in the opposite direction to the way she needed to travel to visit her brother in Woking. Yet he took that, like every puzzling detail, to be a clue. His method was to go over and over and over such pieces of the jigsaw as he had, pushing them around, worrying at them, until they fitted together or suggested a picture or a hunch to pursue.

He wondered if Dagmar's murderer had picked her up in the

direction she wanted to go and then, after strangling her, driven on to London with the body, unloaded his lorry, set off back toward the coast and when no one was in sight dragged her corpse into the hedge. It was a theory that fitted with Simpson's forensic evidence of livid staining on the victim's buttocks caused by blood settling after circulation had stopped. Fabian surmised that the motive might have been robbery because of the missing crocheted yellow bag. But he needed tangible evidence. Tangible clues.

On Sunday 3 November sightseers went to Wrotham Hill to see the murder spot. The weather was milder and dry, though the day was overcast and it was dark by 4.30 in the afternoon. Detectives continued their search of the hedgerows for the puppy and Dagmar's possessions, and went on stopping and questioning drivers and checking paperwork at transport depots.

A twenty-four-hour guard was placed on Dagmar's home. Clothes were taken from her hut and sent to the police laboratory at Hendon for scrutiny, along with strands of hair, a bottle and barbed wire from the murder scene.

On Monday 4 November Fabian, with Superintendent Smeed, visited all lorry drivers' pull-up cafés between Wrotham Hill and London. He issued another press report: the field had thinned out, he expected early developments, enquiries were now confined to the movements of lorry drivers who used the stretch of road where the murder victim was found. He hoped such a seemingly confident bluff might make the perpetrator of the crime panic and slip up.

Next day the inquest on Dagmar Petrzywalski's death was opened by the Tonbridge coroner at the court in Borough Green.

Keith Simpson the pathologist gave evidence, so did Fabian. Joe Hammond who discovered her body attended, and Dagmar's brother Ralph who had identified her. Fabian said he needed more time to investigate. Christmas was coming. Proceedings were adjourned until 7 January 1947.

That same day Fabian drove to Dagmar's sister-in-law Elena Petrzywalski in Woking. He asked if there was a chance she could crochet a string bag identical to the one she had given Dagmar. Elena still had enough of the same yellow string. String was not rationed. It was not to a pattern but she remembered what she had done. She stayed up most of the night until it was finished. Fabian collected the duplicate bag next day. Henry England photographed it and this photograph was published in the *Police Gazette*, the *Kent Messenger* and national and evening papers along with a request for information. If anyone had found or seen a bag like this, would they come forward. Or if they had seen a black and tan puppy or a horseshoe-shaped purse with some silver in it and a Yale key.

The Bag in the Lake

Peter Graham Nash, a fifteen-year-old farm worker who lived in Mill Street in the village of East Malling with his parents, his twin Pamela and another sister Sylvia, had been following the story of the Wrotham Hill murder in the *Kent Messenger* for a week. On 7 November he saw the photograph of the duplicate crocheted bag. He recognised it. It was the same as the bag he had pulled out of the lake in Clare Park some days previously.

At about 10am on Saturday 2 November he had gone to Clare

Park with his friend Eric Bailey. It was private landscaped park-land, with fine trees, a lake and a stable block, the setting for Clare House, an eighteenth-century mansion originally built for John Larking, the Sheriff of Kent. The park was not open to the public but Peter Nash used to go there on Saturday mornings to exercise a pony for the current owner, Lady Peake.

He spied the bag caught on a twig in the lake and fished it out. He hoped there might be some money in it but it was empty. Nothing was to be wasted, everything might have a use, and on his way home he gave it to a family friend, Cora Meacham, a farmer's wife, in the adjacent village of West Malling. She washed it and thought she might use it but when a neighbour, Kate Hessey, who lived in Blacklands Lane, called by she gave it to her.

It alarmed Peter Nash to think the murderer must have struck in that peaceful park. He told his father how he found the original bag. Frank Nash was a policeman before he retired from the force to become a farmer. He sent his daughter Sylvia round to Cora Meacham to get the bag back, then took it to Dorothy Andrews, wife of the local East Malling police sergeant. She gave it to her husband Sergeant Horace Andrews, who gave it to PC Kenneth Freathy, who gave it to Detective Inspector Jenner, who showed it to Robert Fabian, who instructed Sergeant Thrift to drive with it to Glencoe, Triggs Lane, Woking where Elena Petrzywalski lived. Yes, Elena said, it was undoubtedly the bag she crocheted some months ago and gave to Dagmar on 18 October as a birthday present.

Fabian passed the bag to Dr Holden at the Metropolitan Police Laboratory at Hendon. Despite it having been washed by Cora Meacham, Dr Holden found, tangled in the string, hairs 'identical with those of the deceased' as well as black dog hairs, a hair from Mrs Elena Petrzywalski and one or two of Cora Meacham's and Mrs Hessey's too, and those of her daughter Juliet.

Fabian was elated. This, he declared, was a find of the utmost importance, tangible evidence, a clue that might lead him to the woman's killer. He prided himself that inspired policing like this made him a cut above an ordinary detective. He went to East Malling, interviewed Peter Nash and made extensive enquiries in the village. He ordered special search parties to comb the park and nearby lanes and meadows. If the bag had been discarded there was probably other evidence too. Near Farningham, twelve miles away, where Dagmar had been seen hitchhiking, fourteen detectives and other officers searched lanes and hedgerows in heavy rain, knocked on doors, scoured through dense and sodden fallen autumn leaves. They were looking for whatever it was that had been pulled round Dagmar's neck to strangle her. Photographs of a duplicate key and purse were published in the *Police Gazette* and national papers. The hunt went on from dawn to dusk.

Fabian could not understand how the bag had got into a private lake, in a secluded gated park closed to the public, with no roads near by and miles away from where the body was found. He talked to East Malling villagers. He learned the lake was fed from a stream which rose at Wells Street, East Malling, then flowed under the Goldwell cider works which until recently had been a paper mill. Only that year the mill had been taken over and reconstruction work was still going on.

The Goldwell cider works were between a lane known as Badlands and Mill Street. A footpath followed the stream until the stream ran under the works. The East Malling Girl Guide mistress told Fabian how, as children, she and her girlfriends used to put messages in bottles, drop these in the millstream where the cider works now were, then retrieve them from Clare Park lake some hours later.

Detective Inspector Henry England produced ordnance survey maps of the area and photographs of the cider works. The maps showed the lake in Clare Park, the stream, the lane by the mill and its junction with the main road.

Fabian went to the cider works to test the Guide mistress's information. He threw bottles with messages in them into the stream. Three hours later they turned up in the Clare Park lake. Then he launched into the stream the duplicate bag Elena Petrzy-walski had spent the night crocheting. It followed the same route. Walking round the works he noticed a large pile of red bricks stacked in the yard at the back. The foreman told him they had been delivered on the morning of 31 October, the morning of the murder, and were to be used for the construction of an outbuilding. He showed Fabian the delivery note in the company's accounts book. The driver was from a Cambridge haulage firm, M. Dickerson Ltd of Gloucester Street, Cambridge.

Sidney Sinclair's First Statement: Saturday 9 November 1946

Dickerson's journey books had already been checked in connection with the murder at Wrotham Hill days before Peter Nash came forward with the news about finding the yellow bag in Clare Park lake, or the local guide mistress told Fabian of her childhood pastime of throwing bottles with messages in them into the millstream at East Malling.

A few days after the murder, Superintendent Smeed had talked to Dickerson's manager Alan Bell, who told him about the delivery of bricks to the Goldwell cider works in East Malling on the morning of 31 October. The driver was Sidney Sinclair, one of their regular workers, a reliable married man who lived in Little Abington and had been with the company four and a half years.

Smeed telephoned Cambridge county police headquarters and instructed them to investigate further. Sinclair, like dozens of other drivers, had been on the A20 at the time of the murder and his route to East Malling passed Kingsdown and Wrotham Hill.

On 9 November Detective Sergeant Leonard Childerley called at 25 Little Abington. It was Saturday at 7.30 in the evening and Sinclair's wife Daisy was there too. Childerley explained it was a routine check. Nothing about the set-up aroused suspicion in his mind. It was a pretty, well-maintained whitewashed cottage with a thatched roof, a regular family, an hospitable wife, a daughter, a fire burning in the grate, a hot drink offered.

Sidney gave an account of his journey from his home to the cider works. Detective Sergeant Childerley wrote it all down for him to sign:

Statement of Sidney Sinclair, 25 Little Abington, Cambridgeshire, lorry driver aged 45 years who saith:
I am a lorry driver employed by Dickerson of Cambridge and I reside at 25 Little Abington Cambridgeshire.

About 10pm on Wednesday 30 October 1946 I left Little Abington driving an Albion 8 ton motor lorry no. AER 815 loaded with bricks for a cider works at East Malling Kent.

I travelled along the London to Bishop's Stortford Road and stopped at Judd's Café on the London side of Bishop's Stortford. I arrived at this café about 11.30pm and remained until about 3.30 to 3.45am next morning. I know this café well. I frequently use it.

Childerley did not enquire why Sidney chose to spend four and a half hours of the night in a transport café. Nor did he probe as to why Sidney took a whole night making a four-hour journey. It was odd and protracted but did not seem relevant to murder at dawn.

I carried on through Blackwall tunnel, took the left fork along the Woolwich Road to the first traffic lights, turned right, went straight up the hill to the roundabout, turned sharp right to the next traffic lights, turned left, then first right on to the Sidcup by-pass.

I carried on along the by-pass until about 6.30am when I stopped and asked a cyclist where East Malling was as I wanted to get to the cider works. The cyclist told me I was in West Malling and that I had to carry on for a short distance, turn right by the Council yard, then left at the end of the lane and the cider works was at the bottom of the hill.

I carried out these directions and I reached the cider works. At the main gate I saw one of the men going to work. I asked him where the foreman was and he told me he would be in bed and that I would not get unloaded until 8 a.m. I saw this man clock in and as far as I can remember the time was ten minutes to seven by the clock.

I left my lorry just outside the gates and walked into the village to try and get a newspaper but I could not find a shop. I was away from my lorry about fifteen minutes. I waited in my lorry until five minutes to eight, then I had to drive round to the back of the works where they unloaded the lorry. I left the works as soon as the lorry was unloaded. It was just after 9am.

I took the same road back and when I had travelled for about half an hour I stopped at a café on the right side of the road facing London. There were several people in the café and I noticed someone tuning the piano. I remained in this café for about half an hour. I then carried on to Bishop's Stortford and I again stopped at Judd's café. When I got to Stansted Mountfitchet I phoned my boss for orders. It was roughly 12.30pm and I was ordered to go to Chrishall Grange for a load of wheat to take to Bury St Edmunds.

On my journey down to East Malling I did not pick anyone up, no one thumbed me for a lift, in fact I saw no one on the road except other traffic which was fairly heavy in both directions.

I had stopped twice before reaching West Malling, on both occasions it was to fill up the radiator. I can't remember the times or where it was. I am not very familiar with this road.

Statement taken by Detective Sergeant Childerley at 7.30pm on the 9th of November 1946.

For Detective Sergeant Childerley much police work was of this ilk. It was not a lively way to spend a Saturday evening. Sidney Sinclair seemed an amiable and cooperative man with a respectful manner. Checks showed he had no criminal record. He had good recall of his journey, which had been as dull as the directions in a gazetteer The high spots were someone tuning a piano in a café and the water boiling in the lorry's radiator. No foul play was to be detected here. No leering exhortations for unwelcome sex, no screams, no livid bruising or corpse dumped into the bushes. Sergeant Childerley reported back to Detective Inspector Smeed that nothing of consequence had been ascertained. Sidney Sinclair was well regarded both at his workplace and in the village of Little Abington.

Mame Petrzywalski

The life journey which took Mame Petrzywalski to the Houston bungalow on the Hever Estate at Kingsdown followed a spiral downward of her social aspirations. In 1888, when Mame Marshall from Clapham in south London, aged twenty-two, married Jules François Petrzywalski, she thought she was marrying into an affluent, exotic family with status, entrepreneurial flair and European style. But none of her husband's business endeavours succeeded. The family acquired few possessions, put down no roots and, as the years passed, seemed dogged by undue misfortune.

Dagmar's grandfather, Johann Sigmund Petrzywalski, came from Austria to England via Paris in 1858. He was a master fancy pastry cook and confectioner and supplied Viennese pastries –

strudels, tortes and roulades – to Queen Victoria and the Roth-schild family. In Paris he had met and married a hotel cham-bermaid, Salome Ehrhard from Alsace. Their first son, Charles, was born in Paris.

In London their family business prospered and the pâtisserie at 62 Regent Street was mentioned in *The Gentleman's Guide to Europe* as a place that must be visited for the wonder of its cakes. They employed four assistants, all women, kept servants, had a carriage and horses and through naturalisation became offi-cially British with neighbours as affluent and class conscious as themselves. Next door lived a civil servant at the Colonial Office with his wife, family, servants and stables.

The Petrzywalskis had two more children after Charles: Alice, born in Ribeauville in Alsace in 1859, and then Dagmar's father, Jules François Raphael, born 15 September 1865 at the Regent Street address. Salome remained essentially European. Her ser-vants were French, her family from Alsace came for extended visits, she insisted that French be spoken at home and that her children remember their roots. All three were sent to French boarding schools in London.

The Petrzywalskis were arrivistes, socially and materially suc-cessful and ambitious, though European in tastes and style. But in 1874 Johann Sigmund died, aged only fifty-two, from emphy-sema caused by constant inhalation of flour in the bakery. He was buried in St Mary's Roman Catholic cemetery in Kensal Green. Of his three children Charles was seventeen, Alice six-teen and Jules François not quite ten. By the terms of his will his 'dear wife Salome' was to carry on the business as fancy baker and confectioner. This she did with Charles. Jules François was sent away to school and family life ended for him.

Charles was the son who made good and carried on from his father's success. The pâtisserie flourished, he took on more staff, made the business his, started up a restaurant in Langham Street and bought a house in Park Road, Dulwich. As an emblem of Britishness, and with aristocratic pretensions, he kept prize-winning show dogs. In 1883 he was elected head of the newly founded Great Dane Club. Within a year his Great Dane called Charles Sultan the Second became the first champion of the breed.

It was fashionable in society to keep a very large and a very small dog. Queen Victoria kept Toy Pomeranians, inbred to miniature size in Germany. In 1886 Charles Petrzywalski imported a prize-winning black Toy Pomeranian, General Dot, from Stuttgart. The following year, only the second year of Crufts dog show in London, General Dot won second place in the Toy Dog category.

Charles lived with his mother until 1892 when she retired to Lewisham with a French housekeeper thirty years her junior to look after her. Charles married the same year. He was thirty-five. Like his mother, his wife, Amélie, came from Alsace. He bought and moved to the Royal Albion Hotel in Margate, employed a coachman and other servants and exuded an air of prosperity and class. When Salome died in November 1915 she made him the sole beneficiary of her estate.

His sister Alice also prospered. She married an affluent Belgian art dealer and mine owner, Albert Corneille Crom, when she was nineteen. He was old enough to be her grandfather. She divorced him after five years and married an Englishman her own age, Charles Henry Moore. She, like her elder brother, lived in smart houses, travelled in Europe, had a high standard of living and upper-class social connections.

But Dagmar's father, Jules François Petrzywalski, in contrast to his parents, brother and sister, did not succeed in financial or social terms. He was tall, thin, dark haired, cultured, French-speaking and dressed like a well-to-do Victorian, but he did not settle to anything and his business pursuits seldom lasted a year. He married Mame Marshall when he was twenty-three but seemed directionless and without ambition. As the years passed, he and his growing family moved with monotonous restlessness further south-east in London to ever cheaper rented accommodation in nondescript terraced houses, in treeless streets, usually near a railway. He scarcely brought home a wage. They kept no servants, lived frugally, stinted on heating, had little or no social life but kept a façade of class. For a while Mame's sister Alice lodged with them to help with the rent. For holidays they travelled no further than Margate or Ramsgate.

In 1888 he and Mame started married life in rented rooms in the Hampstead Road with him working as a cigar and tobacco salesman. Within a year George their eldest son was born. He was baptised in the Holy Trinity Church in the Marylebone Road. By the time Edmund their second son was born, a year later, Jules François was a warehouseman and the family had moved to Southwark. The following year, when their third child and first daughter Ivy was born, on 5 November 1891, they had again moved and Jules François was trying his hand as a grocer. Ivy only lived a year. Her death compounded the sense of an unsettled family without support from relatives or friends.

They moved to Lewisham, to a leafier road near a bit of parkland. Jules François found work as a soft goods warehouseman and a third son, Victor, was born on 7 October 1893 but only lived a month. Marasmus, the doctor said, was the cause of his death. He fed and fed but wasted away, crying and fretful.

After a four-year gap in childbearing, Mame had a fifth child, Ralph, when she was thirty-one. The family had moved again, this time to Catford, and her husband was in another low-paid temporary job. The following year, on 25 October 1898, in another treeless street near the railway in Catford, in another two-bedroomed terraced house, Dagmar their sixth and final child was born.

Her brothers nicknamed her Dags or Diddles and when she was young sent her teasing postcards in summer from English seaside resorts. 'It's lovely down here,' George wrote in August 1908 from Margate when she was nearly ten. 'On Monday it was about fifty times as crowded as in the picture. I wish you were here. Have swallowed all the water so it's low tide. Love and kisses. Your brother George.'

Their father went on changing jobs, the family went on moving – often round the corner from where they were before, to Tolbeach Road, Holbeach Road, Nelgarde Road and always to the same sort of house. Home was a shifting place and work brought in enough money to keep them poor. There seemed no lucky break, no improvement to their fortunes. At the time of the 1911 census, when Dagmar was twelve, Jules François gave his occupation as a French correspondent and a salesman in the wholesale cloth business.

Dagmar went to local schools until she was fourteen. There was no question of payment for further education. She was dutiful and reliable but expressed no ambition to forge a life of her own and stayed nowhere long enough to make special friends. Her mother showed her no particular affection. The spectre of the daughter who died seemed not to go away. Mame's dissatisfactions were tacit and the mood in the household was civil but cold.

Dagmar left school in 1912 and her father found her a job as an assistant in a drapery firm. Her eldest brother George was working as a warehouseman for a wool merchant. From the money she earned she paid for her keep at home. But such family life as there was began to disintegrate. On 1 February 1912 her brother Edmund sailed to Halifax in Canada from Liverpool on a third-class ticket on the SS *Grampian*. He was twenty-two and wanted to get away to a new life. On board ship he gave his occupation as a farmer. Other passengers were miners, plasterers, waiters, mill hands. It was the last his family were to see of him. In Canada he first found work as a shipping clerk then enlisted as a private with the Royal Canadian Regiment. He called himself Edmund Peters. He was Private Peters, five foot six, fair hair, blue eyes and of the Church of England faith.

Then George, the eldest son, married on 15 September 1913 at Lewisham Register Office. His wife Alice Butcher was the daughter of a master tailor and, like Dagmar, a draper's assistant. They rented a house in Catford and within two years had their son Jules and a daughter Olga.

The two children left at home were Ralph, who was working as a government clerk, and Dagmar.

The Hello Girl 1916

Then came the First World War. Edmund volunteered in August 1915 to fight with the Canadian Expeditionary Force, was sent to France and eight months later killed in an artillery attack at Serre before the Battle of the Somme. He was twenty-six.

To honour their brother and in response to Lord Kitchener's exhortation 'Your country needs YOU', George and Ralph enlisted in 1916. George parted from his wife of three years and two baby children. Ralph served as a private with the Royal West Kent Regiment. (When he himself married and had a son, he called the boy Edmund.)

Dagmar was eighteen and alone with her parents, with one of her brothers dead and the other two fighting in France. She wanted to be usefully employed but had only basic education and few jobs were open to women. 'Mine's a good job & interesting too', advertisements for General Post Office telephonists read. The state had taken over the National Telephone Company in 1912 and it was an expanding industry. To work for the GPO meant a civil service job with security of employment, paid holidays and a pension. She applied for an interview in November 1916.

Applicants had to be single – women who married had to leave – be at least 5 feet 3 inches tall, have a clear speaking voice without accent or dialect, good hearing and colour vision and be accurate in taking down numbers and the correct spelling of towns.

She passed the interview and medical and signed the Official Secrets Act of 1911 swearing not to divulge what her work involved. She was part of a monthly intake, along with Matilda Pearson and Olive Perks. There was a seven-week training, then a civil service examination. Training was strict, with tests each week. Trainees who failed these were sacked. She was taught the five essential requirements of accuracy, courtesy, speed, tact and secrecy, how to have a rising inflection to her voice when answering 'Number please?', how properly to say 'Hold the line please', how to repeat details given by the subscriber. She was drilled in the pronunciation of numbers and their correct pattern: 44000 was double foer oh double oh. She was tested on the standard phonetic alphabet: Q for Queen, S for Sugar, H for Harry, Z for Zebra and V for Victor. She was taught how to connect calls by plugging into the jack socket of the required exchange then dialling the number, how to operate ringing, timing and speaking keys, and a splitting key which allowed her to speak to both caller and recipient. She learned how to deal with personal calls and transfer charge calls and advise on duration and charge of timed calls. No variation in wording was allowed: 'Hold the line please I am trying to connect you' had to be said after a lapse of thirty seconds, 'I am still trying to connect you' after sixty seconds and 'I am sorry, there is no reply' after ninety. Communication was formal and robotic: 'I am sorry, the line is engaged,' 'Please insert two pennies in the box but do not press button A until your number answers,' she and her colleagues were instructed to say. Every three minutes pips would be heard to remind the caller of the expense of passing time. Sometimes calls were obscene. The supervisor then contacted engineers while the operator tried to keep the culprit on the line. Children were a diversion. They called to ask if that was the operator on the line, then said, 'Get off quick there's a train coming.'

Dagmar began on pay of £1 6s a week with annual increments on birthdays. She worked at the HOL and HOP exchanges – Holborn and Southwark. It was an all-female society, She clocked on in the morning, off duty at dinner time, then on again half an hour later. She was issued with a special pencil, rounded at the top for dialling. There was a canteen, a locker room, a rest room. Twelve minutes were allowed for tea breaks. If she needed to go to the lavatory she buzzed the supervisor and was allocated four minutes. Shifts were 8am to 4.15pm or 11am until 7pm. Friday was pay day.

She stayed in the job for twenty-five years and became conditioned by the rules and privileges of quite such secure employment. She was never late, never overran her lunch and was never promoted. She made friends with Gay, Nellie and particularly Pamela Euden. They gave her the nickname Peter. They helped each other out if they needed to swap shifts, and went for walks on Hampstead Heath on sunny days off. At the end of the day she went home to her parents and to a not particularly enthusiastic reception. And so the years passed.

The Obliging Aunt

In 1918 at the war's end Dagmar's brother George returned, traumatised but uninjured. His wife Alice was living with a man called Angus Ross, was pregnant with his child and did not want George back. In an acrimonious divorce he asked that she be denied access to their two children. He said she abandoned him for another man while he was serving his country.

Women had few rights in law and were much scorned for infidelity to their soldier husbands. In 1919 Alice gave birth to a daughter, Lilian. She and Angus went on to have two more children, twins, in 1922. The decree absolute was not passed until 1923 and they finally married in 1924.

George wanted no reminder of his unfaithful wife but was unable to look after his children himself. He remained in the army stationed at Colchester and sent his five-year-old son Jules to live with his parents and Dagmar in Lewisham. Jules was handed over on Westminster Bridge. Mame Petrzywalski did not feel able to take George's three-year-old daughter Olga too, so despite the access ruling Olga stayed with her own mother and saw no more of her father. Jules felt himself to have been given away 'like a parcel of fish and chips'. Home became a bewildering place with his aged taciturn grandparents and his eccentric aunt who had unpredictable moods and suffered with her nerves. Mention of his birth mother was taboo. He was told she did not want him. He carried scant memory of her and never saw her again, though much later, when she was seventy-seven and dying, she phoned him and apologised for abandoning him. He said he would like to meet her but she refused.

When Jules was a child his father sent formal postcards from his army unit: 'Dear Son, Trusting you are getting along alright. Give my love to Grandmamma and Papa. Also Auntie. Love Papa.' In the summer holidays he took Jules to the seaside – to Ramsgate or Southend. 'I bought a trumpet Saturday when peace was signed,' Jules wrote to his grandparents in June 1919. 'I only blow it outdoors. Love and kisses Julie.'

Dagmar, sixteen years older than Jules, acted as his surrogate mother. She took him on outings to museums and the cinema: *The Man Who Laughs*, *Napoleon* and *Ben Hur*. In summer they took trips to the country, usually to Kent, for a walk and a picnic. Jules called his grandparents Mim and Pop. In adult life he described his grandmother as cold and spiteful. He recalled her hitting him for no good reason, said she denied him food and had a memory of her eating walnuts in front of him when he was hungry. He said she was cruel to Dagmar. He said he was brought up by strangers.

Dagmar's other brother Ralph also remained in the army for some years after the war's end. He was usually away but came home to his parents when on leave. Mame and her husband moved to a rented house on Houston Road in Forest Hill in south-east London, a larger semi-detached house with three bedrooms, a bay window and a small front garden and in a leafier road. There was more money, with contributions from Dagmar, Ralph and George.

For her fortnight's summer holiday, Dagmar went to the seaside with Pam and Nellie – to Margate, Lowestoft, Great Yarmouth, Herne Bay, while Jules stayed with his father. Always when away she sent separate postcards to her mother and to Jules, to Dearest Mim and to Julie – inconsequential missives about the weather, the beach, and card games, about not going fishing, and children building sandcastles. She never forgot a birthday. She was dutiful and kind.

As she grew older her brothers thought her a dependable woman, generous and helpful, but moody and solitary, cut off from the usual preoccupations of friendship and romance. It was as if she had no plan in life and sought no relationships outside her family.

Ralph moved out of the Houston Road house when Jules was twelve. He left the army, worked as a government clerk and married Elena Neal, the daughter of an engine driver, on 2 October 1926 in the parish church at Perry Hill in Catford. Dagmar was a witness. He and his wife were both twenty-eight.

She was widowed, her maiden name was Ousoff and she had similar European ancestry to him. They moved to Woking, to Royal Oak Road and to the same sort of Victorian semi-detached bay-windowed house as his parents.

Dagmar was the one who did not marry or leave home. In 1930 George got married for a second time, to Phyllis Wise, thirteen years younger than he was and the daughter of a painter and decorator. He too had left the army and was again working in the wholesale drapery trade. He married in the same church in south-east London as had Ralph, four years previously. Jules went to live with his father and stepmother but he was seventeen and it was too late for him to feel at ease with acquired parents. He courted a Phyllis of his own, Phyllis Purdue, and married her when he was twenty-two. It proved, like his father's, a marriage broken after only a few years by the chaos of war.

Mame and Jules François were in their sixties when their grandson left. Without contribution from their sons there was not enough money to pay the rent and bills on the Houston Road house. They decided to retire and leave London. They bought a plot of land in Kingsdown, where they planned to build a bungalow and spend their old age in the tranquillity of the Kent countryside. Dagmar would have to make her own plans.

Police Enquiries: 12–22 November 1946

Daisy Sinclair was reassured by Sergeant Childerley's interview with her husband Sidney on Saturday 9 November 1946 in their cottage in Little Abington. Childerley seemed a friendly policeman, not in the least suspicious of anything Sidney said.

But Sidney continued to behave oddly. After the interview he cleaned the lorry as it had not been cleaned before, with buckets of soapy water and everything wiped down in the cabin. Then, when he saw pictures in the paper of the duplicate yellow crocheted bag, he seemed to panic the more. He could not sleep and complained to Daisy about his nerves. When she told him not to be neurotic he came toward her with his hands outstretched and made a gurgling noise in his throat.

The police went on searching hedgerows and questioning drivers. On Monday 11 November PC Fred Kirwan of the Kent constabulary found a man's vest, sodden with rain, in grass and leaves next to Winterfield Lane, East Malling. It appeared to have been there some time. Dr Holden at the Metropolitan Police Laboratory in Hendon 'found adhering to the material a large number of head hairs of the deceased'.

Next day, Tuesday, Sidney Sinclair went to see Dr David Burlin in Linton near Cambridge. He told him he wanted to stop driving, he had had an accident that frightened him. He'd gone 'all to pieces' and was not sleeping. He asked for 'something for his nerves' and a medical certificate to give his boss. He gave no details about this accident, but the doctor saw his hand tremor and troubled manner and wrote out a certificate saying he was suffering from anxiety neurosis. Sidney returned the lorry to Dickerson, gave the certificate to Alan Bell and jacked in his job. Alan Bell tried to persuade him to stay, he had been with the firm four years and nineteen days, but Sidney was adamant. He had to leave.

The following day, to Daisy's relief, the newspapers reported that detectives were searching for the driver of a grey saloon car parked for two hours by the hedgerow where the body was found. In the afternoon Detective Sergeant Vessey called on Mame Petrzywalski in her Kingsdown bungalow with the vest. Yes, she told him, it was undoubtedly the woollen vest Dagmar had bought for a shilling at Maidstone market on 29 October; there was the telltale darn on the shoulder.

At 10.45am that same day PC William Davie found a brown attaché case which had had the lid torn off. It was on the bank on the left-hand side of Winterfield Lane, not far from the cider works, 150 yards from the main road, under trees and covered by falling leaves. Four hours later Davie found a lady's glove on the other side of the lane. And then Detective Constable William Wallace uncovered the lid of an attaché case in a mound of leaves.

Inspectors Jenner and Rawlings and England arrived. England took photographs of the case, its lid, the glove, the junction of the lane with the main road. Jenner 'took possession of the lid and removed it to West Malling police station'. It had, he said, 'been crudely torn apart and flung into the hedge, a piece on either side of the lane'.

He passed the case to Chief Inspector Birch at the Fingerprint Bureau who found nothing of forensic significance. Fabian then took the case to Dagmar's mother. Yes, Mame said, it was the little case she had given to her daughter a few months previously.

Next day newspapers reported that the police had found the string bag Dagmar was thought to be carrying and Chief Inspector Fabian of Scotland Yard was satisfied he was now on the track of the killer. He and Superintendent Frank Smeed of Kent CID had talked to more than a thousand people. The place where the bag had been found was kept secret. Fabian told the press, 'It would hamper our enquiries if it were known.'

Evidence accrued, inconsequential detail which only gained significance because a murderer needed to be apprehended, the killing of a woman explained: order forms, snatches of conversation, casual observations by passers-by who had no particular connection to each other. The shards of the past were there to be pieced together. The bag in the lake was the crucial clue. A dozen witness statements were linked to it: Ernest Bennet, a labourer who lived at 16 Council Cottages, Offham, had been on his bicycle on his way to work at 6.30 on the morning of the murder. He was stopped on the A20 about 200 yards from the turning for the village of Ryarsh by a lorry driver. The driver asked directions to the East Malling cider mills. The lorry was loaded with bricks. Bennet told him to take the second turning on the right, which was Winterfield Lane. The conversation was overheard by Stanley Clarke of Breen House from his bedroom window.

There were the statements from the other Bennetts, father and son, both farmers, hailed by a woman, undoubtedly Dagmar, on the A20 road at Farningham Gosse at 5.10am on the morning of the murder. She had something light-coloured around her neck. A heavy lorry with a flat load passed them going the other way about three minutes later and its driver must have seen her.

William Crittenden the lorry driver from East Farleigh saw a woman's shoe at about 7.15am in front of the place where the body was concealed, but had not stopped.

Sidney Sinclair had delivered bricks to the Goldwell cider works early on 31 October. He would have been in the vicinity of Farningham Gosse at about the time the Bennetts saw the woman trying to get a lift. Before 7.15am he would have passed the spot where the body was found, but in his statement to Sergeant Childerley he did not report seeing a shoe in the road. He had also according to his statement driven down Winterfield Lane, where the vest and attaché case were found.

On 16 November detectives questioned workers at the cider factory. Bernard Eldridge who lived in a cottage in the village of Ditton clocked on at 6.52am on 31 October. A lorry, loaded with bricks, was standing by the Time Office entrance when he arrived. The driver, from his cabin, told Eldridge he had been there quite a while and asked where he should put the bricks. Eldridge pointed him to the yard at the back of the works. It was 20 feet from the stream which ran under the factory.

Another worker, Frederick Prudence, saw the same lorry at the works at 7.07am. And Mrs Louisa Davenport noticed a large lorry loaded with bricks backed up to the entrance of the Goldwell cider works at 7.25am. A man was walking to and fro in the road between Clare Lane and the cider works. She thought he looked pale and worried and wished to avoid being seen because as she approached he turned away.

Labourers employed by the cider works helped unload this lorry: Harry West of Beech House, Ryarsh, and Frederick Simmons of The Heath, East Malling. The yard foreman Arthur Blundell, who lived at the Off Licence, Bell Lane, Ditton, signed off delivery note no 6002 for the bricks. All gave their bit of evidence to the police.

Detective Inspector Jenner made a test run from Farningham Gosse, where Dagmar was seen by the Bennett farmers at 5.10 on the morning of her murder, to the Goldwell cider mills, where the lorry delivering bricks was waiting by the Time Office at 6.52am when Bernard Eldridge clocked on. The distance was

$11\frac{1}{10}$ miles. At 30 miles an hour it took Jenner 26 minutes. Fabian calculated that if the driver of a heavily loaded lorry averaged 10 miles an hour, he would have been at Farningham Gosse at between 5am and 5.34am to get to the cider works by 6.52am where he was waiting when Eldridge arrived. If he had assaulted a woman, murdered her, then dumped her body in that interim time the whole process could not have taken long.

Mrs Rose Johnson of the Rising Sun Café in Kingsdown confirmed that a lone lorry driver came into her café at about 10am while her piano was being tuned, as Sidney Sinclair had said in his statement.

On 16 November Chief Inspector Fabian, Superintendent Smeed, Detective Sergeant Rawlings, Chief Inspector Birch of the Fingerprint Bureau and Detective Inspector Law of the Photographic Department at New Scotland Yard, all went to Dickerson's garage in Gloucester Street, Cambridge. The assistant manager Edward Burge looked up delivery note no 6002. Sidney Sinclair of 25 Little Abington, Cambridgeshire had delivered the clay bricks to the cider works in an 8-ton Albion flatbed lorry registration number AER 815 in the early morning of 31 October.

Maurice Dickerson's secretary, Alan Bell, told Fabian how Sidney Sinclair had handed in a doctor's certificate four days previously on 12 November, saying he was suffering from 'anxiety neurosis', and had quit his job. Bell looked up Sinclair's records. He had worked for Dickerson since 1942 and was earning £6 10s a week when he left. Bell had tried to dissuade him from leaving. He was an obliging worker and seldom off sick, though scrapes and accidents with his lorry, apparently due to careless driving, were above average in number. In 1943 he ended up in a ditch at Waterbeach with the lorry upside down on top of him; the following year he knocked a man off his bicycle in Cambridge and drove through a garden wall at Bedford. The company had to rebuild it. And then in July 1946, three months before the assignment to take bricks from Histon to the East Malling cider works, he crushed a man against a wall at West Acton. Fabian noted Sinclair had not suffered ill effects after that mishap, or needed time off work.

Sidney had been cautioned about these accidents and told to stop damaging his wings or he would get his money docked. No criminal charges were made. He offered no particular explanation for the accidents, though he did say he sometimes had headaches and dizzy spells.

Inspector Birch examined the lorry. It was old, a pre-war model, dirty green, with side boards that could be let down half at a time. Fingerprints on the left-hand door of the cabin and by the windscreen belonged to Herbert Mansfield, who had been driving the lorry since Sinclair quit.

Fabian visited Dr Burlin, who had issued the certificate. Burlin confirmed Sinclair was suffering from a nervous upset due to some recent experience and that the certificate he gave him cited anxiety neurosis as a reason to leave his job.

On 22 November a police car was sent to collect Sidney Sinclair from his cottage at 25 Little Abington for further questioning.

3

THE HEVER ESTATE

Kent in the 1930s was a vista of hop fields, orchards, oast houses and parks with chestnut palings. It was a landscape of beauty, a home to nuthatches and turtle doves. Hever Farm stretched over 253 acres of agricultural land. Beyond it were Wrotham and the vast forest of the Weald.

London was overpopulated. There was a squalor to its haphazard urban growth and nostalgia for the era when the city was surrounded by dense forest, and bears, wolves and wild boar roamed. By 1930 Epping Forest, Kenwood and Highgate Woods were remnants of a destroyed landscape.

From the government there was much talk of the green belt and the virtues of healthy rural life. People were encouraged to decant from the city centre to the countryside. In 1927 the Greater London Regional Planning Committee met with an agenda of decentralisation. They advocated open spaces, playing fields and new and wider roads. A girdle of green open space was marked out. The hope was of unified planning, but there was not much money for that. Green Line coaches were introduced in 1930 to transport people from the smoke to the fields. Prompted by this green thinking and pastoral promise Dagmar's parents bought their plot of land in Kingsdown in 1926 while still living in Lewisham.

The selling of Hever Farm was a commercial proposition that cashed in on the rural dream. A land agent, Charles Brake from Fleet in Hampshire, bought the farm in 1925 for £9,044, then carved it into hundreds of small building plots, some with 20-foot frontage to what would be a road, others 'backland plots', accessible only by tracks past other potential dwellings. Selling was in two phases. Plots were advertised in local and national papers. Only a few bungalows were professionally built. Only a few purchasers built solid homes in their spare time. Most buyers, like Jules François and Mame Petrzywalski, with hopes for a better life but little money, put up some kind of dwelling on their 'leisure plot': a rough and ready bungalow, a shack, an old railway carriage, a caravan, a shed. There was scant building control.

The Petrzywalskis were among the first to buy. In their mind's eye they did not envisage the end result. Hever Avenue was no more than a cart track. They arrived to a landscape of cherry orchards and sheep grazing under blossom trees. They could only afford the simplest of dwellings, to the cheapest specification. They ended up with a bungalow, its walls of asbestos packed with straw, made up of two adjoining rooms. It had no chimney or gutters. They heated it and cooked with a paraffin stove, had Aladdin lamps with mantles for light and collected rainwater in butts. There was a lean-to shed at the side and an outside privy.

In its pastoral setting, before a rash of similar dwellings appeared, the crudeness of their bungalow passed as simplicity. Old Kingsdown was lovely: the Saxon church of St Edmund the Martyr, the Manor House tearooms, the pretty settled cottages.

The bungalow promised escape from the disappointment of Jules François' transient jobs and the succession of places that for so many years they had temporarily called home – so remote from the opulence of St James's Place and orders from Buckingham Palace for tortes and strudels. Three of Mame Petrzywalski's children were dead. The other three had independent lives, though Dagmar was to be considered: no husband to provide for her, no place of her own. Her parents encouraged her to buy a plot next to theirs. She paid £12 10s 3d for it in 1930. Her plan was to build on it when she had saved enough money, to have a weekend and holiday place and then, when her working days were done, a home where she could live independently but close to her parents.

At first Mr and Mrs Petrzywalski went to Kingsdown only at weekends. They moved in permanently in 1931. They called the bungalow Houston because that was the last road they lived on in south London. It helped when they collected forwarded mail from the village post office.

As neighbours arrived and the Hever Estate developed, it changed from the tranquil haven of Mrs Petrzywalski's imagination. She was not friendly toward the Taylor family who purchased three plots adjacent to hers. At weekends, Mr Taylor with his wife and two children came down from Peckham on a motorbike with a sidecar and camped in tents on the land they had acquired. He made a seesaw for the children out of bricks and a plank of wood, and put up a shed in which they all lived while they built their bungalow. He was a cabinetmaker and builder by trade. His house-building progress was slow, limited by time to spare and what was affordable. He had reached roof height by the outbreak of the war. He paid the land agent, who lived in a smart bungalow, in monthly instalments. The whole house cost £46.

Residents of old Kingsdown deplored this sell-off of land, the arrival of mainly working-class Londoners, the jerry-built bungalows, huts and shacks given ambitious names like Peacehaven, Meadow View and Sunny Mead. It was their village, their territory. Custom, time and class endorsed their sense of ownership of the fields, farms, manor houses and thatched cottages. They lived in the old houses set in woodland near the Saxon church and the school. Mrs Neal, who owned Neal's Farm, built the village hall. The headmaster of the village school lived at Church Cottage. The vicar married a daughter of Mr Pink, the maker, out of Kent fruit, of Pink's Jams. The four-storey windmill at Pells Lane was a national landmark. There were three shops and that was quite enough. Mr Jessup the coal merchant had a forge and was also the undertaker, blacksmith and carpenter. This haphazard influx of hoi polloi horrified them all.

It became a north–south divide. The green belt was the rough end. Mrs Petrzywalski, or Mrs Peters as she was known, did not like to be viewed as one of the interlopers. 'Oh, you live on the estate' was a humiliating rejoinder. She read the *Daily Telegraph*, equated communism with criminality and kept to a standard with her gloves and hats.

But in the years up to the war, as the estate developed, a community formed among the newcomers: new shops and services started up. Coal and milk were delivered by horse and cart. Barrels of beer came on drays and were lowered on ropes through a trapdoor into the cellar of the Portobello Inn. The rag-and-bone man came from Maidstone to all the surrounding villages, buying and selling junk. The knife grinder went round on his bike and mended pots and kettles too. The baker sold Hovis, milk loaves, steamed bread, Eccles cakes and crumpets. The post office offered 'general sundries, chemistry and stationery', sold Wall's ice cream, and delivered Esso Blue paraffin on Thursdays and Fridays. Hever General Stores sold 'knitting wool, medicines, tobacco, etc. etc.' Dunroamin Stores delivered early-morning newspapers, ran a lending library of sorts, did cycle repairs and sold costume jewellery and Glamour Girl nylons along with groceries and 'toilet requisites'. 'Joan' of Stonecot offered scientific hair cutting, permanent waving and tinting. No job was too small for Ford's the builder and Jessup's delivered cement and bricks. There was no resident village doctor but once a week Dr Hay-Bolton from Wrotham held a surgery. The nearest hospital was at Dartford but the village church of St Edmund King and Martyr was open to all, though the Petrzywalskis never went to its services, harvest festivals, tombolas and raffles.

The Blitz on London 1940–41

Dagmar had her plot of land and her own retirement dream, but her parents' move to the Kent countryside highlighted her isolation as an unmarried woman with modest means in London in the 1930s. Their bungalow in Hever Avenue had only one bedroom so, if she stayed overnight when she visited, she had to sleep on a makeshift bed in the living room.

She kept on as a telephonist without promotion or alteration to her routines. There was a grit about her, a determination. She learned self-reliance and became inured to loneliness. At first she lodged with a Mr and Mrs James in Perry Hill, Catford, in their small terraced house on an unremarkable street of the sort in which she had always lived. She was near her brother George and nephew Jules and it was an area she knew, but it was an arrangement of necessity. It was painful to be in proximity to such strangers. She feared to close a door too loudly or tread on a squeaking floorboard at night.

Her father grew frail and on her days off she went down to Kingsdown to help out, always with a gift: a packet of tea or a scarf she had knitted. But then she became unwell herself; 'internal problems' she called her apparently heavy periods and unpredictable bleeding. She did not go to a doctor. She was reluctant to give voice to such personal symptoms and abhorred the idea of clinical examination.

She was honest, reliable, independent and spinsterish. An outsider. Her pleasure was to visit her married brothers and nephew, who tolerated her but little more. Progress was to move to rented rooms in a bigger house, in a nicer street, with more privacy and an easier journey to work. She moved from Catford to Clapham where her mother had spent her childhood, then, in 1938, to 30 Oakley Square in Camden Town, near shops and Regent's Park and diverse transport. She lodged in the house of an Irish physician, Dr Edward O'Kelly from County Kildare. It was a large cream stuccoed house on four floors. He was a generous landlord and her top-floor room looked out over a garden square. She made her own clothes, cooked her own food, owed nothing to anyone and saved until she had £400 for the day when she might build that home of her own on her Kent plot with her mother and father next door.

Hitler's dream of world domination came like a shadow over all domestic plans. On 3 September 1939 Britain declared war on Germany. By June 1940 Italy had joined forces with Germany,

Paris had surrendered, Paul Reynaud had resigned as prime minister of France and Marshal Pétain had sought armistice with Hitler. German invasion of Britain was thought certain. On 18 June, Churchill, the warlord who had recently become prime minister, prepared the nation for the Battle of Britain. He made the defining speech of his premiership. The survival of Christian civilisation, he said, depended on Britain:

> Hitler knows that he will have to break us in this island or lose the war. If we can stand up to him, all Europe may be freed and the life of the world may move forward into broad, sunlit uplands. But if we fail, then the whole world, including the United States, including all that we have known and cared for, will sink into the abyss of a new Dark Age made more sinister, and perhaps more protracted, by the lights of perverted science. Let us therefore brace ourselves to our duty and so bear ourselves that, if the British Empire and its Commonwealth last for a thousand years, men will still say: 'This was their finest hour.'

The emergency services depended on telecommunications. The telephone exchange where Dagmar worked was a target. More was required of existing staff. More staff were needed. Shifts were made longer for both day and night duty.

The hello girls transmitted messages that were anxious and stark. There was fear of a poisoned gas attack, and at air-raid practice telephonists wore gas masks with inbuilt earphones and transmitters. Forty-four million gas masks were distributed in Britain at the start of the war. Citizens were advised to try them on for fifteen minutes a day to get used to them. For children, the masks were splashed with colour and made to look like eerie elephants with trunks. Bearded men were told in government leaflets to fasten their whiskers with kirby grips before fitting their masks.

Black Saturday, 7 September 1940, a hot summer's day, was the start of the Blitz on London. Hitler ordered it as a prelude to invasion. It was the fiercest air battle of the war. There was the bleak wail of air-raid sirens, then at five in the afternoon the sky filled with bomber planes. Five hundred aircraft an hour for eight consecutive hours. On that first day 430 civilians were killed and 1,600 severely injured. The following day 412 more people died. Over the next months there were constant bombing raids. Two hundred German bomber planes flew over London every night for 57 nights in succession. By the end of September 1940 about 6,000 people had been killed and 10,000 seriously injured. Houses, shops, offices and public buildings were destroyed, railway lines smashed, trolley lines brought down and gas, water, electricity and telephone supplies broken. Churchill wrote: 'At this time we saw no end but the demolition of the whole Metropolis.' In secret session in parliament he warned that the bombing would get worse and the Germans might land half a million soldiers. It was a year before defence against night bombing was found in radar-controlled anti-aircraft guns.

It was the same ordeal, night after night after night: the wail of sirens, the drone of planes, shells that lit up the sky, the crashing of bombs, the sound of heavy guns. Night after night people sat up in shelters. They emerged when the all-clear sounded, viewed the damage, attended to the dead and injured, then queued for the shelter again.

Dagmar kept to her useful job, walked to work past the rubble where houses had been, the firemen who worked night and day to contain the fires, the pall of smoke and soot that hung over London. In October Regent's Park zoo was bombed and a zebra bolted as far as Camden Town where she lived. King's Cross and Paddington were the only two London main-line railway stations still open and St James's Palace and the Foreign Office were damaged by mines dropped by parachute.

The news was of a world engulfed in destruction. Christmas was the gloomiest Londoners could remember. Much of their city was demolished. Seventy-six thousand buildings had been damaged. Over 3,000 bombs were lying around, needing to be defused. Civilians were being killed at a rate of 6,000 a month. On 29 December eight Wren churches were among the buildings destroyed and the GPO's Central Telegraph Exchange in St Martin's Le Grand burned to the ground without enough water to put the fire out. Three other telephone exchanges were bombed that night, making it the worst attack of the war on the capital's telecommunications network. Fires burned all next day. Guy's Hospital at London Bridge had to be evacuated, all of Cannon Street was smouldering, there was rubble as wide as Trafalgar Square around St Paul's, making the whole place look like a builder's yard.

Londoners decamped nightly to public shelters, cellars, Underground stations, crypts, vaults. But there were five more months of intensive bombing to come. People hoped for the German economy to collapse, for America or Russia to join the war on the side of the Allies, for revenge attacks that would turn the enemy away.

Theatre became a diversion from the excessive drama of life.

The remit of ENSA (the Entertainment National Service Association) was to raise morale and keep the nation smiling. George Formby, Gracie Fields, Arthur Askey and Tommy Handley were as much a part of the war effort as Douglas Bader, Hurricanes and Spitfires. Hitler might strut, goosestep and rant about racial purity, but the Allies countered such mania with Charlie Chaplin's *The Great Dictator*.

Musicals and comedy were popular in a way that weightier drama was not. *Me and My Girl* ran for three consecutive years at the Victoria Palace Theatre and the words of 'Doing the Lambeth Walk' became as ingrained in the nation's memory as Vera Lynn's 'We'll Meet Again' and the bluebirds over 'The White Cliffs of Dover'. The Windmill in Soho, with girls in fancy knickers and suspenders 'never closed', and queues were long for *Gone With the Wind* with Vivien Leigh as Scarlett O'Hara at the Ritz Leicester Square and for *The Philadelphia Story* with Cary Grant and Katharine Hepburn at the Empire.

By February 1941 there was still an expectation of invasion. It was not known that Hitler had shifted his focus to the Balkans and North Africa. Between March and May 30,000 bombs were dropped on what was left of London. 'The Big Blitz Back Again' a newspaper headline read on 14 March. A month later, on the night of Wednesday 16 April, came the heaviest raid. For eight and a half hours German planes shuttled bombs from France in 685 sorties. Germany said it was reprisal for the bombing of Berlin on the night of 9 April. There was a full moon and even before fires from burning buildings lit the city, targets were clear: the docks, warehouses, factories around the Thames, the Houses of Parliament, the Admiralty, the Law Courts and St Paul's Cathedral. Eighteen hospitals and 19 churches were damaged or destroyed. Shops in Leicester Square and Oxford Street were blown up, over 2,000 fires burned. 'There is a hot blitz on,' Harold Nicolson wrote in his diary:

> To the south, round about Westminster, there is a gale of fire, as red as an Egyptian dawn. To the north there is another fire which I subsequently see at closer quarters. The stump of the spire of Langham Place church is outlined against pink smoke. I walk on under the guns and flares and the droning of the planes. I fall over a brick and break my glasses. I limp into the Ministry to be told that we have sunk a large convoy between Sicily and Tripoli. This is the news we wanted.
>
> After typing this I go to bed. I get off to sleep all right, but the blitz gets worse and worse, and the night shrieks and jabbers like an African jungle. I have never heard such a variety of sounds – the whistle of the descending bombs, the crash of anti-aircraft, the dull thud of walls collapsing, the sharp taps of incendiaries falling, all around. The British Museum opposite my window turns rose-red in the light of a fire in the University. Every now and then it turns sharp white when a magnesium flare descends. Then rose-red again. It goes on all night.

It became known as 'The Wednesday': 1,108 Londoners died that night; 2,230 were seriously injured. It was the highest toll of any raid thus far.

Among the houses bombed was Dr O'Kelly's house in Camden Town where Dagmar Petrzywalski lodged. The doctor was hauled from the rubble but died two days later at University College

Hospital. He was fifty-seven. Dagmar was in the nearby air-raid shelter and escaped with her life. Her possessions, such as they were, were all destroyed.

Dagmar's Move to The Vic: April 1941

'As far back as I can remember my aunt suffered from headaches and nerves and the bombing brought matters to a head and she retired,' her nephew Jules told Fabian when interviewed in 1946. She went briefly to stay with Ralph and Elena in Woking. She asked if she could live with them until the war was over, but her brother said no. He felt she never forgave him for this refusal and from then on was less friendly toward him, though they never actually quarrelled.

She had nowhere to live and she was traumatised. She went to stay with her friend Pam somewhere in South Ruislip, but the danger and gloom of the war and her precarious relationship with her family took its toll. She had what was called a nervous breakdown. She felt unable to go on with her job or seek new lodgings in London. She wanted to leave the city and build a place to live in, however simple, on her plot of land. She thought she must be safer in Kent, away from the constant peril of bombs and air raids.

She applied to her superintendent at the exchange to take early retirement because of ill health. She had to have a medical examination and admit to fibroids and headaches and how, after Dr O'Kelly was killed and her home bombed, she felt unable to work.

Her pension entitlement was £6 9s a month. Out of her

savings she paid Mr Farrier, who lived near Brands Hatch, to build her a hut on her plot of land on the Hever Estate. She wanted it at maximum speed and minimum cost. Farrier charged her £5 plus materials. The hut he constructed was 10ft long by 7ft 3in wide and 7ft 6in high at the pitch of the roof. It was of creosoted wood with a tarpaulin for the roof. It had no gutters. He put in a triple frame window and the top parts of the glass opened to give air. He added a lean-to shed for gardening tools, and put down stones for a path.

Dagmar made blackout curtains and from Maidstone market bought bits of carpet for the floor, blankets which she sewed together for thickness, oddments of material for a bedspread and cushion covers. She bought a new sewing machine to replace the one lost in the Blitz, acquired a flat iron, a paraffin stove, a divan bed, a chair, little tables, pots and pans, a wireless.

She rented a room in a house in Swanley twenty miles away while the hut was being built. Buses were infrequent and she got into the habit of hitchhiking to check on building progress and to visit her parents. Thumbing a lift was part of making do, the austerity and frugality of wartime. She did not trust private motorists. Not after a driver suggested things she would not repeat. When she became agitated he stopped the car, ordered her out and left her by the roadside miles from anywhere. Lorry drivers were different: friendly reliable men who knew the road, got lonesome and welcomed her company. At times in fine weather she walked all the way from Swanley to Hever Avenue: through Maplescombe Valley past the hop fields, up Botsum Lane, down a cart track to the Maidstone to London road.

As soon as the hut was finished she moved in. It was a home of her own, freedom from a job that had become dull and she was away from the Blitz and bombs, the dereliction, fires, rubble and nightly sense of danger. The Vic brought her independence. She liked lighting the oil lamp, making her own clothes, growing vegetables from seed, collecting eggs from her own chickens.

Restrictions on keeping livestock were lifted in the summer of 1940. Mr Farrier built her a henhouse out of bits of timber and netting. The RSPCA issued a leaflet on the proper care and treatment of hens. Dagmar fed hers on scraps and gave up her own egg ration in return for poultry meal – made up of wheat leftovers and fishmeal. She began with five hens and a cockerel but neighbours complained of the cockerel's morning call, so the butcher wrung its neck. She did not keep rabbits, though it was the most popular source of cheap meat. Mr Taylor next door kept forty in hutches along the front of his garden. He would kill one or two and take them in an old cricket bag up to his relatives in Peckham and Dulwich.

Accustomed to solitude and reticent about the crudeness of her home, in the five years she lived in her hut Dagmar invited no one in. But her austere life was better than lodging in someone else's house in a war zone. She saw the same sunrise as the rich. 'Dig for Victory' the government exhorted and that was her work of the day. She read the leaflets about turning the topsoil, rotating crops and 'How to Make a Compost Heap'. She made her garden grow.

In the Blitz in 1940 the Taylor family, too, were bombed out from their house in Peckham. Thankful to escape with their lives, they made the Hever Avenue bungalow their permanent home. Mr Taylor spent much time in his garden shed, making things.

He built a strange-looking car out of spare parts and drove up to London 'where the money was' to do building work, of which there was plenty given the extent of bomb damage. Mrs Taylor tended her vegetable garden. She had three plots, one just for potatoes, and for money worked as a cleaner 'up at the big house' in old Kingsdown. Her daughter Hilda worked there too on Saturdays. For two shillings she cleaned the brass and silver and peeled and prepared vegetables.

The family were happy with their country life. With her brother Jim, Hilda cycled the lanes, went to the local school and sang in the church choir. There was the Girls' Friendly Society, the Young Men's Christian Society, the Scouts, Brownies, Girl Guides. Mr Taylor belonged to the Working Men's Club. But the Petrzywalskis, parents and daughter, did not join clubs, cycle, or call for tea at neighbours' houses. They kept themselves to themselves.

The War in Kingsdown

War in Kingsdown, though nothing like the bombardment of the city, was war none the less. By leaving London, Dagmar escaped the constant wail of air-raid sirens, roar of planes overhead, sounds of explosion, raging fires and nightly carnage. But Kingsdown was not entirely a safe haven. Nearby airfields were targeted. On 13 September 1940 four high-explosive bombs, mistakenly dropped on the Hever Estate, damaged nineteen houses and the A20 road, and brought down overhead cables and wires. Next month at the bottom of Hever Avenue a woman was killed in her house by a bomb blast.

Free gas masks were distributed by the District Council and Anderson shelters were sold for £7 to people with gardens or without charge for those earning less than £5 a week. Dagmar's parents had a free one. Named after the civil engineer, Dr David Anderson, who designed them, and Sir John Anderson, head of Air Raid Precautions, they were made from six curved sheets of corrugated iron, bolted at the top, with steel plates either end. They measured 6ft high, 6ft 6in long by 4ft wide and were designed to be half-buried in the ground and camouflaged by earth heaped on top. They were dark, damp, tended to flood and did not keep out the sound of bombing. People were reluctant to crawl into them at night or to stay put until the all-clear sounded.

The *Food Facts* leaflet 'What to Do in an Air-Raid' advised on sustenance to take into the shelter:

> If you have a vacuum flask, fill it with hot soup, tea or coffee. Plain biscuits with a handful of sultanas or a piece of chocolate are most sustaining. So are sandwiches made with cheese, sardines or canned salmon. Children need plenty of water to drink. Barley sugar is excellent for them.

When their Anderson shelter flooded, the Taylors, who had more money than the Petrzywalskis, opted for a Morrison shelter. Named after Herbert Morrison, the Home Secretary, and designed in 1941 to withstand the collapse of a house on top of it, it was a large steel cage, 7ft by 6ft, with metal mesh panels round the sides. Mr Taylor assembled his in the back room of their bungalow but the family felt claustrophobic in it, so he then dug a trench in the garden which he covered in sandbags. They felt safer in more open ground.

When the bombing of London began, schoolchildren, mothers with children under five, and pregnant women were packed off to the country to be out of harm's way. Public Information Leaflet No 3 made this evacuation scheme sound benign and generous. Whatever this vicious enemy did, the nation's children were everyone's children and must be spared. So, with their name tags on their coats, little London children were sent off by train to lodge with strangers in unfamiliar homes. Few knew what was going on. Many were scared and homesick. In Kingsdown evacuees were taught in the village hall, separately from local children. The London County Council paid for their education, Kent paid for its own.

Fighting this war enhanced a sense of nationhood and interdependence. Women who had never done paid work ran soup kitchens, joined the Women's Voluntary Service and the NAAFI – the Navy, Army and Air Force Institute. The wireless united the nation. 'Goodnight children everywhere', Uncle Mac said every evening on *Children's Hour*. In the morning the Radio Doctor, Charles Hill, reminded citizens to 'now wash your hands please', cover the leftover lamb with gauze, hang fly papers from the light fittings and eat something green and raw. To spur listeners on and give them courage Sandy MacPherson played the BBC Theatre Organ. *Music While you Work*, at the government's instigation, piped cheerful tunes into the armaments factories to improve morale and increase production. Slow waltzes were banned as soporific; so were songs like 'Deep in the Heart of Texas' which it was thought would encourage workers to bang their spanners on the machinery. *ITMA – It's That Man Again* – spoofing Hitler, was the most popular radio comedy of the 1940s. Its catchphrases cheered the nation: 'I don't mind if I do', 'Can I do you now, sir?', 'It's being so cheerful as keeps me going', 'After you Claude, No, after you Cecil', 'Ta-ta for now', 'This is Funf speaking', 'Don't forget the diver'.

Twiddling the wireless dial found Radio Hamburg and *Germany Calling*. William Joyce, deputy leader of Oswald Mosley's British Union of Fascists, went to Berlin a week before the war. Known as Lord Haw-Haw for his upper-class voice, he broadcast a propaganda diatribe of German successes and British defeats. After the war, convicted of treason, he was hanged by the same hangman and on the same gallows as the murderer of Dagmar Petrzywalski.

In May 1940 all signposts in Kent were removed so that as and when the German army arrived it would be entirely dis-orientated. As were bona fide visitors. Soldiers manned road blocks at the Bull Hotel, Swanley and at Farningham Hill and challenged travellers for proof of identity and to declare the purpose of their journey.

Government pamphlets issued to Kingsdown villagers told them what to do when the enemy arrived. There were seven rules. The first was to 'stay put' in their homes. A commander-in-chief would tell them how and if they were to be evacuated. They must not, like people in Holland and Belgium when the enemy came, flee on foot and by car and bicycle and so block the roads for their own armies and be machine-gunned from the air.

The second rule was not to believe or spread rumours.

If you keep your head you can tell whether a military officer is really British or only pretending to be so. If in doubt ask the policeman or Air Raid Precautions warden. Use your common sense.

Third was to give exact information about anything suspicious.

> The sort of report which a military or police officer wants
> from you is something like this:
> 'At 5.30pm tonight I saw twenty cyclists come into Little
> Squashborough from the direction of Great Mudtown. They
> carried some sort of automatic rifle or gun. I did not see
> anything like artillery. They were in grey uniforms.'

'Do not give any German anything,' was the fourth rule.

> Do not tell him anything. Hide your food and your bicy-
> cles. Hide your maps. See that the enemy gets no maps.
> See that the enemy gets no petrol. If you have a car or motor
> bicycle, put it out of action when not in use. It is not enough
> to remove the ignition key; you must make it useless to
> anyone except yourself.

The fifth rule was to be ready to help the military in every way but not to barricade roads or streets to stop the enemy advancing unless and until told to do so by the authorities. Then civilians should fell trees and wire them together and block roads with cars.

The sixth rule was for every factory, store and workplace to have a system of defence in place against sudden attack: 'Remember that parachutists and fifth column men are power-less against any organised resistance.'

Villagers were told to expect more detailed instructions from military and police authorities and Local Defence Volunteers when the time came. Such instructions, which had to be obeyed at once, would not be given over the wireless as they might convey information to the enemy.

Remember always that the best defence of Great Britain is the courage of her men and women. Here is your seventh rule: Think before you act. But think always of your country before you think of yourself.

The idea was for every village to defend its territory and deny the invading army use of its roads. It was bewildering for the inhabitants of Kingsdown whose routines took them no further than to Maidstone on the bus. The Kingsdown Home Guard tried to be prepared though they were by no means sure for what. Their headquarters were at Knatt's Farm. Their leaders, ex-Captain Pelham who lived at Two Chimneys, Mr Neal from Kingsdown House and Sergeants Thorn and Rand, constructed a shooting range and gave training to local men in ways of attacking motorised transport. This involved firing at a derelict car. Very little was supplied to them in the way of munitions. In 1941 Churchill said every member of the Home Guard must have a weapon of some kind, 'be it only a mace or pike'. For the menfolk of Kingsdown it was more likely to be a shovel. Air-raid wardens checked village houses for infringements of blackout regulations and carried rattles to warn of imminent gas attack.

Kingsdown was at a high point on the North Downs and special wireless receivers were set up in towers in Cooper's Wood. On the night of 22 October 1943 the Kingsdown transmitter started broadcasts designed to interrupt and confuse German night-fighter controllers' orders to their pilots. The staff were Czech, Austrian and Polish. One early success was to talk down a German pilot and persuade him to land his fighter aircraft in a field at West Malling, then capture him, his plane and crew.

But that same year the Taylors' son Jim was killed in a flying accident within months of joining the air force. Recruitment in 1940 was for men aged twenty to forty. In 1943 the minimum age was lowered to eighteen. Jim was seventeen one day, eighteen the next and in the air force the day after. He was buried in the village churchyard of St Edmund King and Martyr.

Sidney Sinclair's Second Statement

Two weeks after being questioned by Sergeant Childerley, Sidney Sinclair was collected from Little Abington and taken to Cambridge county police station on 22 November 1946. It was a Friday. There were gales and wintry showers, a strike of slaughterhouse men and the 10,000th prefabricated aluminium house came off the production line. With the house delivered to a site at ten in the morning, a family could move in such furniture as they had by three in the afternoon.

Chief Inspector Fabian, Superintendent Smeed and Detective Sergeant Rawlings waited for Sinclair. All sat round a table. Fabian had double-checked the records: Sidney Sinclair had no previous convictions. He described his entrance: 'He entered the room boldly enough, a big thick-handed man with a bruiser's face, but there was something about him. "Surely this is an old lag," I thought.' There was something in Sidney's demeanour and expression, something etched into his features and bearing: an aspect of defiance perhaps, or of defeat, mendacity or cunning. Something Fabian could read for he had seen it many times.

Fabian introduced himself and the other officers then said: 'I have seen a statement made by you to Detective Sergeant

Childerley of Cambridge and I would like to go through it with you. I am investigating the murder of a woman at Wrotham Hill on 31st October 1946, the day you say in your statement you were on that road.'

Sidney said he doubted he could help but he would do so if that was possible.

Fabian had a hunch this man was guilty, but in the absence of witnesses or forensic evidence to prove it, he needed a confession. He began his patient technique of going over and over the suspect's account of events, waiting to see if the account changed, was added to or contradicted, or if he could trip him up. He was keen to note discrepancies, revelations, hesitations and to watch like a poker player for telltale clues of feelings. 'What did you say your name was?' Fabian began by asking. 'Sidney Sinclair' was the reply, but it sounded like a lie.

4

THE CRIMINAL

9. **Hagger,** Harold, 27, carman.
   Committed from Highgate, 13 Jan., 1926.
   Received in prison, 4 Jan., 1926.
   Offence—*1st Charge.*—Between 14 and 16 April, 1925, at Hornsey, stealing
   four mirrors, the property of the London & North Eastern Railway.
   2nd Charge.—On 20 and 22 Sept., 1924, at Hornsey, stealing a quantity of
   linen, the property of the Myddleton Laundry
   3rd Charge.—Between 22 and 24 Nov., 1924, breaking and entering the shop
   of the Mirror Laundry and stealing therein a quantity of linen, their
   property.
   Tried before ....
   Verdict or Plea ....

   Sentence or Order of the Court ....

Sidney Sinclair had a deep scar running across his forehead to the top of his nose. He was five foot six and stocky. In February 1940 when he met Daisy Emily Linsdell in Little Abington in Cambridgeshire, she thought him heroic in his army uniform. With his tattooed arms, scarred face and cockney accent he looked a fighting man. In civvies too, he had sartorial flair: his jackets tailored, his shirts clean, shoes polished, a flat cap or bowler hat. He gave her jewellery and was generous with cash, though he did not divulge its source. Such money allowed for treats and extras to the rations and meant Daisy could invest in war bonds by way of saving.

The village of Little Abington, on the north side of the river Granta and about eight miles from Cambridge, was surrounded by fields of wheat, oats and barley. In 1940 much of this land was commandeered by the army, with regiments of soldiers based in camps there. That was how Sidney Sinclair came to the area.

Daisy was thirty-four, of medium height, a slim good-looking woman 'who always had gentlemen friends'. She wore her brown hair in a bob with a fringe that had a white streak in it. She was a widow with two daughters, Ellen and Sheila. She got pregnant with Ellen when she was sixteen while working as a live-in maid for a wealthy family in Bedfordshire. The father was perhaps one of the well-to-do sons. Daisy was sent back home to her parents in Great Abington to have her baby.

Her mother Helena died a few months before Daisy met Sidney. In her teens she too had a child, Leonard, before she married George Oakley, a farm foreman in the village. They went on to have four more children, three girls and a boy. Daisy was the second.

Daisy, in her turn, married a local man, Cecil Linsdell, in 1931 when Ellen was eight. The whitewashed terraced cottage where they lived on the high street, 25 Little Abington, was once the village post office. They had a daughter, Sheila, but when she was six months old Cecil Linsdell died of a liver disease. He left no money and it was a struggle for Daisy to bring up two children on her own.

She was popular in the village, a good-natured friendly woman, a homemaker and housekeeper. In the large back garden she grew fruit and vegetables and kept chickens. She worked for a local farmer and got milk and butter free. She walked and biked eight miles each way to work. Her younger sister Flora lived at Royston and Daisy cycled the fourteen miles there and back in an afternoon to visit her.

The centrepiece of her cottage was the kitchen's large inglenook fireplace. Heat from the fire warmed the upstairs rooms. On bath nights she put the tin tub by it. She made coloured rag rugs to cover the brick floor, had comfortable armchairs, a scrubbed wooden table, a large sink. Opposite the kitchen, on the other side of the hallway, was the sitting room and another fireplace with bellows. A steep staircase led to two small upstairs bedrooms. Daisy had one, her daughters the other. In cold weather she warmed the beds with stone hot-water bottles.

Wooden screens, covered in fabric embroidered by her, stopped draughts from the cottage doors. Off the hallway in a cold walk-in pantry she hung rabbits and pheasants given her by locals. She kept a bucket in there for her and the children to pee in if the weather was cold or wet, or in the night. The lavatory, a hole cut in a wooden box, was in a wooden hut at the top end of the garden. It drained down into the vegetable patch. At the back of the house was a lean-to scullery with a large sink, a mangle and lines to hang washing in bad weather. Next to it was the coal and wood store, liked by slugs. Daisy and her daughters thought their cottage benignly haunted and talked of invisible hands touching their shoulders, a white presence going from one bedroom to the other, and rustlings in the thatch at night.

When Daisy met Sidney Sinclair she was apparently going out with a 'very nice officer' from the army camp who wanted to marry her, but she threw him over in favour of Sidney. She had no reason to doubt what he told her: that he was Sidney Sinclair, aged thirty-nine, a bachelor, a sapper with the Royal Engineers. Her daughters took an immediate dislike to this scar-faced burly man. They thought him ugly, did not want him in their house and were mystified and alarmed that their mother had taken up with him. Ellen, who was sixteen, worked at the nearby RAF base at Bassingbourn, which became a base for heavy American bomber planes in 1942. She was only home some weekends. She always brought her mother extras and luxuries like cigarettes and sweets. Sheila was nine and lived at home all the time.

Sidney and Daisy married on 20 March 1940 at the Cambridge Register Office. Daisy's neighbours, Norman and Minnie Watson, were witnesses. On the marriage certificate Sidney gave his father's name as George Sinclair, a deceased corporation dustman.

'My Right Name is Harold Hagger'

'How long has your name been Sidney Sinclair?' Fabian asked, but received no reply. He, Superintendent Smeed and Detective Sergeant Rawlings scrutinised the man sitting in front of them: his neat clothes, hand tremor, bitten nails, tattooed arms and defensive manner. There was an atmosphere of civility in the room, a fire burning in the grate, a sense of there being all the time in the world to chat. Fabian began to read aloud the statement Sinclair had made to Sergeant Childerley two weeks previously:

Statement of Sidney Sinclair, 25 Little Abington, Cambridgeshire, lorry driver aged 45 years who saith:
I am a lorry driver employed by Dickerson of Cambridge and I reside at 25 Little Abington Cambridgeshire.

About 10pm on Wednesday 30 October 1946 I left Little Abington driving an Albion 8 ton motor lorry no. AER 815 loaded with bricks for a cider works at East Malling Kent.

I travelled along the London to Bishop's Stortford Road and stopped at Judd's café on the London side of Bishop's Stortford. I arrived at this café . . .

Sidney stopped him. 'Wait a minute,' he said. 'You want me to be truthful, don't you?'

'Certainly,' Fabian replied.

'OK. My right name is Harold Hagger, but I've been known as Sid Sinclair for years.'

It seemed he wanted to cooperate. It was hard to know if he felt a need to come clean or had some cunning strategy of his own. Detective Sergeant Rawlings left the room to instruct Scotland Yard's Criminal Record Office to check on Harold Hagger. Fabian asked Sidney if as Harold he had ever been in trouble with the law. Sidney admitted he had been in prison a few times as a civilian and had a bit of trouble in the army, but all for small things and long ago and now he was settled with a wife and two daughters and had turned his life around. Fabian asked him to turn out his pockets. Sidney did so, and Fabian searched him. There was nothing incriminating concealed on him.

Fabian read on. Sidney looked impassive. Apart from the small matter of his name, perhaps he was reassured by the statement's veracity: he was a lorry driver employed by Dickerson of Cambridge, he lived at 25 Little Abington. He left home at 10pm on Wednesday 30 October 1946 driving an Albion 8-ton motor lorry loaded with bricks for a cider works at East Malling in Kent. He drove along the London to Bishop's Stortford road and stopped at Judd's café at 11.30pm and stayed there until about 3.45 next morning.

Fabian asked why he had stayed so long in this café in the small hours of the night. Sidney told him he knew many of the lorry drivers, liked the food and often stopped there. Had Fabian enquired further, he might have found that Judd's café, officially called the Acme Café, was a clearing house for stolen goods and run by a friend of Sidney's, Charlie Judd.

But murder was on Fabian's agenda, not the gallons of petrol, building materials and black-market goods off the backs of lorries that interested Charlie Judd. He continued with Sidney's journey: through the Blackwall tunnel, on to the Sidcup bypass. At about 6.30 that Thursday morning near the village of West Malling Sidney stopped to ask a cyclist where East Malling was. Some ten minutes later he arrived at the cider works. A man there told him he could not get unloaded until eight. He walked into the village to try to get a paper, then waited in his lorry until 7.55. He left the works just after nine.

Fabian wrote it all down. He voiced surprise that it had taken Sidney three hours to get from Judd's café to the East Malling cider works. Had he perhaps stopped for some reason he had failed to explain? Sidney said his account was correct, except he had not included details of two stops he made because the lorry's radiator was boiling and a third stop because of traffic lights.

Fabian continued to show interest in Sidney's account of this unremarkable journey. After he left the cider works, he headed back via Bishop's Stortford, stopped again at Judd's café and at 12.30am made a call from a public telephone in Stansted Mountfitchet to his boss to get instructions for his next job. He saw no one on the road, picked no one up, no one thumbed a lift. It was a routine delivery, just like any other working day.

Fabian then, in his practised urbane conversational manner, mentioned that the crocheted string bag carried by the murdered woman had been found washed up in Clare Park lake and that it could have been thrown in the stream by the cider works because the stream fed the lake.

Sinclair collapsed forward 'as if he had been clubbed', Fabian noted. 'His face had gone yellow.' In an aspect of defeat, he sat by the fire with his head in his hands. It was as if his life stopped with this information. Fabian asked him if he felt all right, or if he would like to see a doctor. Sidney said he was all right. 'I get a bit of a head sometimes.' He said he had seen a doctor not long ago about it and about his eyes.

He went on sitting in front of the fire. Fabian let him reflect. He ordered a hot meal for him from the police canteen. It was rabbit. Sidney declined it, saying he never ate rabbit, and asked instead for a cup of tea and a piece of cake. This was brought to him. Detective Sergeant Rawlings returned with information from the Criminal Record Office; Harold Hagger had sixteen convictions, including one for assault on a woman.

Sidney Sinclair's Second Statement: Friday 22 November 1946

For a while the other police officers left Fabian and Sidney sitting by the coal fire alone. Fabian offered him cigarettes, told him to take his time and, like an attentive sympathetic friend, coaxed information out of him and appeared to believe what he was told. Sidney responded to the invitation from this avuncular or even fatherly man to confide and be helpful. Fabian seemed to sympathise and understand that he, Sidney Sinclair, Harold Hagger, was caught into circumstances for which he could not be held responsible.

After his tea and cake Sidney said, 'Look here, guv'nor, I'm worried to death. I found the attaché case and chucked it away.

When I read in the paper it was the murdered woman's I got the wind up, but true as I sit here I never saw any woman.'

Fabian was adept at concealing pleasure, at showing no surprise. But Sidney had made a mistake of the sort for which Fabian lay in wait. It was such a mistake that professionals who deal in the workings of the mind might have construed it as a need to confess or a desire to be punished. Wide publicity had been given in the press about the missing yellow string bag, but at no time had information been released from the police that the murdered woman had with her an attaché case, or that an attaché case belonging to her had been found by them.

Sidney was not ahead in this process of incrimination. It was a relief to him to be obliging to nice Mr Fabian. He perhaps hoped such apparent cooperation might save his life. Fabian told him a man's vest belonging to the murdered woman had also been found. Was that perhaps in the attaché case too, along with the string bag?

The other officers returned. They again all sat round the table.

'I'd like to get down exactly where you found the case and where you threw it,' Fabian told Sinclair.

'I wish I'd come up before, but I'll tell you exactly what I did,' Harold assured him. This second statement was written down by Detective Sergeant Rawlings, then read out to Sidney for his comment and approval.

I am 45 years of age. I was born on 27 March 1901. At present I am employed as a gardener by Mr Joshua Taylor at Abington. I made a statement to Detective Sergeant Childerley of Cambridge Police on Saturday evening 9 November 1946, describing my movements on the evening of Wednesday 30 October and Thursday 31 October.

The statement I made has been read to me by Chief Inspector Fabian and in the main it is quite true and correct but there are one or two other things I can tell you.

In addition to the twice I stopped because my radiator was getting hot, I also pulled up on the road as I saw an attaché case lying on the verge near the kerb. I can't say exactly where this was as I am not familiar with the road. I do remember that it was after I had stopped at some lights, coasted down the hill and then climbed to the top of a long slope, it was about three miles further on from this point. As I have said when I pulled up and saw the attaché case I got down from the cabin, turned it over and had a look at it. Inside I found a yellow net bag which had some jam sandwiches wrapped up in paper in it; a vest, it wasn't a woman's vest; and a pair of woman's gloves. I picked up the case and took it into the lorry intending to have a look and see what was in it later on.

I continued on the road and didn't stop again until I asked the cyclist, as I said before, the way to East Malling cider works. As I told Sergeant Childerley, I turned right off the main road by the council yard and went down a lane and turned left to the cider works. When I stopped by the main gate, and after I had asked where the foreman was, I sat in my cab and had a look at the things in the attaché case. I decided that none of them were any good to keep. I had a good look at the gloves, and thought if they were any good I would use them for driving, but they were too small, they were women's gloves.

When I drove my lorry to the back of the works, like I'd been told, I went through a gateway on to a concrete road and there was a small stream on my offside. When I got almost to the back of the factory I met one of the cider works lorries trying to get out. I pulled forward a bit off the road to let it pass, and then I jumped out of my cabin and threw the yellow net bag and pair of gloves into the stream which was just nearby. I then shifted my lorry to where they wanted the bricks put, and after they were unloaded I pulled out the same way as I first came in and up the lane to the council yard. About half way down the lane I threw the vest and the attaché case over the hedge on my right-hand side. Before I threw the attaché case over the hedge I tore the lid off. The jam sandwiches which were in the net bag I threw out in the lane near the council yard.

A day or so after I found the attaché case and other things, I saw in the paper that a woman had been found murdered at Wrotham Hill on the day I was there and the police were looking for a yellow string bag they said had been stolen and I got the wind up and decided to say nothing about it. I also read that they were looking for a puppy but I never saw a puppy.

This statement has been read to me and is all correct except that you have left out that it was my offside verge where I found the attaché case. *Sidney Sinclair.*

Statement taken by Chief Inspector Fabian, New Scotland Yard, in the presence of Detective Superintendent Smeed, Kent County Constabulary, written down and read over by Detective Sergeant H. Rawlings, New Scotland Yard, in the presence of Chief Inspector Fabian and Detective Superintendent Smeed.

Fabian was satisfied. It had been a good morning's work. He saw no need to rush matters or be heavy-handed with this man who was so malleable and naive in his duplicity and who seemed to trust him. He would tease further confession from him, of that he felt sure. Sidney as he told his story was halting and vague about just where he had stopped his lorry, where he found the case, vest and bag, why he threw them into a stream and hedgerows. Fabian had heard enough to know that this was not the account of a lorry driver, on a legitimate journey, finding bits and pieces on the road. It was an account, he believed, of a murderer anxiously and clumsily trying to conceal evidence. What he wanted to hear, get down in writing and give as evidence to the courts was that Harold Hagger also known as Sidney Sinclair had murdered Dagmar Petrzy-walski at Wrotham Hill before dawn on the morning of Thursday 31 October 1946.

This was a time of austerity. Everything was rationed or in short supply. Every chance find came in handy. Had Harold Hagger discerned, in the crepuscular light before dawn, a case, bag and gloves lying by some peculiar chance on the grass verge of an arterial road, he might have kept them, however humble they were, might have given them to his wife or stepdaughters. Had he subsequently read a newspaper account of murder, he might have taken the bag and bits to the police. If he feared arousing suspicion because of previous convictions, he might have destroyed such evidence at that point. Then nothing would have been there to incriminate him as the murderer of Dagmar Petrzywalski. As with Sheila Martin, the case would have stayed open and unresolved.

And if the case, the bag, the vest, the gloves had seemed of no use to him at the time, he might just have binned them in a less anxious way. And it would have been a peculiar coincidence for him to have found the attaché case but overlooked the blue shoe, seen by William Crittenden and picked up by Joe Hammond some yards away from where a murdered woman lay in shrubbery.

Fabian and Detective Sergeant Rawlings suggested Sidney accompany them by car over the route from his home in Little Abington to East Malling where he delivered the bricks. It was politely put, but it was not an invitation: it was an imperative and a ploy. Fabian had a hunch the trip might be revealing in small ways that would accrue to large. Sinclair was not charged with anything. He was helping the police with their enquiries. He was not a man to ask to see his solicitor. He had no solicitor to see. There was no trained and wily brain for him to turn to for protection or advice or to guide him to more subtle practice of the art of evasion and skin-saving.

The Therfield Haggers

Harold Hagger's parents, William and Annie, were childhood sweethearts born in the village of Therfield in Hertfordshire in the 1870s. Royston, the nearest town, was a three-mile walk across the fields. Haggers had lived in the village for 200 years and were one of the dominant families.* Others were the Bullards, Gatwards and Andersons. Haggers thought them-

---

* Harold's nephew still lives in the family cottage

selves a rung up from the Bullards, despite generations of inter-marriage between the two families – Annie was a Bullard, her grandmother was Lucy Hagger.

Villagers were agricultural labourers: ploughmen, black-smiths, thatchers. Most cottages were thatched and at harvest time the haystacks too. They lived in tied cottages owned by the gentry, the farming landowners who occupied the manor houses and whose land they worked. If a villager stopped being employed by a particular farmer – not usually through choice – he and his family lost the cottage and all that went with it.

Therfield Victorian village life was hard but with a sense of community and connection to the land that newcomers, in the years before the Second World War, could not achieve. Villagers came from and created families of up to thirteen children, though there were seldom more than seven children of a large family living at home at any one time: one or two would die – a stillbirth, measles, the 'flu, tuberculosis; when they were four-teen the girls 'went into service' as domestic workers, or left to marry when they were seventeen, usually a boy from the same or a nearby village.

It was a bleak village, high up. There were plenty of pubs – the Bell, the Chequers, the Greyhound, the White Horse – where men drank beer, smoked pipes and took snuff. There was a village policeman, the oilman did his rounds with fuel for lamps, the baker delivered loaves, the fish man came on Fridays. There were two general stores and a school. Most villagers were illiterate, owned next to nothing and went to church or chapel at Christmas and for baptisms, weddings and funerals, though among the Hagger clan one dissenter,

Lavender Hagger, voiced unbelief in God and did not have his children baptised.

The cottage where William Hagger grew up was typical of the village. It had three bedrooms: one for his parents, one for the girls, one for the boys. In a shed at the back of the cottage was a copper with a fire under it where the washing was boiled and stirred with an old broom handle. Monday was washday. Afterwards, the hot water from the copper was used for a bath. There was an ample garden for vegetables and with space to keep a pig and chickens.

The railway came to Royston in the 1850s and linked the villagers to a wider world. Other technological advance meant the mechanisation of farm machinery so agricultural workers lost their jobs. Machines created an employers' market. One man could plough a dozen fields. Farmers paid labourers the minimum they could get away with. Men had to leave their communities, look elsewhere for work, move to Cambridge or London to find employment as stokers, railway porters, street sweepers. They became industrial rather than agricultual labourers, the urban rather than the rural poor.

William and five of his brothers migrated to London between 1885 and 1900 in search of paid work. None had been taught to read or write. When Annie Bullard was sent to London 'in service', William used to walk from Therfield to see her at the weekends. It became one of her apocryphal stories of his devotion, for the distance was forty miles. She said he did it countless times. In 1892 they married at All Saints Parish Church in West Ham, known as 'the Cathedral of the East End'. William found work on the expanding railways: he started as a porter, then worked as a general labourer, laying tracks. They began married life at 1 Moreland Street in Islington, in a two-bed-roomed terraced house shared with Annie's sister Emily, who was married to a builder's labourer, Robert Moir. For Annie it was a reluctant migration. Therfield was her home and she did not take to city life. By the time of the 1901 census nine years later, the two families had eight children between them. There was also a lodger to help with the rent. The Haggers' was the most populated house in the street. Their neighbours were plumbers, railway workers and building labourers.

Babies were an inevitable consequence of sex and for Annie Hagger pregnancy was a more or less constant state. She begat a Hagger dynasty worthy of Genesis chapter 4. Her family was her world, she had no life outside of it, but it meant endless provision and it was hard to herald each and every birth as yet another miracle and unequivocal delight. Survival was a struggle. There was no such thing as privacy, and a wash, a change of clothes and a square meal were luxuries. And she pined for the countryside, specifically for Therfield. To be poor in the country meant living simply with the compensation of clean air, home-grown food and the wonder of the lanes and hedgerows. It was easier in the country to feed well. In the city being poor meant squalid quarters, making do and anonymity.

In 1900 a third of urban poor lived close to starvation and in fear of the workhouse. For William Hagger money to provide for his ever-growing family was always a problem. There was not enough of it. There was damp in the walls and there were fleas in the beds. The children scavenged for wood to burn to heat the place, drank from jam jars, had no sheets. Clothes were darned and handed down. A bit of meat was eked out with too many potatoes in the shepherd's pie.

William worked for the railways until 1901, then as a corpo-ration dustman. He was a burly man used to heavy lifting, a regular family man, and working for Hornsey council brought security.

The dustbins, of galvanised steel, had a handle on each side; dustmen tramped through the hallways of houses to the back-yard, hoicked them on to their backs, tipped the motley con-tents of household waste and ashes from fires into a horse-drawn cart, then took the putrid load to the dustyard where it was burned in great chimneys. William wore a hat with a flap at the back to protect his neck. It was dirty, tiring work, his right shoulder stiffened and in middle age he could not turn his neck. But there were perks: a gift of a penny or two on Boxing Day, a tip to take away large unneeded items that could then be sold. And there was a fair amount of prof-itable recycling: dust mixed with horse droppings made manure, ash was used for making bricks, old bottles fetched three shillings a hundredweight, rags, bones, bits of tin, old boots and shoes, paper, all had a value. The shift from horse-drawn to motorised carts in the 1930s meant easier work and promotion for William.

Childhood was not to be lingered over. The pattern was to marry young and move out to rented rooms nearby. The Hagger dynasty became a network of cousins, in-laws, aunts and uncles. They were a close family who looked out for each other in sick-ness and hardship, got by with money, were streetwise and without airs.

In 1906 a Liberal government was elected with a large majority. It introduced welfare reforms: compensation for injuries at work, a state pension of five shillings for those over seventy, insurance for workers in time of sickness. But social reform was piecemeal and uncertain. The Haggers had few rights and no influence in shaping society. Their lives passed unremarked except on censuses and certificates of birth, marriage and death, and records of army service or hospital admission.

William Henry (Bill), the eldest child, born 10 May 1893 eight months after William and Annie married, and named after his father, worked first as a general labourer on the railways, joined the army as a private and married Violet Reeves in Hornsey when he was twenty-seven. They lived round the corner from his parents at 108 Myddleton Road, Hornsey. His first boy, born seven months after he married, did not survive.

Elsie Emily, the second child, born 1895, worked in the laundry when she was fourteen and married Bluey Clear when she was seventeen. Third came Evelyn Lucy (Eva) in 1897. She worked as a domestic, married Dave Haggerty, a plasterer, when she was seventeen and had her first daughter nine months later. Fourth, in 1898, came Percy Frederick, known as Fred, who worked as a milkman and married Kate Spalding when he was twenty-two. Fifth came Harold, nicknamed Woggle, born 27 March 1901. On the 1901 census, four days after his birth, Harold was listed as 'baby' for he had not yet been named. Sixth was Ethel Anne, known as Nancy, for names were a shifting identification, born in 1903. In her teens she had two sons who joined the navy, then in her thirties she married James Simpson, known as Jim, who ran a paper stall at Turnpike Lane. He called out *Star*, *News* and *Standard* and made good money, for as vendor he kept 25 per cent of the selling price. He sold thousands – two hundred quire on a

Saturday night. Nancy had a third son, Barry, with Jim, but she was not much of a mother so her sister Elsie looked after the boy. Nance and Woggle were close and knocked around together as kids. She was good at darts but drank, smoked, got into fights and was altogether wild. Her bad behaviour caused a rift between her and Elsie. Seventh, born in 1905, was Sidney George, known as John, who in his turn also worked as a corporation dustman. He married Elizabeth Balls in 1929 when he was twenty-four.

Two years after the birth of Annie's seventh child her mother, Mary Ann Bullard, died in 1907 aged sixty-one. The family congregated in the Therfield church for the funeral. Annie did not think her father Henry would cope without his wife, but he would not leave the village. The idea of the city was anathema to him. That same year Annie's eighth child, Edith Mary, known as Edie, was born. When she was twenty-six and almost on the shelf by the standards of the household, Edie married Arthur Carter.

Henry Bullard outlived his wife by scarcely a year and died aged fifty-nine in 1908. Again the family congregated in the village church. That same year William and Annie moved to a larger house – it had five rooms – at 28 Campsbourne Road in Hornsey. It was to be their home for forty-five years. William's brother Charles lived with his family at number 25 and also worked for Hornsey Council as a dustman.

Ernest, the ninth child, born 1909, became a milkman but died of leukaemia when he was twenty. Tenth came Arthur Frank, known as Frank, who married Beryl Brewster when he was twenty-three. He was born in 1911. The census that year recorded twelve Haggers at 28 Campsbourne Road – ten children ranging from four months to nineteen years. As ever they also had a lodger, he worked as a night storekeeper for Pickford's removal firm and slept in the boys' bedroom during the day. The rent he paid meant a bit more food. Florie May, known as Flo, born 1912, was the eleventh child. She married Leslie Stokley when she was thirty-two but had no children. Twelfth, in 1915, was Harry Hagger. Perhaps William and Annie forgot they already had a Harold or had used up their supply of names. Also in 1915 William's mother Eliza died. She was seventy and was buried in Therfield of course.

Harry the Second worked as a welder and married Elsie Clarke in Edmonton in 1941 when he was twenty-six. Doris was thirteenth but only lived a year. Last came Ivy May, born in 1917. She married George Taylor, known as Titch, in 1947 and their twins, Susan and Robin, were born the next year but only the girl survived.

William and Annie's family was then complete. For Annie childbearing had spanned twenty years. In middle age she became a big shuffling silver-haired woman who had difficulty walking. She liked to put a pinch of snuff up her nose. They had a dog and she used to give him a pinch of snuff too.

Harold

Harry the First was a problem: a wilful dodgy boy, a feral creature who did nothing right, lied and thieved and bit his nails. He was the fifth child, and there was too much hardship and struggle to try to understand his physical and emotional needs. Discipline was a whack round the head, rewards were as modest as jam on bread. You could not rely on Woggle. If he saw something he wanted he took it. He didn't see the wrong in it, only the gratification if it worked. It was his tactic for survival and a behaviour pattern that became entrenched. He was impulsive, aggressive and anxious and his life quickly became chaotic.

Sigmund Freud had written *Studies in Hysteria* and *Psychopathology of Everyday Life* by the time Harold Hagger was born, but his theories and observations were not of help to a dustman's son in north London at the beginning of the twentieth century.

Half a century later a Stanford professor of psychology, Walter Mischel, did an experiment with 653 four-year-old children that would have resonated with Harold. Mischel was born in 1930 in Vienna. When the Nazis invaded Austria in 1938 his family moved to the United States, to Brooklyn. He was interested in how personality is shaped. In his experiment each child was taken into a room and left alone sitting at a table in front of a plate with a single marshmallow on it and a bell beside it. There was not much else in the room. Mischel told the boy or girl the marshmallow was theirs, but if he or she waited fifteen minutes without eating it, he'd come back and give them another, so then they'd have two to eat. If they couldn't wait, they should ring the bell on the table and he'd hurry in and then they could eat the one in front of them, but they'd forfeit the other.

Mischel spied on each child left alone. Thirty per cent held out and waited for an eternity of fifteen minutes. Often their struggle was acute: they licked the marshmallow, sniffed it, picked a bit off it, squeezed it, grimaced or squinted at it, looked away from it, pulled at their pigtails, rocked back and forward, but earned their double reward when he returned. Of the others, most held out for an average of three minutes, then rang the bell. Some did not wait until he was out of the room before eating the marshmallow.

Fourteen years later aspects of these children's behaviour were followed up. Those who could not or did not delay gratification were more likely to have behavioural problems, low self-esteem and difficulty in passing tests, paying attention and maintaining friendships. Those who waited had better coping skills, were more socially competent, self-assertive, trustworthy, dependable and academically successful.

At no time in his life would Harold Hagger have waited for the door to close before eating the marshmallow. He had no concept of deferred gratification. Nothing in his childhood had led him to trust that a second marshmallow would be forthcoming or to doubt that if he did not eat the first one fast someone else would get it.

He was born at 1 Moreland Street, Holloway on 27 March 1901, the year before his father's promotion from railway labourer to corporation dustman. He picked up reading and writing in so far as it interested him but because of his learning difficulty he was in the bottom class of Park Road elementary school in Crouch Hill. He would not be told what to do or think, to sit down or be quiet, or remember that Reykjavik was the capital of Iceland. He was naughty and disruptive and of low intelligence his teachers said. He saw no point to school, so he truanted. He bunked off on his own or with a couple of boys, thieved cigarettes, picked pockets, stole food, settled grievances with his fists. At home his parents and siblings became intolerant of him. They gave him few chances. Shape up or get out was the message to Woggle. Poor the Hagger family might be, but they viewed themselves as respectable and hard-working and would not give time or room to this troublemaker and slur on their name.

His first job, aged fourteen, was as an errand boy in the Farringdon Road. It suited him and he kept it for two and a half years. It complemented his burgeoning criminal career. But he needed to get away from home. He was not wanted and there was nothing for him, only a stream of puling babies. In 1916 his sister Doris died having only lived a year, his mother was pregnant with her fourteenth child before Doris was buried and there was a war on. Real men were fighting the Boche across the Channel.

Harold got tattooed on both his forearms, and on 2 August went to Mill Hill army recruitment centre to enlist. He said he was eighteen years and four months old and that he was a baker. In fact he was sixteen. He was posted to a training regiment in Luton and five days later charged with using obscene language to an officer and confined to barracks for four days. This set the tone for his army career. Five days after his return to duty he bunked off home without telling anyone. The military police found him at 28 Campsbourne Road, charged him with missing roll-call and deprived him of four days' pay. Two weeks later he overstayed his pass by forty-eight hours and a further three days' pay were docked. Then on 4 October his father, perceiving that his son's military career could only disgrace the name of Hagger, turned up at Luton with Harold's birth certificate proving he was only sixteen and asked for his release. His father may have saved his life. Harold could have found himself on the battlefields of Flanders. He was discharged from the army on 4 October 1917 having served a total of sixty-four days, most of them confined to barracks or absent without leave.

He spent a torrid few weeks at home, then two weeks before Christmas 1917 when caught stealing shoes in Highgate, he assaulted the policeman who arrested him. Charged, he gave his father's name, William Hagger. Harold had become a burden and was not an acceptable person to be. It was the start of a string of shifting aliases: William Hagger, Bill Hagger, Bertie Thomas, William Smith, Fred Hall, William Cook, Sidney Sinclair. He changed his name at a whim to control his life, as a cover for trouble, to avoid apprehension and in pursuit of an identity other than his own. For this first offence he got three months for theft and two for the assault. His father disowned him and forbade him ever to return to the family home. His brother Harry and sister Nance went on seeing him for a while. Woggle might be well off the rails but he was their brother.

In the pubs and cafés Harold liked to appear as a man's man, a regular guy. He swore, bought his rounds, played cards, boasted about girls. But convictions accrued. He was more often in prison than out. His crimes were opportunistic, petty, bungled and solitary: loitering to pick pockets, stealing shoes, shawls, jewellery, cigarettes, cash from a meter, being drunk, assaulting a policeman. His social group became old lags who knew a crooked trick or two: ways to pick a lock or offload stolen goods. In gaol he was known as Basher Hagger. Hitting out was a way to make his presence felt.

Fabian and Harold Go Over the Route: 22 November 1946

The car in which Fabian and Rawlings took Sidney back to Wrotham Hill was comfortable and smart. Fabian made the journey seem like a day out. He and Rawlings were not in uniform. He told Sidney he hoped, by covering the route again, to jog his memory about exactly what happened on the morning of the murder.

They drove through Stump Cross, Littlebury, Newport. The litany of names became a reassurance, like teatime conversation where contentious matters are avoided. At Stansted Mountfitchet Sidney showed Fabian the telephone box where he phoned Alan Bell at Dickerson's at about 12.30 on that Thursday three weeks back and received orders to pick up eight tons of barley from Chrishall Grange. At Bishop's Stortford he pointed out Judd's café – his favourite eating place, where he stopped for about three hours during the night of Wednesday 30 October. They drove through Harlow, Epping, Woodford Green to Stratford, through the Blackwall tunnel to Blackheath, then on to the Sidcup bypass. This journey was the unremarkable one Sidney had meant to make without the screams, the yapping dog, that woman's provocation and wretched death and all the stuff that made his nerves play up so he had to hand in his job. This was the actual journey, not the one to be buried deep and never mentioned.

At Swanley, Sidney pointed out the traffic lights where he waited because the lights were against him. His lorry's radiator first boiled over at the top of Farningham Hill, he told Fabian. What happened? Fabian asked. What had he done? How long did it take him? Sidney had stopped, loosened the cap, topped up with water from a can in the cabin. It took about ten minutes or a quarter of an hour. Fabian's apparent obsession with such trivia was a reassurance. At Farningham Gosse, just before Kingsdown, he showed Fabian the haystacks where for about five minutes he said he again stopped because the radiator was boiling. This, Fabian knew, was where Dagmar was seen hitchhiking, by the Bennett farmers, at 5.10 on the morning of her murder. Sidney did not know they told the police about 'a heavily laden lorry' travelling toward her in the opposite direction to themselves.

Near Kingsdown Sidney said, 'Go easy, it's near here I found the case.' About 200 yards from the Portobello Inn they all got out of the car and he pointed to where he said he had seen the attaché case and stopped and picked it up. A little lane, Forge Lane, forked off beside this spot and Fabian knew in his policeman's mind that this was where Sidney Sinclair had turned off the road and stopped his lorry with Dagmar Petrzy walski in it.

They went on to East Malling with Sidney, the navigator, telling them not quite all they wanted to know. He told Fabian to turn right by the council yard into Winterfield Lane, showed him where he waited by the Time Office at the entrance to the cider works and how he drove round the outside of the works and on to the concrete road. 'Stop here,' he said as if enjoying it all. 'This is where I pulled out to let one of the firm's lorries get by.' They all got out of the car and walked a few paces to the stream that ran through the yard. 'This is where I chucked the gloves and the bag.' It was all so ordinary, this exercise in reconstruction. Murder did not come into it. They were calm, these governors, impassive, they voiced no disbelief, he was

137

helping them, telling them what they needed to know. The details of a workman's day.

They left the cider mill and drove back down Winterfield Lane. 'That's where I chucked the vest,' Sidney said, pointing to a bit of hedge on this journey down memory lane. He and Rawlings got out of the car, the more accurately to determine the spot. 'It's about here I chucked out the attaché case,' he said, a little further on. Again they got out of the car and inspected the hedge.

Near the junction of the A20 Sidney again told Fabian to stop. 'This is where I slung the sandwiches,' he said. Again he and Rawlings peered into the grass. 'I expect the bloody rats have eaten them by now,' Sidney said.

Back at West Malling police station Fabian told him, 'I'd like to get down in statement form the spots you pointed out to Sergeant Rawlings and me.' 'Yes, that's all right,' Sidney said.

Rawlings began transcribing a third statement for Sinclair to approve. Each was quantitatively different from the one before. The route taken was the same, but somehow now there was an attaché case, a string bag, a vest, jam sandwiches. As such quotidian detail accrued, each embellishment and addition brought the noose a little closer to the neck of Sidney Sinclair and his aliases.

Harold's Criminal Career 1918–25

If Harold Hagger saw something he wanted he took it, if he disliked a task he would not go on with it, if angered he lashed out. His second criminal conviction came in June 1918: six weeks for assaulting a policeman in Enfield. He was seventeen. Prison had become a revolving door, his career as a recidivist entrenched. Prison was as much home as anywhere, he gravitated towards it, had no home when out of it and did not seek to avoid it by refraining from criminal behaviour. His attempts to avoid arraignment were not of a reforming sort.

He viewed himself as a victim at odds with the world. Prison was an indignity but no more uncomfortable than his childhood home, and there were men like himself to talk to, play cards with, learn a few tips from. He took the code of honour of prison life. He learned who were the bent screws, how to steal from unattended cars, how to sell knocked-off goods, where to find cheap lodgings and women who did not cost much. He became imprisoned by the consequences of his lifestyle, though exhortation to change glided over him. To confuse the police about his prison record he often changed his name with aliases credible to his class; all the men he became bore an unnerving resemblance to Harold Hagger.

Within weeks of his release he was back inside for three months for stealing money. He then joined the army, the Royal Horse Artillery in Woolwich. He enlisted as William Cook and worked briefly as a driver: he had learned to drive in his father's dustcart, no licence was needed and it was a useful skill for a man who wanted to avoid the police and army authorities.

The military was not a difficult profession to enter. Harold found he could desert from one regiment, then sign up with another under a different name. Eight hundred and eighty thousand soldiers from the United Kingdom were killed between 1914 and 1918. Few checks were made on those who volunteered to serve their country in this way.

He was a committed rather than a cunning crook. Being a soldier was a way to deflect attention from those who pursued him for his misdemeanours. When he deserted he worked as a butcher, a lorry-driver's mate, a labourer, a petrol-pump attendant. He was mainly London-based, but moved to different towns if arrest seemed imminent. Usually he found cheap lodgings and an obliging landlady. Wherever he went he picked pockets at markets, stole from shops, burgled places when owners were out. By the age of twenty he had a string of convictions.

In November 1919 he was given six months for stealing a revolver. What he intended to do with it was not clear. In March 1921 it was a year for stealing shawls from a shop. The sentence was harsh and offended his notion of fair retribution. He appealed against it, unsuccessfully. A year later he got six months for loitering in north London to pick pockets. On his release he was identified as William Smith, a deserter from the East Kent Regiment.

A fatalism set in that villainy was his life. He became careless of detection or punishment, for he had nothing to lose. Stealing was a sport, an addiction and an occupation; turning his head this way and that, maybe he was seen, maybe not. Released from gaol he gravitated toward the street where his family lived, though he was not allowed into their house and sightings of him were kept from his mother. The charges stacked up: in June 1923 it was eighteen months for three cases of shop-breaking in Bedford, in September 1924 three months for stealing linen from the Myddleton laundry in Hornsey, and in April 1925 he pleaded guilty to the theft of four mirrors from the London and North Eastern Railway at Hornsey station.

Harold's Accident 1925

A month after robbing the LNER at Hornsey, Harold was seen 300 miles away on 22 May 1925 stealing a man's overcoat and other clothes from a caravan in Mealsgate, a village near the town of Wigton in Cumbria. He ran off, but was picked up by the police two weeks later, 70 miles away in Preston in Lancashire. He was twenty-four and gave his home address as 28 Campsbourne Road, Hornsey. PC Reginald Troughton was assigned to take him from Preston borough police station back by train to Wigton to be tried at the court there.

PC Troughton was forty, the eldest son of a shoemaker, born in Westmoreland and married for twenty years with six children. Harold was handcuffed to him and they caught the 1.32pm train from Preston to Carlisle. Harold found the proximity intolerable. He told Troughton he had a stomach upset, so twice was taken to the lavatory. In the lavatory, still handcuffed but at least not chained to Troughton, it occurred to him to try to escape through the train window. At Carlisle they changed trains and boarded the 4.35 to Wigton. Harold had been three hours shackled to Troughton and had had no food or cigarettes. As soon as they got on the train, he again said he needed to use the lavatory. Troughton made him wait until the train left the station, then escorted him to the lavatory next to the compartment they were in. He unlocked the handcuff from his own wrist and waited in the corridor outside the door. Harold was in there a few seconds before asking Troughton for some paper. Troughton gave him an envelope he had in his pocket. Harold locked the door from the inside, covered his fist with the envelope, broke the window with the handcuffs and jumped through the window on to the line.

Troughton did not hear the sound of shattering glass over the noise of steam from the engine and the clatter of wheels, but after a minute a passenger facing the rear of the train shouted that a man in handcuffs had jumped on to the track. Troughton pulled the emergency chain, which did not work. He tried another part of the chain but the train did not stop until it reached the next station, Dalston, three miles from Carlisle. The station master alerted the signalman, then Troughton ran back along the track with William James Burrows, a station porter of 17 Scotland Road, Carlisle. They found Harold half a mile down the track with his head and shoulders over the inside rail of the down line and his legs on the four-foot gap between the two lines. He appeared conscious but did not speak. His face was badly bruised and his scalp lacerated. Troughton and Burrows carried him off the line and laid him on the grass. Burrows ran back to find a doctor. Four men arrived and carried Harold to Dalston station on an improvised stretcher. A Dr Doughty dressed his wounds. The station master phoned Superintendent Ernest Stewart at Carlisle county police station and told him a man had jumped from a train and was seriously injured. Stewart sent the police motor-ambulance and a police sergeant to take Harold to Cumberland Infirmary and keep guard over him.

Doctors from the infirmary reported that Harold was severely shocked and concussed, had a large lacerated wound on the top of his scalp and another above his right eye, serious injuries to his body and hands, a fracture to the right side of his pelvis, a dislocated iliac bone and a possible fracture at the base of his skull. They said he might die and his next of kin should be informed.

Stewart phoned the Hampstead police who went round to William and Annie Hagger and told them that in the hospital's opinion it was highly probable Harold's injuries would prove fatal. William and Annie said they could not visit him. They had no money for the fare.

Despite the pessimistic prognosis, Harold was only in hospital for twenty days. On 26 June he was discharged into police custody, taken by police car to Preston police station and put in a cell. He walked with a stick and had a large raw wound on the right side of his head. A week later at Preston Magistrates' Court he was sentenced to six months on two charges of larceny: stealing clothing from a caravan and stealing a gent's overcoat. He was cared for in the prison hospital at Preston until judged well enough to be returned to a cell. By the time of his discharge on 9 December 1925 his head wound had healed into a straggling scar and he was described as fit and healthy. But he maintained that after this accident he suffered headaches, particularly at the front of his head, that these were made worse by noise, that he had dizzy spells, easily became irritated and that his hands trembled.

Harold and the Girl from Bolton 1926

It was prison policy to clear the cells at Christmas time of troublesome but minor offenders like Harold, though in December 1925 he, like many recidivists, had nowhere in particular to go. Prison was a roof and a bed of sorts. Outside, what to do with the days was a problem and occupation of any sort hard to find. Harold moved around the country looking for casual work and things to steal. At Bolton near Manchester, he met a girl, dated her for a few days, spent Christmas with her and promised her everything including marriage. But then in the new year, when he went down to London to do some thieving, he was arrested and sent to Brixton prison for three months.

From Brixton in February 1926 he applied to the court for day release to marry the girl from Bolton. His application was passed to the Secretary of State and refused. His pedigree, the Home Office commented, was 'not edifying'; his sentence was short, he could marry when freed. While Harold was in Brixton his grandfather Alfred Hagger died and the family assembled in Therfield for his funeral.

On his release Harold was immediately reconvicted on three accounts of larceny and shop breaking, committed before his troubles at Preston. He was given a stiff twenty-month sentence in Pentonville prison in north London.

He thought the sentence unduly long and felt resentful and aggrieved. If compelled to do time he wanted it at least to be in Manchester so he could be near the girl from Bolton. On Sunday 11 April he smashed up his cell and injured himself.

'Sir,' James Cater the duty prison officer wrote to the governor:

I respectfully beg to state for your information that at about 4.45pm on 11.4.1926, whilst I was patrolling C. Hall I heard a smashing of Glass which I located on C4/63, the Cell being occupied by No.93 Harold Hagger. When I located him he was hacking at his throat with a piece of his chamber pot which he had broken. I immediately informed the Orderly Officer. The following articles were broken viz:

1 Chamber Lid

9 Panes of Glass

1 Chamber Pot

1 Electric light Globe

1 Pair of Slippers

1 Stool

1 Pillow

3 Blankets

1 Rug

2 Sheets

1 Night Shirt

I am Sir

Your Obedient Servant

James Cater

Harold was despatched to the prison hospital for a report. He told the doctor he was fed up and was going to do himself in. In his report the doctor described him as a 'somewhat impulsive bad tempered man who had in the past given a lot of trouble'. There was, he said, no evidence of insanity and the damage to his neck was trivial.

Three days later, back in his cell, Harold was visited by the prison chaplain. He complained to him of the over-long sentence and the unfairness of his treatment; his 'young lady' lived near Manchester. But, the chaplain reported, in a previous sentence Harold had given much trouble about another girl. 'He is really at heart up against everything and everybody, is bent on a criminal career and to my mind made this attempt only to trouble the authorities. He is a hopeless criminal, though so young.' The chaplain spent his days exhorting prisoners to repent and find salvation through the example and love of Christ, but young hopeless criminals like Harold seemed to have made a pact with the devil.

The governor endorsed the assessment that Harold's violence was not a determined suicide attempt but merely the behaviour of a bad-tempered impulsive man, 'a troublesome man. I knew him at Preston.' Harold was written off as incorrigible. Aged twenty-five he was in deep trouble: he self-harmed, stacked up prison sentences, formed no stable relationships, got into fights, had no friends to turn to, no home to go to, no job. The Governor of Pentonville ruled he be dealt with by the visiting magistrates and punished further for smashing up his cell and damaging prison property. He was brought before them. They told him he had merely scratched at his throat with the broken chamber pot and as punishment increased his sentence and denied him all privileges. Harold had used up his chances. The authorities had had enough of him. He was on his own with his bungling criminal behaviour: look left, look right, smash, grab and run.

Harold's Marriage

The blow to Harold's head did not improve him. By 1927 – the year traffic lights were introduced in England – he had ten convictions and a string of recorded desertions from the army under assumed names. He joined up briefly for a bed and a wage, then returned to his career. On release from Pentonville in September he found lodgings at 25 Campbell Road in Finsbury Park with Jack and Scottie, two ex-convicts. As he often did, he had gravitated close to his parents' home.

The sociologist Charles Booth, at the turn of the century, charted a poverty map of London in which he described Campbell Road as 'lowest class, vicious, semi-criminal'. Also in Campbell Road, a few doors down, was Sophia Cotton who worked in a local café in Hoxton, was twenty-one and alone with her year-old son, Ronald. No father was acknowledged on the boy's birth certificate. Her parents were dead. Her father had been a removal man, her mother had died the previous year. Her parents had rented the house but Sophia could not afford it on her own.

Harold courted her and offered marriage and a way out of her problems. It took him no more than a few days of courtship to make his proposal, for he liked the idea of himself as a married man. The girl from Bolton had lost her chance. But Sophia was also dating a man called Bob Moore. In October Harold beat him up and it was back to Pentonville for a month and a day for drunken assault. He wrote to his younger brother, the one also called Harry, asking him to look after his clothes, boots, shoes and bowler hat until he was out, and threatening vengeance on Bob Moore.

The letter was vetted by the prison authorities. It read: 'I am doing 1 month for hitting Bob Moore but he wants to go away before I come out. I've lost a good job over this, its what you get for loving a girl, but never mind this month will soon go by.' It was considered threatening and Harold was told to rewrite it and only to refer to his clothing.

Harold married Sophia on Christmas Day 1927 at St Anne's Church, Pooles Park, in north London. It was a Christian marriage and Harold made his vows. His brother Sidney and sister Edith were witnesses. For that day at least he was a regular guy, a husband and stepfather.

The boy Ronald took the surname Hagger and Sophia thereafter said Harold was the child's father. But Harold was in prison at any possible time of conception and always said he could not have children. He said he went to the doctor about it and was told his injuries after his leap from a moving train 'weakened his seed'.

For a while it seemed as if marriage might help him. He lived with his family at various addresses in north London and stayed out of prison for two and a half years. But he did not look after Sophia and her boy. 'I was not happy with my husband,' she later said. He gave her money sometimes but did not support her or the child. She had to go out to work, cleaning, and he used to hit her and the boy.

Often he was away. He would disappear and reappear without explanation. In 1928 he went up to Bolton to see the girl he had hoped to marry before he took up with Sophia. He had a dizzy spell, one of his funny turns he called it, and fell and hit his head on the pavement. Mostly he was unemployed. Occasional news of his parents and siblings filtered through from Sidney or Edith or Ethel. In September 1929 he learned his brother Ernest had died of leukaemia in the North Middlesex Hospital at the age of twenty. Harold had hardly known him and anyway what was one brother less or more to him.

Sidney Sinclair's Third Statement: Friday 22 November 1946

Back at East Malling police station after their drive Sidney and the police officers again sat round the table in the interview room. Rawlings got out his pen:

Statement of Sidney Sinclair of 25 Little Abington, Cambridgeshire who saith:

On the 22nd of November 1946 I went in a car with Chief Inspector Fabian and Detective Sergeant Rawlings and took them over the route which I took from Cambridge to East Malling when I delivered the bricks to the Cider Works.

I first pointed out the telephone box at Stansted Mountfitchet where I telephoned my governor about midday on Thursday 31st October 1946 and got my orders to pick up eight ton of Barley at Chrishall Grange. I next pointed out Judd's Café where I stopped for about three hours during the night of Wednesday 30th and Thursday 31st October 1946. The next spot I pointed out was the lights at Swanley where I remembered stopping as the lights were against me. I then pointed out the top of Farningham Hill as the first place I stopped as my radiator was boiling over. I loosened the cap and stopped there about ten minutes or a quarter of an hour. I then travelled on and stopped by some stacks which I pointed out. I stopped there under five minutes. I then travelled on to where I pointed out I saw the attaché case and where I stopped and picked it up. I then took the officers along and showed them where I turned off the main road by the council yard and showed them where I first stopped my lorry by the cider works. After this I showed them where I went round the outside of the works and on to the concrete road and pointed out where I threw the net bag and pair of gloves into the stream. After that I showed them the spots in the lane where I threw the jam sandwiches.

This statement has been read to me and is true.

Sinclair S.

Statement taken by Chief Inspector Fabian, New Scotland Yard in the presence of Detective Superintendent Smeed, Kent County Constabulary, written down and read over by Detective Sergeant H. Rawlings, New Scotland Yard, in the presence of Chief Inspector Fabian and Detective Superintendent Smeed.

Fabian watched, like a spider at the centre of its web, for more hesitation and struggle over detail, a further inconsistency, another revelation unknowable to the innocent. He kept the mood calm and assumed a disinterested air, as if the truth was a bit of a tease and together they must find it. They were both, he made it seem, puzzling over this journey. It was most unlike Sidney or Harold's previous encounters with the police on charges of larceny or drunken assault, when questioning was cursory and he was swiftly and unceremoniously shoved in a cell.

Fabian had timed their journey. He suspected Harold had lured Dagmar Petrzywalski into his lorry by the haystacks at Farningham Gosse, that Forge Lane, where he said he found the attaché case, was where he murdered her and that he had then dumped her body on his way to East Malling.

He told Harold, 'I think it is right for me to tell you that the attaché case and vest have been found where indicated by you and the bag has been found in a lake which is fed by the stream you indicated as the place you threw it. I am going to detain you until I have made further enquiries.' He cautioned him that anything he said might be used in evidence against him. 'That's ok, Mr Fabian,' Harold said to this friendly, affable man with whom he had spent a companionable day. 'If you've found the stuff where I said, it shows I'm speaking the truth.'

That same afternoon at 1.30pm Detective Sergeant Kenneth Thrift from the Kent County Constabulary went to 25 Little Abington with Detective Inspector Jenner and searched the cottage. Daisy, in a state of agitation, suspected this was deep trouble. Ellen was with her, trying to reassure her. Daisy had begun to believe that Sid was guilty: his odd manner, his nerves all over the place, going to the doctor, his agitation at any mention of this murder, giving his notice to Dickerson's, working as a gardener for next to no money.

The detectives were kind. They told her they were just investigating and no charge had yet been made. They asked politely before rummaging through chests of drawers and cupboards, then took away a quantity of Sidney's clothes: two overcoats, one with a check pattern, the other herringbone, his leather jerkin, a jacket, two pairs of blue overalls, a pair of khaki overalls, two khaki shirts, leather gloves, a cap, two pairs of boots and a small case. They said they wanted to have them examined for fingerprints and hairs. From a drawer in the room Ellen used when she was home they took a gold crucifix in a satin bag. She told them Sid had given it to her about three weeks ago as a present, though she had not wanted it. Now she wondered if he had stolen it from the murdered woman.

At the day's end Fabian told Sidney to think over all he had said and remembered and to let him know if he had anything to add. He needed a confession. He suggested Sidney invited the woman into his lorry even though he was travelling in the wrong direction, tried to have sex with her, tried to steal from her and when she resisted strangled her and dumped her body in the hedgerow. He directed that a police officer be in constant watch over him throughout the night.

Sidney was taken down to a cell at East Malling police station. At midnight Detectives Thrift and Jenner helped him out of his jacket, boots, braces, woollen pullover, khaki shirt, over-trousers, trousers, underpants, vest and socks and put him into prison clothes. They took snippings of his hair and sent these and his clothes off for further forensic scrutiny. The clanging of the cell door and turning of the key were familiar sounds to Woggle.

The End of Harold's Marriage

For much of her married life Sophia Hagger had no idea where her husband was. In the early 1930s, after the stock market crash, with the country gripped by economic depression and more than three million people out of work, Harold called himself Bill Hagger or William Hagger and led a vagabond life, tramping the country picking up casual jobs and thieving what he could.

It was in his nature not to feel able to stay, to want to move on from where he was and who he was. In prison he counted the days until he was freed. When out, it was a matter of time before he was caught and put back in a cell.

His thieving got more reckless, the sentences longer, the periods outside prison shorter. From 11 August 1930 to May the following year he was in prison on five accounts of larceny and one charge of assaulting a police officer. He was then out for nine months until, in February 1932, he was caught breaking into a private house in London and stealing jewellery. There was clearly no reforming component to prison and the court belatedly tried the new tack of rehabilitation. He was bound over for two years under the care of a probation officer, Mr Whaite, from the North London Magistrates' Court, who was assigned to help him find work.

It was a time when a national grid of electric power cables was being laid. The ambition was eventually to bring electricity to every home and business in the country. Callenders Cable Company had a contract to construct overhead cables across the Thames at Dagenham in east London. To allow clearance for ships they built two towers 500 feet high with a span of 3,000 feet of cable. For seven months Harold worked as a labourer on this project for £2 5s a week. He reverted to the name Harold Hagger and briefly lived as a husband, father and working man.

But by September men were laid off, as the depression deepened, and he was among them. Mr Whaite commended him for having shown a taste for work and found him another job, as a lorry driver with a haulage contractor, William Rice of Stockwell. The pay was £4 a week, a good enough wage in January 1933. The deal suited Harold. He could supplement a regular income with criminal moonlighting. He held the job for over a year until he was dismissed in February 1934 for striking a woman on the face. It was not the first or last time he whacked a woman and blacked her eyes.

Mr Whaite was out of the picture. Harold lived by thieving for eighteen months, then found night work at Arsenal Garage in Finsbury Park. The wage was half what he had earned as a lorry driver. He was in charge of the petrol station, he was alone, it was night, there was a till, he absconded with the takings. He was caught and for Christmas 1935 the prison gates closed behind him. It was prison clothes, a locked cell, orders shouted, lights out and no prospect of mince pies and brandy butter with Sophia and her son.

Sophia was not pleased to see him when he turned up unannounced in March 1936. She had had enough. She let him know he was a dud husband, out of work and in constant trouble. This was a last chance. Either he straightened up, got a job and lived by some rules or she was moving out. She could not cope with him thieving, disappearing and turning up only when it suited him.

He kept out of gaol for two years but in November 1938 he, or Bertie Thomas as he temporarily was, got caught in Linton in Cambridgeshire stealing cigarettes. He had arranged it so as again to be in prison for Christmas.

Sophia moved out on 13 April 1939. She had 'stuck with him' on, and more frequently off, for thirteen years. 'I was not happy with my husband. He did not support me and I had to go out to work,' she was to tell the police. After a blow too many from Harold she and her boy took lodgings in a single room in Elthorne Road, Holloway. Ronald was twelve. Harold sent no money. He wrote her a letter asking her to have him back, but she did not answer. She wanted nothing more to do with him.

Living in one room with her son and going out to work as a cleaner was more of a life than being with him. She never saw him again. He referred to having 'lost' her. Ten days after Sophia left, Harold Hagger, homeless and disowned by his parents and wife, was caught stealing money from an electricity meter. The next news Sophia had of him came a few years later when Mrs Bartlett, a casual acquaintance of them both who lived in Playford Road, Finsbury Park, told her she had seen Harold in the area and understood from him that he was living with another woman but she did not know where.

When war seemed imminent Harold's parents William and Annie moved back to their village. William's health was bad and London had never suited Annie. With the prospect of bombs and German invasion it was time to return to Therfield. William died there on 5 September 1939, aged seventy, two days after Britain declared war on Germany. He was buried, like many other Haggers, in St Mary's graveyard.

Four years later Annie, herself nearly seventy, married her sister Edith's widowed husband Jack Gatward. There was a pragmatism to it. It was family. She and Jack would look after each other and it meant she had somewhere to live in the village. Jack had been a farm labourer. Edith was twenty when she married him and already had a three-year-old daughter Minnie, father undeclared on the birth certificate. Annie settled into the rented four-roomed thatched cottage where Jack and Edith had lived for all their married lives. She was Mrs Gatward and she never went back to London.

Harold's War

Harold at the outbreak of war was out of work, unreconciled to his dying father, and his wife had made it clear she would rather penury and social stigma than married life with him. He displayed patriotic fervour and a desire to bash the Hun and on 16 November enlisted, using his birth name, as a private with the Queen's Regiment. He lasted sixty-five days, then deserted on 20 January 1940.

In 1939, defence regulations, issued out of fear of German invasion, imposed numerous obligations on citizens. The state had power to requisition any property: a house, a boat, a railway, a railing; it could imprison without trial any individual thought to be a threat to public safety; it punished with up to fourteen years' imprisonment 'any omission on the part of a person to do anything which he is under a duty, either to the public, or to any person, to do'; it told farmers what crops to grow, landowners which trees to fell, citizens how much cheese they could eat, what time they must be off the streets, what documents they could publish.

The blackout was imposed on 1 September 1939. No chink of light must come from any window, no illuminated signs or street lights were to be switched on, there must be no unmasked lights from torches or vehicles. Electricity companies reduced voltage, the world became gloomy and it was easy quite literally to get lost. For the old and unagile, 'blacking out' windows was difficult and accidents in homes increased. In the first four months of the war more than 4,000 people were killed on the roads, twice as many as in the previous year. In 1940 300,000 people were taken to court for blackout offences.

But for a seasoned villain like Harold Hagger obligatory darkness was a devilish boon – as was the black market. 'Black markets exist for black sheep,' the nation was told. 'Ask yourself these five questions:'

Do you ever try to get more than your ration? Or accept more if offered?

Do you ever shop-crawl? That is, go from shop to shop trying to buy a little here and a little there of some food which is scarce?

Do you ever pay more than control prices, or pay unfairly high prices for foods that are not price controlled?

Do you ever waste food of any description?

Do you neglect to produce all the food you can or to preserve foods whilst they are plentiful?

Women were told their frugal honest housekeeping would see the nation through to victory. Though seven million of them did paid work in the forces, in civil defence or in industry, they were reminded their essential place was in the home: fires should be lit, rooms cleaned, meals cooked, shopping done for when their men came home. 'See that your emergency store is always in order,' the Ministry of Food told them. They should have a total of sixty-four cans of soup, fish, meat, evaporated milk, jam or marmalade, pudding and cheese, share their bathwater and protect their food supplies from bomb dust:

Never leave food uncovered. Thick dust which settles after a blast due to a bomb explosion frequently renders food unfit to be eaten. This dust penetrates cartons and wrapping. Cover any food which is not in boxes or tins with a thick cloth or dust-sheet. This will also keep out fine splinters of glass.

The idea behind such instruction was pursuit of the common purpose and the common good. The exhortation was to play fair and avoid even trivial transgressions. Long queues formed for matches, prunes or a bit of fish. To jump the queue was as much an offence as to swindle with coupons. It was illegal to give unwanted rations to friends or neighbours 'whether by sale, barter or gift'. Few citizens took much offence at the swapping of food for clothing coupons or the sale of sweet coupons by a hard-up family, but inspectors mingled in the queues disguised as civilians and in the first three years of the war 57,794 people were convicted of infringing food regulations. A Gallup poll in January 1942 recorded 85 per cent approval for sending black marketeers to prison without the option of a fine. Thefts from docks or government stock could lead to fourteen years in prison.

Police manpower was focused on evacuation, billeting, enforcing restrictions on lighting, sales and purchases. All of which meant there was little time or manpower to spare for tracking down a crook like Harold Hagger, an army deserter, moving around the country under assumed names and under cover of darkness, siphoning off tanks of petrol, stealing bags of sand, offloading stolen goods at black-market prices.

Lack of police resources and the blackout created wonderful opportunities for Harold to thieve without detection. The war for him meant an unusually long stretch out of prison. The scarcity of virtually everything opened a keen market for anything he stole: petrol, clothes, food. And when he had money, he knew where to buy the sugar, meat and tobacco denied to those who lived within their rations.

Harold Hagger was unpersuaded by ideas of restraint, citizenship and the notion of pulling together for the common good. He had no allegiance to family, no empathy, no moral core. He was the blackest of black marketeers and sheep. If his eye alighted on an unguarded item he might shift for profit, he took it, be it a crucifix or a kipper. Not to do so would be to miss a trick for such a determined if unstrategic crook.

Enter Sidney Sinclair

Private 28467 Harold Hagger of the Queen's Regiment was wanted for desertion. Harold Hagger was a problem to himself: no wife, in and out of prison, in trouble with the army. It was time for a change of identity and a fresh start. On 22 January 1940 Sidney Sinclair enlisted at the army recruiting centre in Holloway. Sidney was the name of one of Harold's younger brothers. Sidney Sinclair sounded like a man who would wear the same clothes as Harold Hagger, go to the same pubs, play the same games of cards, but be free of Hagger's baggage and problems.

At his interview Sidney Sinclair perjured himself creatively. He gave a false home address in south London, said he had served four years and two months from 1917 to 1921 with the 6th Inniskilling Dragoons under the name Fred Hall and as a civilian had worked as a coal porter. He was unmarried, had no criminal convictions and his religion was Church of England. He was a practical and handy man willing to do any job and ready to serve overseas if needs be.

He was given grade A1 for his health and assigned work as a stevedore with the Royal Engineers. His unit, the Mobilisation Company 16th Depot Battalion, was based near the village of Little Abington in Cambridgeshire, where the army and air force had commandeered much of the surrounding land. Sidney Sinclair, known as Sid, became popular with the regulars in the local pubs. He bought a generous round and liked to play cards and boast of his sexual conquests.

Sidney wanted a home and a wife. Within days of meeting Daisy Emily Linsdell he proposed to her. He seemed an affable soldier, friendly, convincing. He gave her presents without explaining their provenance and declared himself unmarried. Had she known anything of Harold Hagger, serial criminal, wife beater and army deserter, she might have thought again about allowing him into her pretty cottage. Sid told her nothing of him, or of Bertie Thomas, William Cook or Bill Smith. He explained the straggling scar on the right side of his forehead with a story about falling from a moving train and fracturing his skull. He had been unconscious for a fortnight and in hospital six months. It added vulnerability to his manliness. He needed looking after. He told Daisy that his parents were dead, he had never been married because he had not found the right woman until he met her, he had no family and he could not have children because of the accident.

He wasted no time. He was nearly forty and needed to leave the bad luck of Harold Hagger behind him. On 20 March 1940 Sidney Sinclair, bachelor, married Mrs Daisy Emily Linsdell,

widow, at the Cambridge Register Office. The marriage was not
bigamous in Sidney's view because he was not Harold Hagger.
That Sophia Hagger was very much alive was no impediment
to Sidney Sinclair. She was not alive to him. Daisy would be a
good wife, it was a small matter that her two daughters disliked him. This friendly sleepy village was like Therfield, the
tranquil place nineteen miles away his mother had always
yearned for as home. It was just the place to start afresh. Sidney
took a week of honeymoon after his wedding, then returned to
his army unit. He was confined to barracks for seven days for
being absent without leave from 15 to 28 March and made to
forfeit fourteen days' pay.

Sidney Sinclair's War 1940–42

Sidney Sinclair's army career quickly came to resemble Harold
Hagger's. He preferred thieving and being at home with
Daisy to working as a stevedore. In April his pay was stopped
for being AWOL for eight days. In May he went AWOL for
seventeen days and was locked up for two weeks when he
returned to his unit. To his annoyance he was then posted to
Dunfermline in Scotland. He bunked off for seven months,
was declared a deserter and all his pay was stopped. When
eventually picked up in London in February 1941, he was sentenced to three months' detention. In September he went to
the army doctor and said he felt ill. Nothing was found to be
wrong with him but he was downgraded from A1 to B2
because of varicose veins. Three months later, in December,
Sidney was sent to serve in Iceland. He did not know where

Iceland was. It sounded cold and foreign and he did not want to go there.

Iceland held a strategic position along the north Atlantic sea lanes. Though officially neutral in the war, it cooperated with the British and American forces. German presence there alarmed the Allies and when German U-boats damaged and sank Icelandic vessels, Britain first supplied the Icelandic coastguard with weapons and ammunition, then, on 10 May 1940, invaded the island and stationed 25,000 British troops on it.

Iceland did not suit Sidney at all. He was expected to work as a docker. Everything was unfamiliar. There was nothing to nick and nowhere to go outside the army base. He felt entirely displaced. He made an appointment with the army medical officer and became quite hysterical about his headaches, nerves, dizziness from the noise and cold, his insomnia and searing scalp and how he kept falling over and trembling. He gave a startling account of his 'accident' twelve years previously. He said he had been unconscious for fourteen days and in hospital for six months with a fractured skull, pelvis and left arm.

Sidney's health was further downgraded to C and after fifty-nine days he was invalided home as unfit for service and sent to Longmoor in Buckinghamshire to be examined by an army psychiatrist. Sidney apprised him of his accident and fractures, told him how he trembled, coughed, could not see in the dark, was deaf in his right ear, unable to perform his duties or do anything that involved climbing or noise and showed him an additional scar on his forehead which he said dated from when he collapsed in Bolton in 1928 because of a dizzy spell.

The psychiatrist wrote his report. He thought there was a hysterical component to this ever-increasing mass of symptoms and that Sidney's main problem was an anxiety neurosis.

This is a case of hysteria occurring in an individual of poor intelligence and low educational level. This man is of low morals and in my opinion is making the most of his symptoms and the fact that they are based on a severe physical injury. Psychiatric treatment is not indicated.

In my opinion this man is totally unsuitable for any form of military service, a result of his condition and marked hypotension.

He asked for a second opinion: 'If you concur, I will arrange to have him medically examined.'

A second psychiatrist gave his view: 'I concur. In my opinion this man is suffering from the after effects of cerebral contusion with a morbid anxiety neurosis superadded, and is totally unfit for any form of military service. Will Medical Specialist please see?'

Sidney had put on the performance of his life. He had found Iceland far more punishing than Brixton or Pentonville. A physician, Captain Ingham, gave him a medical examination and wrote a full report: The patient Sidney Sinclair, a sapper, aged 42, was 5 feet 6¼ inches tall, his hair was brown, his eyes grey, he weighed 12 stone 3 ounces, had a fresh complexion and tattoos on both forearms. His physique was moderate to obese, his teeth good, his lungs clear, his pulse rate normal, there was no sugar in his urine. He had slight varicose veins behind his left knee, his heart was slightly enlarged, he had a coarse tremor in his hands, cerebral contusion, post-concussional headaches and deafness as a result of an accident at Carlisle twelve years previously when he fractured his skull. Clause 22 of army medical rules read, 'If there is evidence that the disability is due to serious negligence or misconduct on the part of the man, such evidence will be recorded here.' Captain Ingham wrote, 'There is no such evidence.' For Sidney Sinclair fell from a train. He did not, like Harold Hagger, jump through a lavatory window when handcuffed and under police escort, to escape custody. Sidney Sinclair had never been in prison. He had served in Iceland from December 1941 to February 1942 as a docker. He told Captain Ingham that before the war he worked as a coal porter and a coal merchant but was frequently off work through sickness. The Carlisle accident occurred before he joined the army so he was not entitled to an army pension. He said he had a pension policy with the Prudential Assurance Company.

Captain Ingham downgraded his health to E on 25 May 1942 and advised his permanent discharge on medical grounds. Sidney Sinclair was discharged from the Royal Engineers on 27 May 1942 having served two years five months and six days, many of them AWOL. He was declared 'totally unsuitable for any form of military service'. So ended his military career, which had been as ignominious as Harold Hagger's. Sidney viewed this discharge as a triumph. He was out of the army. Free. The ruddy war could fight itself. He knew other ways of getting by.

Ellen Linsdell and the Americans

Initially America wanted to remain neutral in the Allies' war with Germany: involvement in a European conflict had no electoral appeal. But by December 1940 Britain had run out of money to pay for weaponry and planes. Winston Churchill sent President Roosevelt a desperate appeal for heavy bombers 'to shatter the foundation of German military power'.

On 29 December 1940 Roosevelt came up with the lend-lease plan. Ships, tanks and war supplies would be 'loaned' to Britain, though no one was quite sure how they would be given back. Churchill saw the plan as a free and unlimited supply of hardware to fight Hitler's regime. Roosevelt hoped it was a way of avoiding committing American lives, though by September 1940 military service for men aged between twenty-one and thirty-five was compulsory in the USA.

It was not just bombs the Americans sent under the lend-lease plan. More popular for the villagers of Little Abington, Kingsdown and Therfield were the cans of pilchards, beans, condensed milk and treacle made available under a points system. Lord Woolton, Minister of Food, explained it all in a wireless broadcast on the Home Service on Sunday 2 November 1941:

Our friends in the United States have been helping us very generously ... You can buy these new goods where you please and when you please within a four-week period. You're free to spend your points on any foods that you choose on the list and you can go to any shop you like to

165

make your choice. Everyone doesn't want the same thing every week. We want variety.

It was help at arm's length. A year later, on Sunday 7 December 1941, Japanese aircraft attacked the huge US naval base at Pearl Harbor in Hawaii. Churchill was joyful. He wrote of the event, 'I knew the United States was in the war, up to the neck and in to the death.' As a result of Pearl Harbor the United States declared war against Japan. Four days later Germany and Italy declared war on the United States.

General Dwight Eisenhower was to be Supreme Commander of the Allied forces in Europe. Within a month US troops sailed to Britain from Boston or New York on transport ships and ocean liners. They were coming to launch a cross-Channel invasion to defeat the enemy. They brought bombs, guns and ammunition. Churchill offered use of RMS *Queen Mary* and RMS *Queen Elizabeth*.

The GIs – so called because 'General Issue' was stamped on their uniforms, guns, boots and blankets – had little idea of what was wanted from them or what to expect. They were issued with *A Short Guide to Great Britain*. It warned them the whole country was no bigger than Minnesota. The British did not know how to make a cup of coffee, drove on the wrong side of the road, had an impossible accounting system for their money, drank warm beer and loved to hunt, fish and bet on horse races.

The first GIs arrived in spring 1942. Their ships docked at Liverpool and Clydeside and they were met on the quays by women from the Red Cross who gave them cups of tea, and by British army bands playing 'Shoo Shoo Baby' and 'I'll Be Seeing You'. They were importuned for cigarettes, sweets and fruit.

They went where they were told to go. Some were billeted with private families, and might be sent to a cottage like Daisy Sinclair's or a manor house. They were classified, trained in military discipline, camouflage techniques, map reading, marching: 'We fired M1s, charged strawbags, bayonetted them, uttering ear-splitting yells as we did so. We crawled through ditches and under barbed wire with live ammunition zipping overhead and shells exploding . . .'

The US Army requisitioned buildings to set up camps and depots. Several thousand American airmen were stationed at Bassingbourn, seventeen miles from Little Abington. It was a flagship US Army Air Force base, home to huge bomber planes like the B-17 Flying Fortress, named the Memphis Belle by its pilot Captain Robert Morgan. These heavy bombers, big birds they were called, needed vast airfields and concrete and steel runways. Tracts of surrounding farmland, pastures and fields of wheat and barley, were commandeered. At Bassingbourn the main runway was 6,000 feet long and camouflaged to make it look like agricultural crops. From these runways the Flying Fortress and other big bombers flew into occupied Europe and Germany to blast the enemy to smithereens. At the end of May 1942 aircraft from Bassingbourn took part in the 'thousand bomber' raid on Cologne, codenamed Operation Millennium. A thousand aircraft flew in a stream for ninety minutes over the city, dropped 1,455 tons of bombs, started 2,500 fires, killed or injured 5,500 civilians, bombed out 45,000 homes and destroyed seventeen churches, sixteen schools, ten historic buildings, fourteen public buildings, seven banks, nine hospitals, six department stores and more.

Daisy's elder daughter Ellen worked at Bassingbourn, so she did not see too much of her unwelcome stepfather. She worked as a parachute packer. It was a job on which lives depended and each parachute had to be inspected and packed to a safe standard. Another of her tasks was to return to their families the belongings of American servicemen and women killed in action. She felt privileged to work at the base with all the perks of food, clothes and luxuries. She briefly became engaged to a US fighter pilot but he was killed on a bombing mission. She visited her mother regularly and gave her supplies from the American camp. One time she went home and Daisy had a black eye and badly bruised wrists which she tried to pass off as an accident. Ellen warned Sidney if he did that to her mother again she would tell the police.

Among the villagers, the GIs were viewed as heroes with their gifts of candy, tinned fruit, cigarettes, chewing gum, soap and nylon stockings. They were popular with the girls and not just because they used aftershave and smelled nice. They were affluent, well fed, well dressed and generous. They gave parties for the local children, held dances and could afford to get drunk in the pubs and leave huge tips.

But there was resentment too. The GIs arrived at the same time as British men of call-up age left to fight overseas. In 1942 a private in the British Army was paid 14 shillings a week. His US counterpart earned £3 8s 9d. For civilians there was the Blitz, blackouts and austerity. A slab of butter had to last a month. It was said that a British family could live for a month on what was scraped into the garbage can after any meal at an American base. To many, these young Americans seemed unacceptably swanky, with their gum chewing and familiar manners. It was all right for them to flash their money about and curry favour with the girls: 'Overfed, overpaid, oversexed and over here' was one adage much bandied about. 'Up with the lark and to bed with a Wren' was another. 'Heard about the new utility knickers? One Yank and they're off.'

And for the young American men the displacement was hard. They were used to T-bone steaks, blueberry pie and maple syrup, not Brussels sprouts, powdered egg and Spam. This island the size of Minnesota was cold and inadequately heated. It offered mud, rain and heavy dark bread. GIs were supplied with a booklet: *Instructions for American Servicemen in Britain 1942*. In it, they were warned not to drink the milk because it was unpasteurised and not to eat much if invited into someone's house for a meal because their host had frugal rations.

Life was open to misinterpretation. Often GIs could not comprehend dialects, and lessons in vocabulary were needed on both sides. If they used the word bloody it was a swearword, if they said someone looked like a bum it meant they looked like a bottom and if they asked for a rubber they got an eraser. For the Brits, when an American spoke of the hood of a car he meant the bonnet, when he said vest he meant waistcoat, when he said undershirt he meant vest, when he said crackers he meant biscuits and when he said biscuits he meant scones. To bridge the hospitality gap and ease homesickness Ambrose Heath published *Simple American Dishes in English Measures*, in 1943. In his recipes chowder transmuted into baked bean soup, and fishcakes Creole fashion were fried in damp custard powder because of the scarcity of eggs.

Sex and the GIs vexed the authorities. The three million American servicemen who passed through Britain between 1942 and 1945 fathered about 24,000 children outside marriage. The area of London's Mayfair where prostitutes worked became known as Little America. 'Bad apples', Fabian of the Yard called prostitutes: 'There is a big brown bruise on their souls, of self indulgence and selfishness. I do not think there exists in London any such person as an honest prostitute. They taint any flesh they touch.'

In 1942, 70,000 new cases of venereal disease were reported to clinics. Warning notices were pasted up in public lavatories and a defence regulation in January 1943 required that a suspected carrier be compulsorily examined and treated if named by two witnesses. In May the US Forces newspaper *Stars and Stripes* had a cartoon of a GI canoodling with a girl against a wall, captioned with V for Victory crossed through and VD in its place.

Wartime austerity fitted into an existing mindset of denial. The sexual reserve of the Petrzywalskis reflected the repression of the times. There was still censorship, with D.H. Lawrence's *Lady Chatterley's Lover* and Radclyffe Hall's *The Well of Loneliness* viewed as too filthy to publish. Some parts of the body were too private to mention, rape was viewed as violation rather than violence and for many women, including Dagmar, menstruation was an embarrassment. Euphemisms were substituted: 'time of the month', 'the curse' or 'on the rag'. Sanitary towels, as they were called, were packaged in plain covers and kept under the counter at the chemist's. 'Women of refinement dislike to ask for so intimate an article by its full descriptive name,' Kotex wrote in a trade publication. 'Not once, in any advertisement to women, have we described Kotex as a sanitary napkin.'

Nine out of ten parents did not talk to their children about sex. At the BBC, Lord Reith did not allow divorcees to work for the Corporation. Nurses, like telephonists, had to leave their profession if they married, the Church preached that fornication was a sin, such sex education books as there were, wrote of the importance of chastity before marriage, and doctors and clergymen warned that masturbation led to blindness, stunted growth and insanity.

Statistics on Britain's changing sexual mores during the war alarmed politicians and the Establishment. They did not release them, out of concern for Britain's image abroad. Of the 5.3 million children born between 1939 and 1945, more than a third were illegitimate and a third of these births were to married woman. In pre-war Britain most petitions alleging adultery were filed by women. By the war's end two out of three applications were filed by husbands against their wives and by 1945 there were five times more divorce petitions than in 1939.

Contraception was a difficult topic. Condoms were hard to get because there was a shortage of latex and the government gave priority to teats for bottle-feeding babies. Those that could be found were of a thick rubber and meant to be washable. But American condoms were readily supplied to GIs.

Perks from Bassingbourn, of both essentials and luxuries, found their way into Daisy's house. Ellen was friendly with two of the cooks at the base and they gave her butter and corned beef, tins of cream and peaches which she took home for her mother. Daisy liked to share these goods with families in the village. When Sidney got hold of such extras, he was adept at offloading them, be they slabs of butter, condoms, nylons, scented soap or cigarettes.

Maurice Dickerson

For some months after the ignominious end to his career as a professional soldier Sidney Sinclair was unemployed, but the blackout, black market and life with Daisy suited him. She tried to help him with his strange moods and nerves and thought of him as a good husband, generous with money and gifts of an eclectic unpredictable sort, though his temper was to be feared. Her younger daughter Sheila saw and heard the violence of it. She was nine when Sidney arrived at 25 Little Abington. In later years she said she remembered little of the time he lived with them and what she did remember she would prefer to forget. All his attention to her was unwanted.

In October 1942 he got a job as a lorry driver for Dickerson in Cambridge. Maurice Dickerson had a reputation for keeping his lorries on the road until they fell apart. He began his haulage firm in the 1920s with a lone 1-ton Ford truck, worked hard, was his own boss, said yes to any job, made a profit and saved from what he earned. As an economy, he did his own repairs. When he got a puncture delivering a load of flowers to Manchester he stuffed the tyre with hay from a nearby field.

In a few years he saved enough to buy 30 acres of gravel-pit land near the village of Great Shelford, south of Cambridge by the river Cam. He bought two horses, Pansy and Snowy, both drays. His eight-year-old son John looked after them, fed them, brought them up from the village, harnessed them to a 1-ton skip, then led them down the pit incline to Joe, the digger-man at the bottom. Joe dug the gravel with a spade and flung it on to a mesh screen on the skip for the sand to filter through. It took all day to fill one skip. John then whipped the horses up the incline to a lorry at the top.

A family business grew. By 1937 Maurice Dickerson had earned enough to buy a Priestman mechanical excavator with steel steering wheels and runners, a crane, five lorries and the Teversham Corner Garage in Cambridge. He started a company making lorry parts, a motor repair business and a vehicle recovery service. Contracts came for road building and demolition work. He and his family began to live in style.

Then came murmurings of war. The Ministry of Defence wanted an airfield at Waterbeach, six miles from Cambridge. Dickerson had bought up nearby land where gravel could be extracted. He got the contract to build the Waterbeach runway. For him, the war was a period not of austerity but of great profit. At its outset he had ten 5-ton lorries, by the end a fleet of thirty-two. The government contracted him to transport munitions and bombs from the Midlands to the East Anglian docks. The high fees paid were commensurate with the danger involved. The munitions factories and the docks were targeted by the enemy. One night seven of Dickerson's drivers were killed in a bombing raid.

Alan Alderson Bell, a thin man with glasses, false teeth and problems with stomach ulcers, was the firm's company secretary for all his working life and Maurice Dickerson's longest-serving and most trusted employee. In 1942 he employed Sidney Sinclair, as he now was, married with two daughters and residing in the nearby village of Little Abington. Alan Bell was based at Dickerson's main office in Gloucester Street, Cambridge. He lived in rented rooms in Cambridge and his landlady gave him his meals and did his laundry. He had a girlfriend, Gladys, whom he delayed marrying until he was sixty-five. He died soon after the wedding ceremony and in his will left all he possessed to his brother. Gladys then wrote to John Dickerson pleading penury and asking for financial help.

Sinclair was one of the rough men, the workers, prepared to drive a load of bombs, shells, guns, gas canisters, gravel, sand, bricks, hay or whatever from one part of the kingdom to another. Sidney did not care what was on the back of his lorry as long as he got paid. It was dangerous work but it did not seem like that to him. There were extras in it, that was the main thing. He knew how to sell on the share of petrol, sand and gravel he took for himself.

He told Alan Bell he had driven heavy goods vehicles in the army. That was recommendation enough. No special licence was needed, no tests or checks were made. The work suited him, alone in the cabin of his lorry with no prison guards or army officers barking orders at him and meting out punishment. In the lorry there was just the road and his own time. He could take the route he liked, stop when he wanted. He always carried money for petrol and emergencies. Expenses, Dickerson called it. And the work tied up well with thieving. He knew where to look out for things, where to offload stolen goods, where to pick up a woman if he fancied it. You could get anything if you had money.

Much of what he knew he learned in prison. You couldn't do time in Brixton and not come out knowing where to pass on what you nicked or where to find a woman. Sometimes they'd stand by the road wanting a lift. There were plenty of them in Bolton. But you had to watch your wallet, they were after the money. A few of them gave him trouble and he'd hit out. They'd not gone to the police, not like that woman when he was driving a lorry at Stockwell, who cost him his job. And Daisy's daughter Ellen threatening to squeal on him. He didn't hit Daisy. Only when she went on about where had he been and where stuff had come from and the trouble he'd get into. She'd made him hit her. Just to shut her up. She knew about his nerves and his funny turns. And that other girl of hers, the young one, who wouldn't be in the same room with him.

'A Clearing House for Thieves'

Judd's café near Bishop's Stortford was Sidney's favoured place for offloading stolen goods. Its formal name was the Acme Café but regulars called it Judd's place. Charlie Judd defined it. He could shift anything. Five years younger than Sidney, he had been its proprietor since 1939. Before that he was a haulage contractor. It was a useful elision of interests, as Sidney Sinclair knew.

The café, a long low building, led out at the back to the towpath of the river Stort. Judd lived in The Boathouse, not far downriver, with his wife Dulcie, two daughters and two sons. The house had outbuildings and a garage and when goods were brought in to the café, mostly at night when the police were not about, he loaded them on to a boat and took them downstream to be stored.

Sidney viewed Charlie Judd as a friend among friends. Men in the same trade. Charlie knew about Harold Hagger. He ran a good café with a welcoming atmosphere. There was a juke box with popular songs: 'Zip-A-Dee-Doo-Dah', 'You Make Me

Feel So Young', 'That Old Black Magic', 'I Got the Sun in the Morning and the Moon at Night'. Sidney liked the food: pie and mash, roast meat and veg, not Spam or rabbit.

There was a swagger to Charlie Judd. He was fearless but every so often got hauled in. In March 1941 he was given twelve months by the crown court at St Albans on five charges of receiving property 'well knowing it to have been stolen'. Between August and December the previous year, the court heard, he received 240 gallons of petrol, 'Property of His Majesty's Government', cases of matches stolen from United Match Industries Ltd, 1,000 sandbags that belonged to the Government, three geese which belonged to Susannah Hitchcox, and jars of jam and boxes of lard that were the property of the Cambridge and District Cooperative Society. The total value of the stolen goods was about £200.

Seventy-two gallons of the petrol had come from George Edwards, a sergeant in the Royal Air Force stationed at Bassingbourn. He had borrowed £13 10s from Judd to buy a car and could not pay him back, so he stole the petrol from the airfield and delivered it to him in drums.

The cases of matches were valued at £63. A man named Springham, who worked for the haulage firm used by the United Match Company, loaded an extra three cases of matches on to his lorry. Judd paid £2 10s a case for them, though the wholesale price was £21 and the retail price £24.

'I describe this café', said Mr Frederick Levy, the judge, 'as a clearing house for thieves, where every variety of property is brought in and literally accepted.' Which was what it was and why Sidney liked it. There was none of this condemnation of black sheep. The black market was trade and livelihood. The art was to get away with it. By March 1941 there were 178,000 indictable offences in England and Wales. Almost anything seemed to be a crime: a chink in the blackout, a stolen bag or two of sand, but that same month 4,259 civilians were killed and 5,557 injured in bombing raids.

Charlie Judd did his time, made a few new contacts, then started up again. The following year he got off with a caution when the police raided the café after a tip-off. They found no stolen goods but said he was using it as a gaming house because he had two fruit machines there. Both Charlie Judd and Sidney Sinclair thought it a trumped-up charge.

5

MURDER AT
WROTHAM HILL

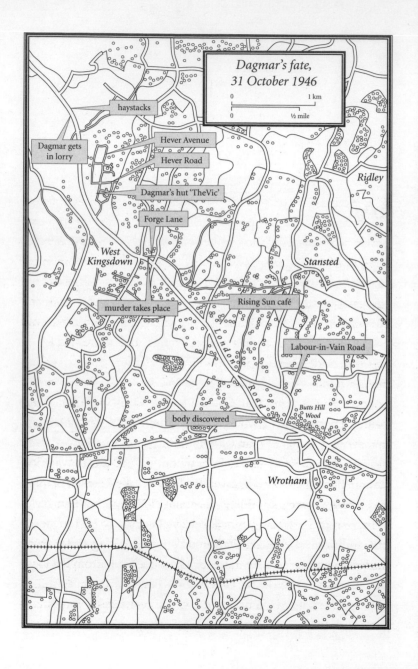

Dagmar's fate,
31 October 1946

haystacks

Dagmar gets
in lorry

Hever Avenue

Hever Road

Ridley

Dagmar's hut 'TheVic'

Forge Lane

West
Kingsdown

Stansted

murder takes place

Rising Sun café

Labour-in-Vain Road

London Road

Butts Hill
Wood

body discovered

Wrotham

Wednesday 30 October 1946 was a cold day. Shortage of electricity caused a power cut and the ministry of fuel and power warned people to 'go easy on coal'. Stalin's minister of foreign affairs, Vyacheslav Molotov, called for a prohibition on atomic bombs and described Winston Churchill as 'a prophet for aggressive imperialists who embarked on hazardous military adventures for the sake of achieving world domination'. The vicar of St Oswald's Church in Preston, Lancashire, wrote a letter to *The Times* deploring capital punishment as an offence against human rights, Hedy Lamarr starred in *The Strange Woman* at the London Pavilion, and at Coleshill, Warwickshire, Ellen May Young, a paint sprayer, was committed for trial for her subterfuge in marrying, in the Roman Catholic church in the village of Baddesley Clinton, Irene Mary Palmer whom she had met at Waterloo station. Ellen had posed as an ex-RAF pilot, called herself Stanley and written more than thirty passionate letters to her fiancée.

In the morning Sidney Sinclair drove his lorry to Histon, north of Cambridge, to collect Dickerson's East Malling order from the brick-making factory there. Bricks were made from the local clay. Crooked Histon he called the village with its winding village street. It was famous for the Chivers factory that made jam using fruit from local orchards. Sidney's instructions from

Alan Bell were to take the bricks next day to Goldwell's cider works at East Malling in Kent.

The lorry he was driving was an 8-ton Albion, dark green and battered, registration AER 815. The governor's name was painted on the front and sides: M. Dickerson Ltd. It had a split windscreen and one little wiper on the driver's side. In cold weather it took some cranking to get it started. There was no passenger seat, the engine cowling went through the cabin and Sidney had to carry a large water can for when the radiator boiled going uphill with a heavy load.

He helped load the bricks and secure them with a tarpaulin and straps. It was a full load, so the going would be slow. At four in the afternoon he called at Dickerson's office in Cambridge and told Alan Bell he'd take the loaded lorry home to Little Abington, have his tea, then deliver the bricks first thing in the morning.

He planned to rest up, then set off at about 10pm. That would leave him plenty of time to stop off at Judd's place. He had quite a few things for him: bricks, petrol, tinned food. And Charlie wanted him to help take goods downriver: loading and unloading, stacking and storing.

Daisy gave him tea and sponge cake, then went to bed. He dressed in a khaki shirt, trousers and braces, blue overalls, a woollen pullover, boots, a herringbone jacket and a flat cap.

The night was frosty with an east wind. At the northern end of the High Street he turned left to the Fourwentways round-about, then on toward Bishop's Stortford and London, past Stump Cross, through the villages of Littlebury, Quendon and Stansted Mountfitchet. He watched out for road signs but knew the way so far. The road was clear, though it was hard to reach 20 miles an hour even on the flat.

Dagmar Petrzywalski

The road to Wrotham Hill 31 October 1946

The corpse in the hedgerow

Detective Superintendent Smeed arrives at the crime scene

A dark blue shoe found
on the grass verge by
Joe Hammond, a lorry driver

The duplicate yellow bag
crocheted by Dagmar's
sister-in-law Elena Petrzywalski

Maurice Dickerson's fleet of lorries. Second from the left is the dark green
Albion 8-ton lorry AER 815 driven by Sidney Sinclair

Motorists are stopped: a manhunt begins

The second marriage of Dagmar's brother George Petrzywalski to
Phyllis Wise in 1930. Dagmar, far right was bridesmaid. Jules, her nephew,
George's son, sits in front of her. Standing far left, her mother Mame. Seated
far left, her sister in-law and brother Elena and Ralph

Inside 'The Vic'

The only photograph of Harold Hagger. He wears a flat hat and is under arrest

Daisy, deceived
into a bigamous
marriage by Harold

His mother Annie holding on to her hat on a
day out with one of her sisters

The murdered woman

Dr Cedric Keith
Simpson, Home
Office pathologist

Albert Pierrepoint,
executioner, with
his wife Anne

Albert Pierrepoint and Robert Fabian after an execution

It took him an hour and a half to get to Judd's café. Parked lorries lined the forecourt. Inside, Sidney was among familiar faces: men he knew from prison at Pentonville, Preston, Brixton, men who knew him as Harold, Bill or William, who knew the trade and tip-offs. They mingled with the regular drivers. They had a certain look, like nothing could touch them, nothing could faze them.

Charlie Judd gave him cash for his goods and Sidney had his dinner, a steak pie and greens. You had what you liked at Charlie's, none of this two ounces of this, four ounces of that and a scrape of the other. Then he worked for three hours helping Charlie take goods by boat to the storehouse and load up a couple of lorries. It was raining on the river and there was no moon.

Sidney left Judd's café at 3.30 in the morning. His wallet was in his jacket pocket and stuffed with money which was how he liked it: £17 10s. He had a full tank of petrol and a false receipt for it for Dickerson. The lorry held 30 gallons. Ten gallons cost 15 shillings. He was flush. This was real money. Close on three weeks' wages. He could have what he wanted with that. Anything. The sun would come up at seven. He'd be at the cider works by then. If he was early he'd have tea in a café and read his paper. He drove on through Spellbrook, Sawbridgeworth and along the London road, through Thornwood, Epping and Epping Forest. Most of the trees were bare. It rained on and off but he didn't mind. Rain and wind kept the engine cool, though it was hard to see in the dark with one little wiper that smeared the windscreen. There were only heavy lorries like his on the road with deliveries to be made.

It had been a good night. Six years now he'd been married

to Daisy. She didn't probe. He wondered if she carried on when he was away. She was fond of the men. She didn't know about Harold Hagger and Mrs Hagger or about the women he could buy when his wallet was full. Those girls of hers were moody. Didn't call him dad. Didn't call him anything. The young one didn't like him near when he tried to go up and say goodnight to her and be nice to her. He let her know there'd be trouble if she told her mother.

On he went to Buckhurst Hill and Woodford Green, through Leytonstone, Maryland and Stratford, then under the Thames through the Blackwall tunnel, built for horses in 1897. It was a tight fit now for two lorries like his to pass each other. On to Greenwich, up Westcombe Hill, on to the Sidcup bypass and through Swanley. The traffic lights were against him in the town, he swore as he waited for what seemed an age. And the radiator kept overheating. Dickerson never serviced his bloody lorries. At Farningham Hill, Sidney loosened the cap, waited five minutes for it to cool down and topped up the tank. Then on to Gorse Hill, called Death Hill or Farningham Gosse, near to Kingsdown, where Dagmar Petrzywalski and her mother lived in their separate simple dwellings.

Dagmar Petrzywalski: Thursday 31 October 1946

Dagmar got up at 4am on Thursday 31 October 1946 after very little sleep. Hedy had yapped and whined all night and would not stay still.

There was no hint of dawn, the morning was cold. Dagmar dressed in layers of clothes bought from the market or that she had made herself. Though unconcerned about how she looked, she wanted to be warm. She made a towelling pad because of her wretched bleeding and fixed it to a flannel belt. She contrived a suspender belt out of a skein of pale blue wool and elastic and fastened her brown lisle stockings to it with four large buttons. She put on a pink woollen vest, light green woollen knickers, lock-knit combinations she had crocheted herself, a beige tussore-silk slip with sleeves and a frilled hem. She had no expectation that her makeshift inelegant lingerie would ever be seen. Over it she put a dark blue sleeveless rayon frock and a blue and beige jumper she had recently knitted. She made an Alice band for her hair out of a skein of blue wool, fixed it in place with kirby grips, then kept it neat with a hairnet. She put on her size 6 blue Oral shoes and the thick blue-grey coat she had made from a blanket bought in Maidstone market and lined in orange satin. Up her sleeve she tucked a white handkerchief wrapped round a little orange Bakelite container of ointment for when her nose and lips got sore from the cold, and round her neck she wrapped the man's white vest she had bought for a shilling. The way she folded it no one would see the darn or know it was not a scarf, and she could tuck Hedy in it if the dog got tired or nervous.

She had made a lead out of string for Hedy and into the small battered attaché case her mother had given her two months previously had packed her week's ration of cheese as a present for Elena, jam sandwiches for the journey home, her horseshoe-shaped brown leather purse with 15 shillings in it, the keys to her hut and her mother's bungalow, her identity card and ration book and the yellow crocheted bag Elena had made for her. She expected she and Elena would shop for bits and pieces, and

185

usually Elena gave her something to take home, a pie for her mother or a pan.

Last time Dagmar went up to Woking, on Friday 18 October, a week before her birthday, it had been cold and overcast too. It was the day Hermann Goering's body was cremated and his ashes thrown away. He had poisoned himself in a prison cell at Nuremberg so as to avoid being hanged. And the Duchess of Windsor's jewels had been stolen from Lord Dudley's house in Sunningdale. Thieves climbed up a drainpipe, took the large black box with £25,000 worth of jewels in it and got away unnoticed in the mist while the Duchess was having tea.

And it was the day Elena gave Dagmar the yellow bag. Dagmar arrived at her house just before eight in the morning. The manager of Hill View garage in West Malling, nice Mr Wells, gave her a lift to Elephant and Castle, then she took the tube to Waterloo and the train to Woking. Mr Wells often went up to London and several times she'd had a lift with him. Twice she had tried to pay the equivalent of the bus fare, but he refused so emphatically she stopped offering.

Dagmar had a sense of anticipation as she set off, with everyone else still sleeping, the sky dark and the air fresh and sweet. She tucked the note on which she had written OUT in red ink into the fence by her mother's gate and set off down Hever Avenue. There was no lighting but she did not need a torch. Her eyes soon got used to the dark. She felt safe and purposeful with the little dog trotting beside her. They went down the centuries-old flint path. In summer the track filled with grasses and meadow flowers. At the top she passed the garage villagers referred to as The 21 because outside it was a milestone marked '21 miles to London'.

When she reached the London road, the A20, she tucked the puppy into the vest in her coat. In the containment of warmth and dark it settled down. There was very little traffic but she knew lorries would be using the road. She walked towards London for some hundreds of yards. Her method was to walk and put up her arm for any passing lorry. It was too cold to stand still. She walked briskly and had reached the haystacks at Farningham Gosse, a clear bit of road, before a lorry came down the hill behind her. She turned to hail it. There were two men in it, but it did not stop. She always felt a momentary disappointment but she was not disheartened. Sometimes it took two or three or even five tries before she was lucky. In the end out of kindness someone would give her a lift, someone who knew the lack of early-morning buses and the need to help out if they could. But the driver of that lorry, Henry Norris Bennett, never stopped for strangers, though he did wonder about a woman on her own in the dark at this time of the morning. He could not see her clearly but she did not appear young. He noticed she had something light round her neck. The next thing he noticed was an old lorry with a heavy load coming the other way uphill. The driver of it saw the woman trying for a lift but not succeeding.

The Murder

It was as if they had a date with each other. Two loners, two outsiders. Like characters by Samuel Beckett. In 1938 Beckett was stabbed in a Paris street by a pimp named Prudent. He visited him in prison and asked why he had done it. '*Je ne sais pas, monsieur,*' Robert-Jules Prudent replied, '*je m'excuse.*'

It was still dark at 5.20am. Sidney saw the woman turn and try to flag down the lorry heading for London, driven by Henry Bennett and his father. He caught her in his headlights, saw the rebuff, saw them overtake the small, shadowy figure walking towards him. She did not try to thumb a lift from him. He was going the wrong way. He drew up alongside her, wound down his window, leaned out, called to ask where she was heading. She wanted to get to London. He told her he was going there too, he just had to drop these bricks off, he'd give her a ride. She said she wanted to reach London by eight because of getting a cheap early-morning ticket for Woking on the train, so she'd wait for a lorry going her way. He said it wouldn't take him half an hour to drop this lot off. He'd get her to London before eight. Easy.

She believed him. It was too dark to see the colour of the lorry; maybe it was a dirty blue or grey, it looked old. She saw the name Dickerson painted on the front of it. She saw a stoutish man in a jacket and flat cap. He seemed a cheerful sort, disposed to help her. They were so kind, these lorry drivers. She went round the front of the lorry, he leaned over and opened the nearside door, she clambered up. There was no spare seat; she sat on the engine cowling, her back to him, Hedy tucked inside her coat. It was good to get out of the cold and drizzle. He drove off. The niceties were few. She told him her name. It sounded foreign. She said she was going to visit her brother in Woking. Oh yes, he thought, believe that you'd believe anything.

Within moments Dagmar felt alarm. The atmosphere was wrong, the way he eyed her. She had her back to him but when she turned her face she saw the scar that ran across his head. It looked as if someone had tried to chop his head off with an axe.

Worse than that were his eyes. They walked over her. The dog would look after her. She tried to be calm. She asked if he was sure they'd be in London by eight. She thought she'd prefer to get a lift that was going straight there. It would be all right, he said. It wouldn't take long. She'd be there in time.

It had bored him, the long drive through the night. It was hard to keep awake. He could do with sex. He had the money for it. Daisy didn't want it. That side of things didn't last. Sometimes, once a month or so, when he'd had a few beers. But there were plenty of women. This one must be up for it if she was out on the road in the dark at 5.20 in the morning on her own. He noticed the little brown attaché case and wondered how much was in it. He'd get money off her or sex of a sort. Or both. She was in his lorry to do what he wanted with her. Everything was an opportunity.

He drove along. A lane forked off not far from the Portobello Inn, about a mile from Labour in-Vain Road. It was a narrow track called Forge Lane. No one would use it at this time. He pulled in, turned off the headlights and the side lights too. Outside was darkness, the shapes of trees, no sky. The silence was absolute after the noise of the engine. They were out of view from the road. He got his wallet out from his jacket pocket. Tried to make her turn to face him. Tried to show her a wad of money. Told her what he wanted if she was to get some of it. Asked her how much she charged. She whimpered. He supposed she was playing hard to get. He grabbed at her. She was silent. Frozen with fear. This was evil, this was mortal danger. She lurched toward the cabin door, he pulled her back, trapped her with his arm, forced her around. In the dark of the cabin she saw his thick hands and that scar again. He pushed his hand up her coat and dress. It was more anger he felt than lust. And he liked to make her afraid.

And then she screamed. A shrill high scream that pierced into his head. He grabbed at her as she tried for the door, slapped her across her face, tore at her clothes, shoved his hand up her coat and dress, muttered about her having the rags on, said she could still play about with him. She could smell him, hear his breathing. She screamed the more, desperate screams, crazed with fear, screamed for help, for the police, the police. The puppy yelped, a hysterical high-pitched sound. It was a dog that knew nothing of these people or where it was, or where it belonged. The sounds hit Woggle, Harold, Sidney. She should have known how noise brought on his funny turns. Someone might hear. He'd shut her up. He'd do what he wanted with her. She was in his lorry. She was a whore.

They were two isolated people quite beyond safe relationship. She was naive, he was vicious, she was trusting, he was depraved. She repressed any mention of sex, he assumed she was lewd. Daisy would not be on a dark road alone before dawn. No decent woman would be. This one was asking for it. Whatever his name, Harold, Sidney, Bill or William, he spent his life watching out for easy prey, something to pounce on, something to take, something that was his. Nothing he took was worth anything. Nothing he took was enough. He had nothing, he was a loser. People could say what they wanted about him. None of it was his fault. All he wanted was to be wanked off by this broad who looked like rubbish, who was flaunting it, standing by the road in the dark at five in the morning. He'd give her a quid for it if she was nice to him.

He had a mind if not to rape her then to get her to comply.

Dagmar Petrzywalski was, as Keith Simpson the pathologist put it, *'virgo intacta'*; as Fabian put it, 'this middle-aged frail maiden lady who declined his advances'; as her nephew Jules put it, 'I cannot remember her ever having a male friend. I would not describe her as a "man hater" but she did not have much room for men.' Keith Simpson's post-mortem showed she had fibroids, which caused her to bleed. She did not go to the doctor or mention these. She referred to her 'internal troubles'.

Sidney Sinclair was not troubled by such niceties. His assault was not protracted but for Dagmar it was for ever.

She lurched to the door and kicked it open. She went on screaming for help, gulping, jabbering about the police. He hated her. The dog jumped out and ran trembling into the bushes. Taken from its mother, caged in a market and now this terror. Dagmar screamed for the dog and tried to follow it. She had something round her neck. He pulled it tight from behind her as she struggled for the door. To shut her up, keep her in the cabin, keep her from the police and him from prison and all the stinking mess of it: his mother who wouldn't let him through the door, his sister Edie who never said a good word to him, his father whacking him round the head, that Sophia droning on at him, PC bloody Troughton with his handcuffs, the chaplain telling him he was a sinner. He pulled the white scarf thing so tight her back arched over the engine cowling. He only pulled it for a few seconds. Just to shut her up. Enough to fracture the right horn of the thyroid cartilage. Enough to make her go quiet and still.

Absolutely quiet and absolutely still. He held the scarf in both hands and she lay over the cowling like a spilled sack. He held her there, then blanked out. For twenty minutes he sat in the silence of this country lane, his mind closed off, beyond thought. When he came to there she was, this lump, arched back over the cowling. He was still holding the scarf thing in both hands. He lifted her head, shook her. She was a goner. Dead. Someone might see. He pushed her into a sitting position on the floor. He had to get rid of her, get her out of his lorry, out of his life and get on with his day. He did not know who she had been. She was anyone. Nobody. She was, in a way, in a place he wanted to be – beyond anxiety, failure or anger. Out of it.

Harold Hagger, Sidney Sinclair had now gone beyond the boundaries of his own wrongdoing. This wasn't six months or a year. This was where Woggle's anger and thieving had led him. He was a murderer. It would take some guile to keep this one under cover. It was her fault for screaming. At least he wouldn't hear those screams again.

This was not how Sidney Sinclair had planned his day. He got out and closed the nearside door. There was no sign of the bloody dog. He started the engine, switched on the lights, backed out to the road. He drove for about twenty minutes toward East Malling. The woman sat propped against the engine cowling, blood settling into stains where her backside bounced against the hard lorry floor.

Halfway down Wrotham Hill there was no traffic in either direction. He had a clear view of the road. He got out, went round the front of the lorry, opened the nearside door, looked each way, dragged her out and across the verge, hoicked her over the barbed wire and dumped her behind the hedge. No one had seen. She was out of his lorry and he felt better. Felt nothing. A bit shaken up but it was over. None of it had happened. None of it. He could shape life how he wanted it. He still had her case. There might be something in it though it didn't look much, mended with string. The sky was lightening. He had work to do. He did not want to be late with the bricks. There was that barley order for later in the day. He released the brake and let the lorry coast down the hill to start the engine

It was about ten more miles to the cider mills. At West Malling he stopped a cyclist, Ernest Robert Bennet, a labourer who lived at 16 Council Cottages, Offham. 'Good morning, sir. Where's the Goldwell cider works, East Malling?' Sidney asked in his cheerful, respectful way. This Mr Bennet was thirty-six, born in Clapham, the third son of a solicitor's clerk. He told Sidney he was nearly there, he should carry on, take the second turning on the right by the council yard. 'It's called Winterfield Lane,' he said. Stanley Clarke of Breen House was getting dressed and overheard the conversation from his upstairs bedroom window. He wondered what was going on at the cider mill that they needed all those bricks

Before 7am Sinclair pulled up outside the gates of the cider works by the Time Office where the factory workers clocked on. He turned off the engine and headlights, and opened the case. There was 15 shillings in a brown horseshoe purse, a couple of Yale keys, a piece of cheese, a wrap of sandwiches – all that was in them was a scrape of jam – a pair of gloves and a yellow string bag. Sinclair ate the cheese, ripped the lid off the case, ripped the case into two, then put the gloves, purse and bag in his pocket and sat waiting.

At 7.07 a machine hand, Frederick Prudence, who lived in a council cottage in the village of Larkfield, arrived on his bicycle. As he clocked on, Sidney called to him from his lorry that he had a load of bricks for the mill, he didn't bloody well want to wait all bloody day and where was the bloody foreman. Still in bed, Prudence told him. Sidney would have to wait until he heard the starting whistle at eight. He thought Sidney seemed a cheery sort of bloke, though he swore a lot.

Sidney left his lorry outside the gates and walked into the village to try to get a paper. He could not find a shop. Everywhere was closed. He went back to his lorry, sat in the cabin and waited.

At between 7.30 and 7.45 Mame Petrzywalski went down the path outside her bungalow to collect her *Daily Telegraph.* She noted Dagmar's piece of paper tucked in the fence with OUT written on it in red ink.

In the cabin of his lorry Sinclair dozed and idly watched men arriving for work and clocking on. It had been a tiring drive. At 7.45 Frederick Simmonds, a labourer, a local man who lived in East Malling, clocked on. Sinclair told him he needed to get away, he had another job waiting, he'd been hanging around this bloody fucking place since ten to seven. Fred Simmonds said he'd be attended to as soon as the whistle blew, but he would check matters with the 'outside' foreman, Arthur Blundell.

At about 7.55 the chief foreman arrived in a private car. Sinclair was shown to his office by a workman, Bernard Eldridge. He 'swore quite a bit about being kept waiting'. The foreman told him the bricks were to be unloaded on waste ground at the back of the mill, he should take his lorry round through the back gates. Sidney drove round the mill to get there. Another lorry blocked his path to the waste ground, so again he had to wait.

He was eight yards from the stream which went under the cider works. He got out and threw the yellow string bag and

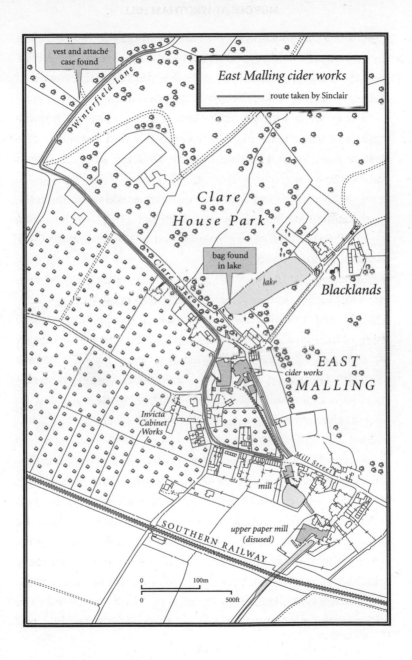

East Malling cider works

————— route taken by Sinclair

vest and attaché case found

Winterfield Lane

Clare House Park

bag found in lake

lake

Blacklands

Clare Lane

EAST MALLING

cider works

Invicta Cabinet Works

Mill Street

mill

SOUTHERN RAILWAY

upper paper mill (disused)

0   100m

0   500ft

gloves into the stream, then paced up and down. The day, like his life, was not turning out well. Louisa Davenport, who lived in Dumb Clock Row, saw him and thought he looked nervous and pale. Born and married in Malling, she knew the area. Her father had been a stoker when the mill was used for paper-making. Now she worked in the canteen at the Willet & Robinson coal yards in Hart Street, Maidstone. She always walked from her house to catch the firm's lorry which stopped at the Rising Sun in Mill Street to pick up workers for the coal yard. She had the impression Sinclair did not want to be seen. He turned away when she passed him. She looked back. He seemed agitated, there was something suspicious about his manner.

Again Sinclair sat in his lorry, then drove on to the waste ground and helped Fred Simmonds and another labourer, Harry West, get the bricks off the lorry. 'We got unloaded just after nine.' So much for his promises to get Dagmar Petrzywalski to London by eight. Arthur Blundell, a foreman with the firm for two years, signed the delivery note Sinclair handed to him and gave a copy to the storeman.

And so a trail was laid: signed slips of paper, snatches of over-heard and idle conversation, the names of strangers, casual observations by passers-by, the mundane occurrences of everyday life, only to be remembered, retraced, reconstructed and to gain significance if interlocking facts were needed, if quotidian detail required forensic scrutiny in order to ascertain, with certainty, what precisely occurred when, where, in what way, and by whom, when murder, the ultimate crime against humankind, had taken place.

To get his empty lorry out through the back gates to the cider mill, Sinclair had to keep reversing and turning. He drove down Winterfield Lane to the main road. As he drove he chucked the vest, then the bits of the attaché case, then the jam sandwiches, into the grass verge and hedgerows.

And that was that. All done. Finished. It was still early and he was rid of it: the bricks, the woman, the bag, the case, the sandwiches, the lot.

At the other side of Wrotham Hill, at 10am, he went into the Rising Sun café near Kingsdown for a mug of tea, a couple of cakes and a cigarette. It was one of the cafés he liked. There were several people in there. It was run by Walter and Rose Johnson. Rose was having the piano tuned. She was fifty-two, born in Hackney, a milkman's daughter. She had married Walter, a milkman's son, thirty years previously and they had five children, a girl and four boys. In 1927, in a sale of land belonging to South Ash Manor Farm, Walter bought three acres and built the Rising Sun and several bungalows. He was not a stranger to prison cells. In August 1940 he was charged with making a false insurance claim against Sun Insurance. Two detectives came to arrest him at the café. Walter got out his shotgun. There was a struggle. In a cell at Dartford police station he tried to kill himself, then appeared in court with his head bandaged and said he didn't understand the charges.

Sidney stopped for half an hour at the Rising Sun, then drove on to Bishop's Stortford and had his dinner in Judd's café. At 12.30 he phoned his governor for the next order, from the call box at Stansted Mountfitchet. He was told to collect the barley from Chrishall Grange and take it to Thurston, near Bury St Edmunds. He called at Dickerson's yard to get the invoices and paperwork for this assignment. Alan Bell said when he had finished that job he could take his waggon home to Little Abington. He had done enough work for one day.

Sidney Sinclair's Fourth Statement: Saturday 23 November 1946

Sidney could not sleep in the prison cell at West Malling police station on the night of Friday 22 November 1946. The police watched over him like he was a killer. He wanted Fabian to believe him, he wanted a story he could believe himself. In his mind he went over the route yet again and thought up another version. Fabian had to believe what was true: he hadn't meant to kill the woman. He just had to stop her screaming. He would have let her out the lorry if she'd kept quiet, been nice to him and asked normally. He didn't mean to strangle her with the bloody scarf or vest or whatever it bloody was.

Next morning at 8.20 he asked Detective Constable Cyril Bailey to light a cigarette for him, then enquired, 'When will that Inspector Fabian get here?' Bailey told him, 'He usually arrives about nine thirty.' Sidney asked the time, then said, 'I've hardly slept for over a fortnight. I want to tell him what happened. I'll tell him the truth that I picked the woman up and what happened.'

Bailey was triumphant. He phoned Fabian who arrived at the police station within a quarter of an hour and was even more calm and friendly than usual toward Sidney. 'I've been told you wish to see me,' he said. Sidney replied, 'Yes, I want to tell you all about it. I must tell somebody.' He had, he said, thought the whole business over all night and he thought it better to tell the truth about what actually happened.

Fabian gave him tea and another cigarette and told him he need not say anything unless he wanted to, and what he did say would be taken down in writing and might be used in evidence against him. Did he understand that?

He took him to an interview room and again asked, 'Do I understand you want to make a statement?' 'Yes,' Sidney replied. Fabian, courteous and solicitous, asked, 'Would you like to write it yourself or would you like Sergeant Rawlings to write it?' 'Let the sergeant write it, he's written the others,' Sidney said.

> *Statement of Sidney Sinclair of 25 Little Abington Cambridgeshire who saith:*
> I have been cautioned by Chief Inspector Fabian that I need not say anything unless I wish to do so and what I do say will be taken down in writing and may be given in evidence.
> *Signed Sinclair S.*
>
> I have asked to see you because I have thought this business over all night and feel it is better for me to tell the truth about what happened.

But the truth was an elusive concept for Sidney and he had no practice at telling it.

> What really happened was that when I was driving along the road after my second stop because my radiator was boiling I saw a woman on my offside and she held her hand up for me to stop. I pulled in and she said 'I want to get to London.'

This was not a good beginning. That was not the truth about what had happened. He had seen the woman hold her hand up for the Bennetts who were going to London. She had not held up her hand for him. He was going the wrong way. It was he who had stopped because he was predatory and opportunistic.

I said to the woman, 'I shan't be going back to London till between nine and ten.' She said 'Where are you going then?' I said 'I've got to take these bricks to East Malling' and she said, 'All right I'll come with you.'

She got up into the cab and put an attaché case on top of the engine cover. When she got in she said something about a puppy, but I didn't see one. She must have put it down by her side or had it tucked inside her coat. I started off and drove a little way when the woman said, 'Will you pull into the little fork turning just along the road as I want to talk to you.' I said, 'I will pull in for a few minutes if you like but I haven't got much time. What do you want to talk about?' By this time she had pointed to where she wanted me to pull in and I pulled up and switched my headlight off.

'Which headlight was that?' Fabian asked with his obdurate and insatiable enthusiasm for seemingly irrelevant detail. 'It was the one on the nearside,' Sidney replied. Fabian let him get on with it. He watched his face: the look in the eyes, the hesitancy in his voice, the overemphatic persuasion of a man who lied. What was it that allied him so irredeemably to falsehood, wrongdoing and evasion? No reference to be made to the squalor of his intention: that Dagmar knew within seconds she had made a mistake, that she sat on the engine cowling with her back to him, the puppy tucked in her coat, that he could not see a bag or case without thinking to steal it, that she pleaded with him to stop, said she wanted to get out, that he pulled into Forge Lane, turned off the headlights, leered at her, that even before he did anything to her she started screaming, the dog yapping.

Fabian was the better actor. He feigned belief, gave away nothing of his pleasure that this old lag was making life easy for him and as good as had a noose around his neck. Didn't he know he was giving this eyewash to Detective Inspector Robert Fabian, whose business for twenty years had been crime and murder, who had sent brighter murderers than this one to the gallows and put uncounted homosexuals, prostitutes, drug addicts, thieves and all manner of rotten eggs behind bars?

Fabian asked polite, encouraging little questions and let Sidney make one gaffe after another. Sidney, unlike Fabian, was not good at his job. To be good at a job meant attention to detail, tenacity, vigilance, application. Had Sidney put the evidence – the vest, case, bag – into one of his father's dustbins, he most likely would never have been apprehended. Had he pleaded guilty he might have invited better defence counsel than with such evident lies. He had not learned much in his career as a criminal. Fabian knew Dagmar Petrzywalski wanted to get to London before eight in the morning. No court would believe she asked to stop in the dark, down a deserted lane, going in the wrong direction, to chat with this scar-faced villain.

I said, 'Now what you got to talk to me about?' She said to me, 'Have you got any money on you?' I said 'I always carry plenty of money about with me on this job' and she said, 'I haven't got any money and I want to get some to get to London.'

Fabian knew from her mother that Dagmar had at least 12 shillings on her. He had witness statements describing how she left the equivalent of the fare on the passenger seat when she hitchhiked, was thrifty but generous, never arrived at her nephew's or sister-in-law's house without a gift and had saved some £400 to supplement the Post Office pension that arrived every Friday.

She then said, 'If you give me any money you cannot interfere with me as I have got the rags on.' She said, 'How much money have you got on you?' and I said I had about £17 in my coat. Then she said 'If you give me some money I will play about with you.'

That was as near as Sidney Sinclair could get to admitting the squalor of his intention, his sordid view of sex. It seemed this forty-eight-year-old virgin who worked for twenty-five years as a telephonist, cared for her aged mother and lived alone in a shed, who was too reticent even to articulate the words sanitary napkins or consult a doctor about vaginal bleeding, and whom no one saw naked, had the alter ego of a frenzied harlot. It would not have helped his case to say he would have given her a quid if she'd wanked him off and what was she doing on the road at five in the morning if she wasn't a slut. He perhaps had not got the measure of his victim as he pawed at her, stuck his hand between her legs, made a lewd remark about the rags on, swore at her.

While she was talking she must have been messing about with my jacket and the next thing I saw was that she had my wallet in her hand and was putting it down her breast. I turns round to her and said 'So that's your bloody game is it?' and with that I hit her round the side of the face. She started kicking and screaming.

Fabian let it all pass without comment. Sinclair's lies suited him. Judge and jury would take a view. 'Where was your jacket?' was all Fabian asked Sidney, who told him it was hanging on a hook at the back of the cabin. But the early morning was cold and wet, it was late October and the cabin unheated. Would he not have had need of a jacket?

As I went to get hold of her round the neck something came away which turned out to be a vest which she must have been using as a scarf. With that I went to pull the scarf and I must have pulled it too hard and the next thing I saw was the still body of the woman and this frightened me. I shook her and she just slumped down.

It was true he had pulled the vest too hard. To stop her screams and the dog yapping and because he was vicious and wasn't getting what he wanted, had never got what he wanted or anything of worth. But Fabian had what he wanted. An admission of killing. No jury would believe the story about the wallet. Sidney Sinclair had had it. Had he told the truth there might have been a faint chance of manslaughter. No defence would wash with this yarn. Better that he was going to plead not guilty. It would go as hard as hell against him.

In the struggle the woman had kicked the cab door open and I got a bit panicky and I closed the door, backed out on to the road and drove on towards East Malling. I travelled on for a distance and half way down a hill, which turned out to be Wrotham Hill, I stopped, got out, went round to my nearside, opened the door, had a look to see if anyone was coming. I then lifted the body out of the cabin, carried the body across the verge and laid her behind the hedge. I then went back to my lorry, shut the cabin door, went round to the offside and got into my seat. I let my brake off and let the lorry coast down the hill to start the engine up. As I was driving away it was getting day break. I found the attaché case was still in my cabin and I then saw the vest the woman had was in the cabin too.

It was all right now. He could say it as it was. He did not have to say how he sat there, in the cabin, for twenty minutes in awe of what he had done. He did not have to lie any more. Not when he was telling Fabian about the road and the sign posts and the traffic lights. Fabian seemed just as interested in those matters. Did he drag the body? Fabian asked. No, Sidney told him, he had lifted it and carried it across the verge and laid it behind the hedge. That seemed a gentlemanly way of putting it. After all, she had been a woman. Not that he had lugged her out the cabin, dragged her dead weight across the verge, her legs trailing so she lost a shoe, dumped her in the bushes, the brambles and barbed wire ripping her stockings so her foot stuck through, tearing the net out of her hair. Not that he covered her face with her coat because she was as dead as a fucking dodo and he didn't want her looking at him with her accusing dead eyes.

I then went back to my lorry, shut the cabin door, went round to the offside and got into my seat.

It was nice and reassuring the way Fabian wanted to know about the nearside and offside. All the sequential manly detail calmed the story down, bleached it, turned it into the recounting of a mundane day's events outside the reach of right and wrong, the law and retribution.

I let my brake off and let the lorry coast down the hill to start the engine up. As I was driving away it was getting day break. I found the attaché case was still in my cabin and I then saw the vest the woman had was in the cabin too.

Sidney saw it now, the grey unpromising dawn, the pathetic case fixed with a bit of string, the white vest with a darn in the shoulder. He should have burned them. That was a big mistake. Careless. What use were they to him or Charlie Judd or Daisy?

I drove on to West Malling and asked a bloke on a bike the way to East Malling. He told me to carry on and turn right by the council yard. I kept on and turned right as he told me and went down the lane, turned left at the bottom as he told me, went down the hill, turned right at the bottom and into the cider works yard. I pulled up outside the gates of the main entrance. I switched my headlights and engine off, still being shook up over what I had done. I made up my mind to get rid of the attaché case.

He was telling the truth. Surely Fabian could see that. Turned right, turned left, kept on, turned right, pulled up, switched the engine off. The rest was bad luck inflicted on him because he was a victim. Who wouldn't be shook up if that lot had happened to them? If Fabian was unconvinced he did not show it.

I opened the attaché case and saw what was in the case was a yellow net bag with a parcel of food what turned out to be jam sandwiches and a pair of gloves.

He didn't mention Dagmar's ration of cheese, which she was taking as a present for Elena and which he had eaten with ungentlemanly appetite, or the purse with the keys to her hut and her mother's bungalow and the 15 shillings in silver in it which he had pocketed.

I put the gloves and string bag into my pocket. I got out of my cabin. As I was getting out there was a man, who turned out to be a workman, going in to clock on. I asked him where the foreman who is in charge was and asked him what time they started. He said, 'We have two times here, 7 o'clock and 8 o'clock.' He said to me, 'I'm afraid you'll not get unloaded until 8 o'clock.' I said, 'That's a pity. I want to get back early to pick a load of barley up.'

With that I came back to my lorry and then I walked up a narrow passageway by the side of the factory and walked right the way round back to my lorry again. I opened my door, got in and sat in my lorry for a while. I see time must be getting on as the other workmen kept on coming in and clocking on. I said to one of the workmen through my window, 'Who is the foreman in charge to where these bricks have got to go?' He said, 'He is not here at the present but he should be here any time now.'

I waited a short period, a little private car pulled up between the wall and my lorry by the gate, a man got out of the car and he went to walk into the gates. I said to him, 'Who is the gentleman in charge to where I have to take these bricks to?' He said, I forget the name he said now, 'So and so should be in the office now, I'll go and have a look for you.' I follows behind him to the office, he goes in and he said, 'He'll be out in a minute.' I goes in, see a gentleman sitting at a desk and asked him where these bricks was going. He said they would be going out through the other gate on to a bit of waste ground at the back and said, 'By the time you get your lorry started the gates will be unlocked.' I gets my lorry started and pulls round the back. I could not get straight in, I had to back on to a bit of ground at the back. I goes through the gate on to the concrete road. I drives along the concrete road and I found that one of their own lorries wanted to get out. I pulls off the road a bit for him to get by and in the meantime I got out of my lorry took the net bag and gloves out of my pocket and threw them into the stream which runs through the cider works yard and into the cider works.

Murder might take fifteen to twenty seconds. Disposing of the body another sixty, destroying the evidence another three, the whole dismal episode over in a couple of minutes, an unimportant life snuffed. Surely Fabian could see that the important thing, the honourable, manly thing, was manoeuvring an 8-ton lorry into a cider works. Doing it right, deferring to the foreman, waiting for the gates to be unlocked, obeying orders. Surely Fabian could see that Sidney, Harold, Woggle was deep down a sensible fellow, a hard-working man and this mess was a passing misfortune.

When I got back to my lorry I managed to turn round and managed to take the bricks to where they wanted them put. Two of their workmen started to unload and I helped. We got unloaded just after nine. When I was unloaded I went over to the foreman to get my ticket signed. He signed it and I started out the way I came in.

He didn't have to help unload, it wasn't his job, but that was the kind of man he was: helpful, obliging. Fabian should see this was an ordinary working day, distorted and confounded by this depraved hitchhiker.

I turned right outside the gates. I couldn't get out in one turn and had to keep backing. Eventually I got going.

I followed the road back on to the lane, turned up the lane, turned right to get back on to the main road. Proceeding down there I threw the vest out on the offside going down. Going a little further down I threw parts of the attaché case away, which in the meantime I had broke. A little further down I chucked the jam sandwiches away. Then I turned left on to the main road and proceeded on my way home. I stopped at a café just the other side of Wrotham Hill and had a cup of tea and a couple of cakes.

Sidney liked his tea strong with two sugars and his preference was for plain sponge cakes, nothing fancy. Daisy's Victoria sponge was best.

I then drove on to Stortford where I stopped at what they call Judd's Café where I had my dinner. After my dinner I proceeded on to Stansted Mountfitchet where I phoned my governor up for orders. I was told to go to Chrishall Grange and pick up eight tons of barley and take it up to Thurston near Bury St Edmunds. I carried out my orders and had to call into Dickerson's yard at Cambridge for the invoices for the barley on the way. After I had got my invoices and got filled up the guvnor's secretary told me it would be all right for me to take my waggon home that night, so I took my waggon home. I carried on working for the firm, but this business worried me, so I went to the doctor, the Czech doctor who works with Dr Brown, to get something for my nerves. After that I went all to pieces and packed my job up. That was on the Monday. I was out of work for nearly a week and then I got a job with Joshua Taylor of Abington as a gardener. That was where I was working when the officers came to see me.

Fabian then produced Sidney's wallet. It had been examined by Chief Inspector Birch at Scotland Yard's Fingerprint Bureau to see if Dagmar's fingerprints were on it, but nothing showed up. Fabian asked Sidney if it was the wallet in contention, then Rawlings brought the statement to an end.

The wallet you have shown me is the one I had in my jacket in the cab of my lorry and is the one the woman took.

This statement has been read to me and is true.
Sidney Sinclair
Statement taken by Chief Inspector Fabian, New Scotland Yard in the presence of Detective Superintendent Smeed, Kent County

Constabulary, written down and read over by Detective Sergeant H. Rawlings, New Scotland Yard, in the presence of Chief Inspector Fabian and Detective Superintendent Smeed.

Fabian went to his office. He had paperwork to do. Sidney Sinclair was again cautioned, then formally charged with murder by Detective Inspector Jenner of the Kent County Constabulary.

'The Statement What I Confessed to This Morning is True'

It was the Crown prosecution versus one miserable man. Fabian sent telegrams to the Commander and Deputy Commander of Crime at New Scotland Yard and to the Press Bureau:

Sidney Sinclair, age 45, a gardener, of 25 Little Abington Cambridgeshire, has been charged at West Malling Kent with the murder of Dagmar Petrzywalski on 31 October 1946 and will appear at the Occasional Court this afternoon.

23 November 1946

By that evening and the following morning the information was on the front page in national newspapers. At The Cinema, Ashford, Laurence Olivier and Joan Fontaine starred in *Rebecca*, illegitimacy in Kent had risen from 5.41 per cent of births in 1941 to 8.28 per cent, and Christmas rations were to be increased: an extra 1½ pounds of sugar for period 6, an extra pennyworth of meat for period 8. This bonus did not apply to Sidney Sinclair, who had forfeited his ration book and whose meals were now provided by His Majesty's Government.

At West Malling police station he was again measured, weighed and documented. This was a recurring feature of being processed by the system. On forms it was again recorded that he was 45, 5ft 6in, fresh complexion, brown hair, grey eyes, scar on forehead, tattoos etc. On Saturday afternoon at a special sitting of the Malling Police Court he was charged with the murder of Miss Dagmar Petrzywalski, 48, known as Miss Peters, at Wrotham Hill on 31 October. He pleaded not guilty. At this first stage the only evidence, given by Detective Inspector Jenner, was that at noon that day, when formally charged, the defendant in response had said (with disarming mendacity), 'The statement what I confessed to this morning is true.' Sinclair was granted a certificate for legal aid and remanded in custody. The date for the preliminary hearing of the case was set for 13 December. He was taken to Maidstone prison, admitted to hospital there and kept under observation for what was left of the weekend. He kept saying to the prison doctor, Dr Methuen, that he had had enough and wanted to kill himself. On the Monday afternoon, following instruction from Methuen, he was transferred to Canterbury prison, which was larger and had more resources than Maidstone. At Canterbury he made a botched attempt to achieve his wish to be gone.

Daisy's Plight

The talk in the village of Little Abington was of the crimes of Sidney Sinclair and the fate of Daisy, whose plight was extreme. Now she did not even have a name. And she was pregnant. She was forty. It was unclear if Sid was the father. Daisy, as her daughter Ellen put it, had all sorts of suitors, rich and poor. Six years into what she thought was her marriage, she and Sid did not have sex often and he had told her he could not have children, but it seemed that most of what he had said and done was a lie. Sid was not Sidney Sinclair at all but Harold Hagger, thief, army deserter, bigamist and murderer.

Daisy's biggest worry was her marriage status. The certificate was worthless. This Harold already had a wife whom he had never mentioned and apparently a son too, called Ronald. As for money, now there would be none coming in. She had often wondered and feared where the extras he brought home came from, but he resisted all questions. The war bonds bought with the cash he erratically gave her were under a false name, his ration book was worthless, so was his life insurance policy with the Prudential; and her widow's pension from her bona fide husband, Cecil Linsdell, small though it had been, had stopped when she married Sidney Sinclair. Or thought she married him.

Daisy could not absorb all the police told her. Sid was accused of murdering an innocent woman who only wanted a ride in his lorry to visit her brother. He had tried to force sex on her. He was brutish and lewd. It was a capital charge, a hanging offence. And yet, when she and her daughter Ellen travelled the hundred miles to Canterbury to visit him in prison, she felt sorry for him. He seemed so down, so pathetic. She could not view him only as a criminal, knowing as she did his childlike anxiety and temper displays, his pride when he brought a wad of money from his wallet to give her, his appreciation of her home cooking, her stews and cakes, soups and pies, his handiness around the house, his pleasure in getting dressed up in snazzy clothes. Deep down he might be a villain, but they had declared love to each other. The whole business made her ill and she was admitted to hospital in Cambridge with depression and problems with her unwanted pregnancy.

Mame Petrzywalski and Dr Hay-Bolton

Mame Petrzywalski could not cope in the days following her daughter's murder. Ralph and Jules came to help with practical things: shopping, getting rid of the hens. Mame wanted to leave Houston but felt she must stay until after the trial. She needed to be there to help the police and answer questions, but she could not sleep and sounds in the night made her afraid. When she looked across at The Vic she expected to see Dagmar. When she heard footsteps she wondered if they were hers.

She saw Dr Hay-Bolton at his weekly surgery in the village. She was not a woman who talked about feelings, confided or asked for consolation, but she cried when he asked her how she was. He prescribed the barbiturate Luminal for her to take at night and an amphetamine, benzedrine sulphate, to alleviate her anxiety in the day.

The murder, certifying Dagmar dead at the roadside, the inquest and impending trial, aroused painful memories for Dr Hay-Bolton. He did not tell Mame that he too was the parent of a daughter declared murdered. Twenty-five years earlier he had been an army doctor in Shanghai. In June 1921 he brought his family home on leave to England. He, his wife, their three-year-old son and nine-month-old baby daughter Susanne, stayed with his wife's mother, Mrs Horsfall, in Chipping Norton in the Cotswolds. A Japanese amah, Otoki Sakabi, travelled with them to look after their baby girl. On 21 June the baby was found drowned in a brook near his mother-in-law's house. A verdict of murder was returned against the Japanese amah, who spoke no English.

Dr Hay-Bolton and his wife were visiting friends when their daughter died. They had employed Otoki Sakabi on the recommendation of the manager of the Astor House hotel in Shanghai, a colonial hotel where tea dances were held and customers wore formal dress for dinner. Dr Hay-Bolton's mother, Jane, was staying there at the time. The manager told them Otoki Sakabi was a 'travelling' amah who had been to Europe before. She was with the Hay-Boltons for five weeks before they sailed to England. She was forty-one and widowed. Dr Hay-Bolton gave her £20 to buy uniforms and agreed to pay her £5 a month. During the whole time on board ship 'she was in every way satisfactory'. She got on well with the baby, who seemed very fond of her.

In the early afternoon of 21 June 1921 she took Susanne for a walk. At eight in the evening a woodman on the Heythrop estate found the child lying face down in a nearby brook. The brook was 10 or 11 inches deep, 7 or 8 feet wide and down a sloping bank. The baby was dead. The perambulator lay on its side under bushes. The nurse was covered in mud and wet from head to toe, with one of her muddy shoes by the bank, the other in the stream. On the opposite bank the police found five £1 notes, a ten shilling note, a shilling, keys, a comb and some scissors. They were identified as belonging to Otoki Sakabe.

Norman Hay-Bolton's cousin, Alfred Bolton, also a doctor,

certified the child dead. Death was by drowning. He said he was sure the baby was alive when she entered the water and a wound under her chin was 'too severe to be caused by her own nails, but not enough to cause any particular damage'. It could have been caused by the nurse's scissors.

Otoki Sakabi was taken to Chipping Norton police station and charged with the murder of Susanne Alathea Hay-Bolton. At her trial, Professor Shunda Tachibana, a Japanese academic living in Oxford, interpreted and translated into Japanese the unconvincing evidence given by the prosecution. 'The prisoner appeared excited, and talked volubly in her own language.' The jury found her guilty of murder. She was sent to Dartmoor prison, the hardest and most severe in England, where violent offenders were incarcerated. No one there spoke Japanese. She was released after ten years in 1932 and deported to Japan.

Dr Hay-Bolton did what he could to calm Mrs Petrzywalski. She was his last patient of the day. He then went home to Wrotham. His daughter Susanne, had she lived, would have been twenty-five. But her death, the fate of the Japanese nurse and the murder of Dagmar Petrzywalski were small misfortunes as measured against the punishment inflicted on the people of Japan in the summer of 1945 at the war's end. 'We have discovered the most terrible bomb,' President Truman wrote in his diary on 25 July:

It may be the fire destruction prophesied in the Euphrates Valley Era after Noah and his fabulous Ark. Anyway we think we have found the way to cause a disintegration of the atom. An experiment in the New Mexico desert was startling to put it mildly. Thirteen pounds of the explosive caused the complete disintegration of a steel tower 60 feet high, created a crater 6 feet deep and 1,200 feet in diameter, knocked over a steel tower half a mile away and knocked men down 10,000 yards away. The explosion was visible for more than 200 miles and audible for 40 miles and more.

This weapon is to be used against Japan between now and August 10th. I have told the Secretary of War to use it so that military objectives and soldiers and sailors are the target and not women and children. Even if the Japs are savages, ruthless, merciless and fanatic, we, as the leader of the world for the common welfare, cannot drop that terrible bomb on the old capital or the new.

On 6 August 1945, in agreement with Britain and to lead the world for its common welfare, the United States dropped an atomic bomb codenamed Little Boy and weighing 9,700 pounds on Hiroshima. Three days later Fat Man, weighing 10,213 pounds, was dropped on Nagasaki. Paul Tibbets from Illinois piloted the B-29 bomber that killed 140,000 people in Hiroshima. He saw the city disappear under a blanket of smoke and fire. In interviews he said he had no regrets. 'My one concern was to do the best job I could.' He was made a brigadier general and lived until he was ninety-two. Charles Sweeney piloted the B-29 that bombed Nagasaki and killed 70,000 people in a day: 'I just wanted the war to be over so we could get back home to our loved ones,' he said. Albert Einstein's equation $E=mc^2$ was the theoretical basis for nuclear fission: 'If only I had known, I would have become a watchmaker,' he is thought to have said of this particular application of it.

6

THE TRIAL

Fabian was well satisfied with progress on the Wrotham Hill murder case, but he wanted unequivocal victory. He allowed no relaxation of effort and spurred his team on to formulate evidence for the prosecution.

The day after Sidney Sinclair was charged, Detective Sergeant Thrift and Detective Inspector Jenner went round to The Vic, Dagmar's erstwhile home, at 11.15 in the morning and removed three pieces of carpet, two pieces of folkweave material, two blankets and a sheet. All this was given to Dr Henry Holden to scrutinise for hairs or blood.

Sophia Elisabeth Hagger told Detective Sergeant Rawlings that if necessary she would gladly give evidence against her husband for committing bigamy. She was living comfortably in Holloway in north London at 8 Scholefield Road with Francesco Paolo Ferrigni, a divorced Italian painter and decorator employed by Islington council.

Detective Superintendent Smeed sent letters to all working on the case, letting it be known that Sidney Sinclair alias Harold Hagger CRO no 23511/17 were one and the same man and that the said man stood remanded in custody by West Malling (Kent) Magistrates' Court until his next court appearance at 10.30am on

219

Friday 13 December on the charge of murder at Wrotham Hill in the County of Kent Against the Peace.

Fabian gathered depositions from thirty witnesses. Sworn statements were taken from:

- Joseph Henry Hammond, the unfortunate lorry driver who found Dagmar's body
- Sergeant Thomas Frederick Pettitt, the first police officer at the crime scene
- Dr Norman Hay-Bolton, who certified Dagmar dead
- Inspector Henry England, who photographed her body and the hedgerow where she was found
- Dr Cedric Keith Simpson, who carried out the post-mortem
- Dagmar's mother, Mame Petrzywalski, who went to the police after reading in the *Daily Telegraph* of the discovery of a body and fearing it was her daughter
- Ralph Peters, her brother, who identified her corpse
- Elena Peters, her sister-in-law, who crocheted at Fabian's request a replica yellow bag of the one she was carrying on the morning she was murdered
- Henry Norris Bennett, the farmer on his way to London with his father at 5.15am, who thought of stopping to give Dagmar a lift but did not do so
- William Crittenden, the lorry driver who saw Dagmar's blue shoe on the verge of the road at 7.15 in the morning but did not stop to investigate
- Alan Alderson Bell, Sidney Sinclair's boss at Dickerson's haulage firm in Cambridge

- Sergeant Childerley, who went to 25 Little Abington and first questioned Sinclair in a routine check on lorry drivers
- Peter Nash, the farmer's son who found Dagmar's yellow bag in the lake at Clare Park when exercising a horse on a Saturday morning
- Cora Meacham, the housewife who washed the bag after Peter Nash gave it to her
- Sylvia Nash, Peter's sister, who ran round to Mrs Hessey's to get the bag back after Peter saw the picture of its duplicate in the *Kent Messenger*
- Ernest Bennet, who gave Sidney Sinclair directions from West Malling to the East Malling cider works
- Stanley Clarke, who from his bedroom window overheard Sidney asking the way to the East Malling cider works
- Bernard Eldridge, the workman at the cider works who showed Sidney to the foreman's office when he was waiting to deliver the bricks
- Harry West, the labourer who with Sidney's help unloaded the bricks from the lorry
- PC Fred Kirwan, who found the vest Dagmar had bought at Maidstone market in bushes in Winterfield Lane
- PC William Davie, who found pieces of the torn attaché case Sinclair threw into the bushes in Winterfield Lane
- Detective Constable William Wallace, who found the lid of the case

The names behind their depositions were like credits in a show. Each man or woman helped reconstruct a nefarious event that occurred on an autumn morning in 1946. The intention was to prove the guilt of a criminal beyond reasonable doubt and to ensure his punishment according to the law of the land. All swore before Almighty God they were telling the truth, then signed their depositions in the presence of Mr W.E. Dedrick, justice of the peace for the County of Kent. On 7 December Fabian forwarded these depositions, his report, the defendant's statements and a folder of photographs to the director of public prosecutions for use as evidence at Sidney Sinclair's trial.

Morling Prepares the Defence

Sidney Sinclair's legal aid was paid for by the state. No nationwide scheme for such aid was formalised until 1949 but William Beveridge's welfare state included access to justice and the right to legal representation.

Edward Alexander Morling of 5 Granada House, Maidstone was hired as Sidney's defence lawyer. He was forty-three and had been brought up with his two sisters and brother – he was the third child – in a three-roomed flat in Wimbledon. His mother Annie, from County Galway, widowed young, raised them as a single parent and worked as a council office cleaner to pay for their education.

The Kent constabulary passed relevant documents to Morling. His client's case did not look promising. It seemed Sinclair's only plausible chance of reprieve from the gallows was for him to be deemed clinically insane: off his head, and not responsible for what he was doing.

The definition of insanity was semantically awkward. To qualify, the defendant had to comply with the M'Naghten Rule.

In 1843 Daniel McNaughton, a Glaswegian woodcutter, shot dead Edward Drummond, secretary to the prime minister Robert Peel. His intention was to murder Peel but he got the wrong man. He believed himself the victim of an international conspiracy masterminded by the Pope and the Conservative government. Found guilty of murder but insane, under the Criminal Lunatics Act of 1800, he was sent to the state criminal lunatic asylum at Bethlem Royal hospital. On his admission papers was written 'Imagines the Tories are his enemies. Shy and retiring in his manner.' Twenty-one years later, in 1864, he was transferred to the newly opened Broadmoor hospital and spent the rest of his life there.

His sentence prompted public protest at such a display of state leniency. The House of Lords then drew up the M'Naghten Rules for when insanity could be accepted as a defence. Broadly, the defendant had to have a psychotic mental illness and be so deluded he did not know what he was doing or, if he did know what he was doing, not know it was wrong. No matter how alarming, menacing and unusual his personality, the man who knew what he was doing and that what he was doing was wrong was, according to the law, sane. The problem then, as ever, was of definition, diagnosis and the assigning of conditions to mental and physical states that were not understood, did not lend themselves to medicalisation and for which there was no known cure. Medical experts were practitioners of a most imperfect art. A diagnosis of paranoid schizophrenia might decriminalise the perpetrator of the murder, even though few schizophrenics were or ever have been killers. A diagnosis of manic depression might scrape by; obsessive compulsive disorder, where the defendant knew what he was doing and

223

that what he was doing was wrong but could not stop himself, would not.

There was a wide grey area for guilt. And there was no particular scrutiny of why Harold Hagger seemed compelled to behave as he did or why all the retribution and expense of the criminal justice system failed to transform him one jot. If he was not M'Naghten mad he was, faced with the law, sane. If he was sane he should be killed for killing, if he was mad he should be spared. The irony that the killer of the killer must be deemed sane did not come into the equation.

Another slim chance for Morling's defence of Sidney Sinclair was a plea of manslaughter. It was arguable and almost certainly true that Sinclair had not intended to kill Dagmar Petrzywalski. In his textbook of forensic pathology Keith Simpson described how quick and unintended strangulation could be, but the law was unremitting: if there was intention to rape or rob it was murder.

Sidney showed no inclination to swerve from his account of himself as the victim of assault. Morling could see his client's farfetched fantasy would be blatant perjury and was not going to hold up before judge, jury or anyone capable of rational thought. He asked Scotland Yard for sight of the correspondence relating to the Preston business, the train accident of 1925 and the treatment of his client in Carlisle infirmary. It was possible a skull fracture might have left Sinclair physiologically mad, M'Naghten mad. But it was hard to argue that Harold Hagger's behaviour before he jumped from the train was less criminal than Sidney Sinclair's after. They seemed much the same man now as then, though perhaps more so now. And Preston prison had closed in 1931 with its records transferred to Liverpool prison, which was badly bombed in the war. The room where records were held 'suffered from blast, incendiaries and water and most were lost'. All the Liverpool governor could now find about Harold Hagger was one case paper: it stated on admission to Preston prison hospital from Carlisle Infirmary he walked with a stick and had a scar to the side of his head but he had been released on 9 December 1925 'fit and well'.

Fabian sent an officer from Cumberland and Westmorland constabulary to the Carlisle Infirmary to glean medical details about Harold Hagger's injuries in 1925. The hospital would not disclose such records to the police without written request from Fabian as officer in charge of the case and written permission from Harold for information to be released. After delays, then acceptance that the request could come from Morling, the report arrived. It showed no evidence of a fractured skull. Harold had not been unconscious long and was discharged after twenty days.

Morling also requested details of Harold's suicide attempt at Pentonville in the faint hope that might define him as M'Naghten mad. The prison commissioners' report said he attempted to injure himself in April 1926 but this was not regarded as a genuine suicide attempt. He was punished for smashing up his cell and cautioned regarding the 'feigned attempt' at self-harm.

Morling's defence did not look promising, but he was free to hire psychiatrists of his own choosing to give their opinion about Sidney Sinclair's sanity. It was possible that, for money, a persuasive case might have been made, but Morling was reluctant to run up high bills for a client on limited legal aid when the case for the prosecution was persuasive and the case for the defence looked weak.

Preliminary Hearings

On 13 December the defendant was brought from Canterbury prison to West Malling Magistrates' Court. 'Sinclair sat with his eyes closed throughout the proceedings and on his behalf Mr Morling pleaded not guilty and reserved his defence,' the *Kent Messenger* reported.

The Crown prosecution case was outlined: Miss Peters, as for convenience she was called, a forty-eight-year-old recluse, was found strangled about four miles from the wooden hut where she lived. Strangulation was by forceful pressure maintained for at least fifteen or twenty seconds. Sidney Sinclair, when first interviewed at Cambridge in a routine police check on all lorry drivers using Wrotham Hill on the day of the murder, denied seeing a woman hitchhiker on the road but three days later handed in his notice to his employer and produced a doctor's certificate citing anxiety neurosis. His statement to Fabian of Scotland Yard, made on 23 November, admitting he killed Miss Peters, was read to the court. Edward Morling said he would contest the murder charge on the grounds of insanity or manslaughter.

The case was adjourned for a week until 20 December after disclosure that the army, on hearing of the court case, now had an arrest warrant for Sidney Sinclair who, as deserter 28467 Private Harold Hagger, had absconded from the General Service Corps. The officer in charge of army records in Cambridge had a muddle to sort and updating to do.

Sidney was returned to his cell at Canterbury prison. Christmas was close, there was snow on the roads and he was a hundred miles from Daisy and home. On 20 December the court briefly reconvened. Sidney stuck to his version that Dagmar proffered sex and tried to rob him of his wallet. Notices were served on police officers and witnesses to attend his trial at Maidstone assizes on 24 February 1947. Dr Brown from Canterbury prison hospital asked that he be transferred to Brixton hospital for observations on his mental state until this date. This was agreed.

Those free to do so hurried away for seasonal festivities. Dagmar Petrzywalski's body was taken from the mortuary fridge and buried not far from her father in the graveyard of St Edmund's church in Kingsdown. There was no headstone. Around the edge of the tomb was chiselled 'Dagmar Petrzywalski passed away 31 October 1946 aged 48'.

Mame Petrzywalski went to stay with Ralph and Elena in Woking. She planned to sell her bungalow, Houston, leave this scene of such wrongdoing and misfortune, and live with them as soon as the trial was over.

One hundred and seventy-six Christmas trees stolen from government woodland near Eastbourne were ordered to be distributed among the poor by a local magistrate and Odeon cinemas throughout the land showed the Marx Brothers in *A Night in Casablanca*.

Sidney Sinclair in Brixton Prison

Incarcerated in Brixton for Christmas and with his future as bleak as the weather – it was the start of the coldest winter for seventy years – Sidney again talked of suicide. Dr Frederick Hayden Taylor, the prison's medical officer, kept him under observation and prepared a detailed report on his mental state: a report on which Sidney's life depended. Taylor studied his medical records, his depositions to Fabian, accounts of his conduct in Maidstone and Canterbury prisons, his army reports, the opinion of the army psychiatrists.

Sidney tried to convince Taylor of his blackouts when driving: the stifling cabin, the noise of the engine, his head in a deluded twirl. But the prison officers said they witnessed no blackouts. Sinclair was well behaved, clean and tidy except for one afternoon when he attacked another prisoner who accused him of cheating at cards.

Daisy came out of hospital but was scarcely managing. She visited Sidney with Ellen and wept for his plight and her own. Dr Taylor interviewed her but she did not know what usefully to say to protect her so-called husband from the gallows. She knew nothing of the M'Naghten Rule and thought it would help if she presented Sidney as a nice man. She told Taylor she had never witnessed any blackouts or heard Sidney complain of them. He often had headaches, particularly after a long drive, was nervous, restless, irritable and perhaps sometimes bad-tempered, but never violent. She kept quiet about the blackened eyes and bruised wrists observed by her daughter.

On New Year's Eve Dr Denis Hill carried out an electroencephalograph on Sidney and recorded the results as mildly abnormal: 'The abnormality suggests a constitutional rather than an acquired disorder. There is no evidence for epilepsy and the EEG does not indicate any previous traumatic dysfunction.' Quite what that meant no one asked, but it was unlikely to save Sidney's neck.

Dr Taylor wrote up his professional opinion for the court: Sidney Sinclair was unstable and neurotic because of cracking his head on a railway line in 1925. His headaches were relieved by mild sedatives. Neither the headaches nor his dizzy spells would stop him knowing what he was doing or that what he was doing was wrong. In his opinion Sinclair was not insane and was fit to answer the charge of murder.

On New Year's Eve a fifteen-page letter was passed to Sidney from 'A Citizen, a Sinner saved by Grace'. It informed him the Lord was near and Christ died for everyone and would wash him in His precious blood. If Sidney repented he would be saved. 'What is your answer to be? Are you going to accept the Saviour or will you reject Him, knowing that in doing so, you have to meet Him as Judge?'

It was no help or consolation to Sidney, who wanted more tangible rescue and whose trial drew near. Throughout January formalities were sorted, procedures followed, forms completed, dated and stamped. Mr King, governor of Brixton, asked if Canterbury had the 'necessary equipment for performing executions'. The governor of Canterbury asked head office for instructions as to where Sidney should be sent if convicted of the capital charge. He was told according to resolution A545/26 it had been decided to return to pre-war practice and divide all London capital cases between Wandsworth and Pentonville. If Sidney was sentenced to death he should be removed to Wandsworth prison.

Two days before his trial Sidney was shunted back to Canterbury 'for production'. The governor of Wandsworth was warned to expect him at the end of February. The diary of the country's principal executioner, Albert Pierrepoint, was consulted for a convenient date.

Rex Versus Sidney Sinclair

The trial was billed as Rex versus Sidney Sinclair. On 27 February the defendant Sidney Sinclair, CRO no 23511/17, was arraigned before Mr Justice Byrne at the Kent winter assizes, Maidstone. The charge was murder. This was Byrne's first judgement on a capital charge. Mr Derek Curtis Bennett KC and Mr E.J.P. Cusson appeared for the Crown prosecution and Mr Melford Stevenson* and Mr W. Scrivens for the defence.

The judge opened proceedings. He told the jury there was no doubt Sidney Sinclair had strangled Dagmar Petrzywalski, with the vest she was wearing as a scarf, in the early morning of 31 October 1946 on the main A20 road, somewhere between the haystacks at Farningham Gosse and the spot where the body was found on Wrotham Hill. Sinclair had admitted this. The yardstick they must apply was: did he know what he was doing and that what he was doing was wrong.

Vows of truth-telling were made and God invoked as the all-seeing eye and ultimate arbiter of truth and justice. Defendant and witnesses were cross-examined, depositions read out, exhibits and photographs shown.

The jury of twelve, guided by the gowned, bewigged upholders of the law, observed Dagmar's respectable relatives: they saw her old broken-hearted mother in hat and gloves, who

---

* Melford Stevenson, nine years later, defended Ruth Ellis, who shot her lover. He had no success and she was the last woman to be hanged in England. He went on to become a judge with a reputation for severity. In 1969, four years after the death penalty was abolished for all crimes except treason and piracy, he handed down the longest prison sentence in English legal history, life sentences with a minimum of thirty years each, to the Kray twins, sensational criminals in London's East End during the 1950s and 1960s

had gone with her daughter to Maidstone market to buy a puppy and told how her daughter worked as a Post Office telephonist for twenty-five years but retired early because she was not strong; they saw Dagmar's kindly sister-in-law who crocheted a yellow bag for her birthday present, and they saw Sidney Sinclair, or was he Harold Hagger, recidivist and compulsive liar, of bullish build with a scar that straddled his face and with thick hands and the vocabulary and speech cadences of a dustman's son.

In the court before his eyes was all the squalor and disarray of Harold Hagger's life: his bigamous wife whom he denied even the right to a name; the dead woman's relatives whom he insulted with lewd lies about her behaviour; the army and prison psychiatrists he tried to deceive and who did not have a good word to say about him. And the police, Fabian and his team, into whose arms he returned as if to his natural home, who gave him tea, cake and cigarettes and treated him with courtesy, whom he had tried to oblige as he reconstructed, as if among friends, the ordinariness of that October day, but who now sought no less than his death in the service of justice and their own job satisfaction and hoped-for promotion.

Curtis Bennett for the Prosecution

Mr Curtis Bennett for the prosecution was on sure ground, precise with detail, his testimony measured. He told the jury that though when charged Sinclair had said, 'The statement what I confessed to is true,' they should not take the word 'confessed' as meaning he was confessing to murder. He was not.

He read out Sidney's last statement with all its naive and incriminating fantasy: 'Even if somebody steals your wallet,' he informed the jury, 'you are not allowed to strangle that person.' And anyway the contentious wallet, exhibit 15, had been found at the defendant's house.

'I think you should know', Curtis Bennett told the jury, 'that this woman had not been outraged.' But, he said, in view of Miss Petrzywalski's age, the fact that she was a virgin, her past history and the testimony of those who knew her, it was unlikely the defendant's story of what happened immediately before this fatal assault was true. There was no evidence to put before the court to show that the deceased woman had behaved in an immoral manner with other lorry drivers who had given her lifts on previous occasions.

Dagmar, he told them, was a mild-mannered recluse who lived in a hut she had built on the Hever Estate. He described her buying the man's white darned vest in the market, the marks of ligature round her neck when dead. He went over plausible times and distances of that Thursday morning: at 5.15am on 31 October a farmer going to London saw a woman on the left-hand side of the road waving for a lift. He did not stop but saw a heavily laden lorry coming in the other direction. At 6.30am the defendant asked the way to the East Malling cider works. At 6.58 he had been waiting at these works quite a while to unload his lorry. The victim's body was eight miles from the cider mills where the defendant was delivering bricks, and five miles from where she had beckoned for a lift. Curtis Bennett showed the court the vest found in the Winterfield Lane bushes, exhibit 5, the bits of attaché case, exhibit 6, the yellow bag in the Clare Park lake, exhibit 7.

That the defendant was a liar was as much beyond dispute as

the fact that he had killed this woman. When he wanted to leave the army he embellished his 1925 train accident and told the military authorities that after it he was in hospital for six months and unconscious for fourteen days. In fact he was in hospital for twenty days followed by two years in prison. Since 1925 he had been in prison seven times for dishonesty. He was discharged from the army in 1942, suffering the 'after effects of cerebral contusion with marked anxiety neurosis added' and declared unfit for any form of military service. But soon after that he was apparently fit enough to drive lorries and was regarded as a good worker. Was it not interesting, Curtis Bennett posited, that the defendant went to a doctor three days after his interview with the Cambridge police officer who was questioning all lorry drivers on the A20 on the day of the murder? 'For the first time for many years Mr Sinclair was again found to be suffering from anxiety neurosis following a recent shock.' Perhaps the shock had been accounts of murder in the newspapers and a visit from the police officer.

If a defence of insanity was made he, Curtis Bennett for the Crown, would call prison and army psychiatrists to rebut it. And if a defence of insanity failed and a second defence of manslaughter was sought, that too he, Curtis Bennett for the Crown, would refute.

Keith Simpson

Witnesses were called and cross-examined. The pathologist Dr Keith Simpson was a seasoned court performer. His fees were £3 3s for each day he attended a trial. He justified this because he had performed an autopsy, written a report on it and given evidence. He enjoyed the formality and dignity of the court, the wigs, robes and process. He called the judge My Lord, used the familiar stock phrases: 'I formed the opinion that . . .', 'the findings were consistent with . . .'. He anticipated questions, was prepared with answers, had all his records with him and never tried to memorise. He stood erect, spoke clearly, listened to the question, only answered what was asked, never evaded, admitted if he did not know, answered without heat, dispassionately, and avoided taking sides or sounding emotive.

He confirmed to the court that it was he who carried out the post-mortem on the deceased. Her height was 5 feet 3 inches, she was of medium to small build, not strongly built but healthy apart from fibroid tumours that caused bleeding of the vagina. There was nothing to suggest sexual attack. The deceased was a virgin.

The cause of death was asphyxia due to strangulation. There was no evidence of struggle but, yes, minor injuries on the cheek and left eyelid were consistent with a blow on the side of the head struck by the prisoner's hand.

Death was at about 7am or earlier and yes, was consistent with the time the defendant was on the road. Groups of marks across the front and sides of her neck were firmly impressed into the skin. At the back of the neck the impressions faded. They were in keeping with tight constriction by a folded cloth applied from behind and yes, the marks could have been caused by exhibit 5, the vest. Very considerable force would have been required for at least fifteen to twenty seconds. The constriction was sufficiently tight to have fractured the voice box and caused extensive bruising behind it.

Sidney Sinclair Cross-Examined

Sidney Sinclair was no strategist, but in his career had learned something of the cat and mouse procedures of the law. He knew he needed an explanation beyond a sleazy fancy for sex, or theft of this woman's meagre possessions. He liked to play cards in prison and at Charlie Judd's and now was a player in a game in which he needed to score on two out of three fronts: he was innocent, he was mad, and he did not know what he was doing.

He performed in an effort to save his life. It had worked to get him out of the army. Maybe it would get him out of this hole. He made much of his injuries from that jump from a moving train, told the court he had a fractured skull, concussion, a fractured pelvis, spent eight months in hospital. The length of time he was hospitalised lengthened with each telling of the story. He showed the jury the scar on his head, told of blinding headaches, giddiness, blackouts, trouble with his eyes, funny turns – twelve in the last four years, the same in number as those in court summoned to judge him. And his blackouts: Dickerson knew of them, his wife was always telling him to go to the doctor about them. She'd never seen them because she didn't drive with him. In the village of Waterbeach in 1943 he found himself upside down in a ditch. He crawled out after twenty minutes and was taken to hospital in Cambridge with a bruised spine. He was off work for a fortnight, or was it a week. Same thing in 1944 near Bedford. Blackout. Went through a garden wall. Again at Acton in June, or was it July 1946 when he crushed that man against a wall. 'The pains come on if I get excited or overdone with work, or anything like that.' Head colds, long journeys, being a coal porter in the army, all that did it too. Pains that made him lose conscious ness. He didn't feel them coming on. They descended in seconds.

As for that Thursday, 31 October 1946, which they all were so anxious to reconstruct . . . He went over it again. He had re-iterated it so often it seemed more true than the truth. It had become as rotelike as the Lord's Prayer. A woman at the side of the road . . . signalled to him to stop . . . asked for a lift . . . suggested going with him, then on to London. He told her she could please herself . . . sat on top of the engine cover, her back to him . . . said will you pull in off the road I want to talk to you. He told her he hadn't long to stop. He pulled into a lane. He switched the lights off, turned the engine off. She asked if he had any money. He told her he always carried plenty of money on this job . . . She had the rags on. She said, 'If you give me money I'll play about with you.' He told her, 'I didn't give you a lift for that. I was just trying to help you out.' His coat was hanging to his left behind his head. 'The next thing I saw was that she had my wallet in her hand and was putting it down her breast. I said to her is that your fucking game and I hit her on the side of the face. She started hollering, screaming and kicking. When I tried to get the wallet away she tried to scratch my eyes.'

He was, he suggested, holed up with a vixen. But the hairs on our head are counted and scratches leave traces under finger-nails. He got the wallet off her, tried to get hold of her neck, 'this vest which she must have been using as a scarf came away in my hand and I remember putting it round her neck.'

'I think that is the last I remember 'til when I come to.' He was still holding the vest. He let go and she was lying over the engine cover. He went to lift her and as he did so she rolled over again. 'I took the scarf away to see if she was still alive but I found she was gone.'

His narration and turn of phrase did not endear him to the court. With questions and scrutiny the lie deepened, his voice became hesitant, his tension acute. Did he know Miss Petrzywalski? No, he'd never seen her before. Was she a big woman? She was a smallish woman. Not tall. Why did he really pull off the road? Because she asked him to, to see what she wanted. Why did he switch off the engine and all the lights? All the lights had to go off together, the headlights and the side lights. It was bad wiring. What was it she wanted to tell him? She said if he gave her money she'd play about with him. Where was she sitting when she said this? Where was his wallet? She was sitting with her back to him. His wallet was in the inside pocket of his jacket hanging up. He was wearing a boiler suit. She turned round and reached across to try to reach it. He didn't know how he put the vest round her neck. He admitted he had got the wallet back before he put the vest round her neck. He now had no doubt he strangled her. He put the vest round her neck to stop the shouts and screams. Why was she shouting and screaming? He didn't know why she went on screaming and hollering. He couldn't say how the vest round her neck would stop her screaming. He was afraid someone might hear. He remembered holding the scarf in his two hands, remembered putting it round her neck. He didn't remember tightening it.

Curtis Bennett asked, 'How would a scarf round her neck stop her screaming unless it was tightly drawn?'

'I can't say.'

'How could you stop her screaming with the vest unless you partially throttled her?'

That he did not know.

Was he insane at the time?

He didn't know what he was doing. It was his turns.

But Sidney Sinclair/Harold Hagger remembered those screams that were to throttle his life as well as hers. She had made him do it. Why couldn't they see he wasn't himself when this thing happened? When this scarf somehow got round this woman's neck and throttled her. Why couldn't they see he could not help himself or keep to a resolve to change his behaviour, that right and wrong and consequence were all a muddle in his mind?

He told them anxiety over it had made him go to the doctor. But it seemed he could not convince these toffs in wigs and long coats that none of it was his fault, that he was a victim of headaches, blackouts, injuries, that jumping from that train and being unconscious all those days, weeks, months, had these after-effects, this woman had upset him with her screaming, it wasn't his fault she screamed, wasn't his fault he stole things, compulsively lied, married bigamously, leered at Daisy's daughter. He was only trying to get by, live his life, get something for himself, something that eluded him.

Questioned about his actions, he fabricated and justified. His story did not reveal a pleasant view of female motivation: that women demanded sex and money from strangers who only wanted to help them out. It was indeed a challenge to persuade anyone in the courtroom that this forty-eight-year-old pensioned telephone operator, a virgin troubled by fibroids, with no previous interest in sex of any kind, had on that dark and dismal early morning changed the reticence of a lifetime and fought for sex with him in exchange for his money and then tried to steal his wallet when he was the unwilling partner. But what was true or not true or right or wrong did not matter to Sidney. He did not care if he was in a courtroom, a barracks or a bar. Instant gratification without thought of consequence was the need that ruled and doomed his life. It harked back to the deprivation of those childhood years. Take it quick, the slice of cake, the coppers on the sideboard, or you lost your chance. What mattered now was to say anything, be anyone, so as to get out of the almighty mess this woman had got him into, though he knew, with the desperation of defeat, his performance ensured that not a vest but a rope would be pulled with very considerable force for at least fifteen to twenty seconds around his own neck.

Melford Stevenson for the Defence

Melford Stevenson in defence did not pursue the idea that Dagmar Petrzywalski met her death in the course of Sidney's determined effort to retrieve his stolen wallet. He endorsed the account of his client's jumping from the moving train, his mental blackouts and mental instability. He told the jury, 'You are not here dealing with an ordinary man . . .' Sinclair had no motive to desire Miss Petrzywalski's death. He did not desire to kill her. He did not intend to kill her. 'Where is the material on which any man or woman can come to the conclusion that he intended to kill that woman?' Melford Stevenson asked. Jurors would have to conclude that here was a case of manslaughter or a state of insanity in which Sinclair did not know what he was doing.

'Did you ever at any time desire to kill this woman?' he asked Sinclair.

'Never in my life.'

'Did you ever intend to kill her?'

'Never.'

But insanity needed psychiatric diagnosis for its plea to be upheld and manslaughter needed less reprehensible circumstances than Sidney Sinclair could convincingly offer.

Colonel Loughman as Witness

Colonel Loughman, President of the Army Medical Board at Aldershot, told the Court that in May 1942, after Sinclair's psychological and medical condition was investigated, he was permanently discharged from the army. He should never have been accepted in the first place. Sidney Sinclair or Harold Hagger suffered from hysteria which should have been perceived from the start. His mental capacity was not of a high order and he had a 'psychical disorder of the mind'. He was sane in 1942 but his hysteria manifested itself in deafness, headaches, rapid breathing, coarse tremor of the hands and unreliability. The Colonel could give no opinion of the defendant's mental state at the time of the killing, but in general he thought his was a typical case of hysteria which was a disorder of behaviour rather than a disorder of the mind.

Dr Frederick Hayden Taylor

The semantic niceties of the law, the foundation for justice and punishment, were not helping Sidney Sinclair's plight. If he knew what he was doing on that murderous Thursday, and knew it was wrong, but could not prevent himself from doing it, even though he also knew that the punishment was the gallows, then he had no defence. There was, it seemed, agreement that there was something wrong with him, but it was not enough to deem him insane.

Mr Justice Byrne questioned Dr Taylor, the Brixton medical officer: 'You have had the man under your observation from 20 December last year until two days ago. Is he in your opinion suffering from defective reason caused by disease of the mind?' Taylor told him he could not say whether the functions of Sinclair's mind were upset on 31 October but in his view the prisoner was not now suffering from hysteria. Sinclair had reported a mental blackout while in Brixton but he, Taylor, had not seen it. In his opinion Sinclair was suffering from post-traumatic neurosis following concussion of the brain from 6 June to 26 June 1925, but he had found no evidence of a disease of the mind which would cause him not to know that what he was doing was wrong. His powers of reasoning were not impaired by his mental instability. So far as he could ascertain the prisoner had not suffered a fracture of the skull in 1925 but only concussion which induced a neurosis. In his opinion Sinclair was sane. Hysteria, he said, did not upset the balance of the mind, though the defendant would be more prone to acts of violence than a person not suffering from it.

Melford Stevenson asked Dr Taylor if there was any doubt that the defendant was mentally unstable. Taylor replied, 'No, there is no doubt at all.' But in his opinion hysteria did not affect the whole mind and the effect of it on the function of the brain was not such as to prevent the prisoner realising what he was doing. The prisoner's brain was disturbed to the extent that he would become more liable to lose his temper, but he could still control his mind.

Sidney's life depended on the diagnosis of psychiatrists and the conceptual analysis of lawyers. He was disturbed, hysterical, neurotic, unstable, abnormal but that was not enough to mitigate punishment for doing what he knew to be wrong. Semantically, conceptually, there was an assumption that he could have acted otherwise and that he understood the consequences of not doing so, though why this made his behaviour more rational than someone who did not, the law left unexplained.

Nor could it be argued that the gallows were a deterrent to others of the same disposition if they, like him, could not, unaided, change their behaviour. Were he insane he would not be able to help himself. He was not insane, so other words applied: bad, evil, wilful, wicked, guilty.

Daisy Sinclair

Daisy was pregnant and unwell. Despite Sidney's lies and the humiliation of his having a wife from whom he was not divorced, in spite of his criminality, picking up women in lorries and now, it seemed, murder, she would have liked to save his life and have him home. She knew him as a troubled man, but her man. He brought home money, worked a bit in the garden. It was painful to see him manacled like an untrusted tethered dog. He had put on weight, she supposed it was lack of exercise and stodgy prison food. She did not know what she ought to say in court to save his life.

She said she had lived with the prisoner as his wife for seven years, this was the first she knew of his already having a wife from whom he was not divorced, the first she knew of his picking up women in his lorry. Yes, she had told Dr Taylor, the medical officer at Brixton, that she had never seen her husband have a blackout, but he had complained of them the night he returned from Peterborough after an accident with his lorry and, she said, he often complained of headaches, particularly after a long drive. When he had these he was very quiet and reserved. He never did say much but he was much quieter when he had his headaches. Yes, he had a bad temper but no, he was never violent. She told them about his 'funny habit of coming to me with his hands like that', and she made a strangling pose with her hands that might not have helped her putative husband's cause. He'd make 'a funny noise in his throat' as he approached her. A gurgling. Perhaps akin to the gurgling his victim made as he choked her to death. What Daisy appeared to enact was murderous intent. She said she'd tell him not to get neurotic. But this behaviour was only periodical. He was, she told the Court, 'the best of husbands, honest, sober and industrious'.

The Verdict: 28 February 1947

The trial lasted two days. On 28 February Mr Justice Byrne reviewed the evidence, summed up, and told the jury the verdicts open to them were that Sidney Sinclair was guilty of the murder of Dagmar Petrzywalski at Wrotham in Kent on 31 October 1946, that he was not guilty of murder but guilty of manslaughter, or that he was guilty but insane. He reminded them of the distinction between neurosis, hysteria and insanity where the perpetrator could not be held responsible for his actions.

The jury retired for thirty-five minutes' deliberation, then the foreman returned to ask for a photo of Dagmar Petrzywalski. Dagmar's face looked open, bespectacled and guileless, her demeanour modest. Back in the courtroom the jury rejected both defence submissions and returned a verdict of guilty of murder. They made no recommendation for mercy. One of the women jurors was in tears.

The judge called Sidney Sinclair to the witness box and asked him if he had anything to say as to why sentence of death should not be passed on him. Sidney swayed, ran his tongue over his lips and said, 'No.' The judge put a black cap on top of his wig and pronounced: 'Sidney Sinclair, also known as Harold Hagger, you will be taken hence to a lawful prison and from there to a place of execution where you will be hanged by the neck until you are dead and thereafter your body buried within the precincts of the prison and may the Lord have mercy upon your soul.'

It was over to the Lord for the mercy which human society in the name of justice felt obliged to withhold. It was over to the Lord, too, for mercy or not upon the souls of the lawful killers of Sidney Sinclair, who were not insane under the M'Naghten Rule, nor abnormal, hysterical or suffering psychical disorders of the mind.

Sidney Sinclair in Wandsworth Prison

After the verdict, at 3.45 on that Friday afternoon Sidney was taken to Wandsworth prison, equipped as it was with a gallows. Wandsworth, a category B men's prison, built in 1851 and originally called the Surrey House of Correction, was designed to house 700 prisoners in individual cells each with their own toilet, but in 1870 all the toilets were removed to make room for more prisoners and slopping out was introduced. The gallows were in a room in E wing known to prisoners as the cold meat shed.

A Home Office memorandum detailed strict procedure from time of sentence to execution. It was thought humane to get the deed done within a reasonable time frame. For Sidney this was three weeks. His execution was fixed for 18 March 'subject to any variation'. That meant any appeal for clemency had to be considered and decided on within that time.

The governor of Wandsworth reported Sidney Sinclair's arrival to head office: he was prisoner 10171, his crime was murder, his sentence death, there was no recommendation for mercy, he had previous convictions, a medical report would follow. The governor also applied to the prison commissioners for 'a list of candidates competent for the office of executioner, together with copies of the records as to the conduct and efficiency of each of them with a view to their transmission to the High Sheriff'. He wanted, too, 'a copy of the memorandum of instructions for carrying out the details of an execution; also for a copy of the table of drops'. Albert Pierrepoint was recommended as executioner with H.B. Critchell as his assistant.

The army records officer in Edinburgh asked Scotland Yard for particulars of the sentence passed so he could continue his struggle to update his muddled files.

Sinclair's defence counsel doubted there was anything in the judge's summing up to prompt the Court of Criminal Appeal to revise the sentence. None the less they put in a half-hearted request for death to be commuted to 'penal servitude for life'. They asked for a full medical enquiry 'before the Secretary of State decides whether or not the law should take its course'. They said that though Sinclair was not a man of good character, had six-teen previous convictions for shop-breaking, larceny and assaults on the police, it was agreed he was neurotic and of unstable mind and this crime was not premeditated. He had met Dagmar Petrzy-walski accidentally while in the course of his employment and he regretted what he had done.

Pending the outcome of this appeal and possible medical enquiry, Sidney was housed in the condemned suite at Wandsworth prison and denied contact with other prisoners. The cell was double the ordinary size, with chairs for the two officers who guarded him night and day. A basin and lavatory were in an adjacent cell and there was direct connection to the execution chamber: the Cold Meat Shed. The governor, medical officer, chief prison officer and chaplain visited him twice a day. He wore prison clothes, did not have to work, was allowed visits from friends, relatives and lawyers and to write and receive letters. He was given newspapers, books, cards and dominoes. Prison officers joined him for such games. He was allowed to smoke in his cell, given ten cigarettes and a pint of beer a day and put on the hospital diet, which meant better food than for less imminently mortal prisoners.

7

THE EXECUTIONER

Albert Pierrepoint was a man of principle, a hard-working dependable Yorkshireman who took pride in his craft. His career as an executioner began in 1932 when he was twenty-seven but even as a child he knew that was what he wanted to be.

He recounted his moment of vocational epiphany in his autobiography *Executioner: Pierrepoint*. He was eight and waiting outside a pub in Bradford for his alcoholic father:

'This is my eldest son,' my father said. 'And one day he will be the Official Executioner.' I looked up at my father and my mind was suddenly very clear. My mission, my one-man expedition, I knew what it was. And I knew what it needed. 'Our Dad,' I said, 'can I go into long trousers?' He looked at me with all the pride in the world. 'Yes, our Albert,' he said. 'You can. I'll speak to your mother about it.'

'It's in the family really,' Albert wrote. His uncle Tom was an executioner and so was Albert's father Henry, until he got the sack. They all referred to 'the firm' and viewed themselves as public servants. Albert's mother, 'a typically patient and hard-working woman of her time, with perhaps more of the virtue of loyalty than some women cherish in these times', was reserved and undemonstrative, worked in a munitions factory in the First World War and never spoke of her husband's occupation or her eldest son's.

Albert said his father's prophecy 'resounded in his ears'. His father too wrote an autobiography, serialised in *Thomson's Weekly News* in 1916. Henry Pierrepoint wrote:

> The word 'hangman' almost invariably evokes a shiver in over-sensitive persons. They imagine him a morose, bloodthirsty sort of villain. Well I have a charming wife and a family of young children and I would refer you to them as to whether I am anything in the way of a brutal villain.

Albert did not say his father was a brutal villain, only that he had a 'sometimes fiery temperament' and made his mother unhappy. Nor did he reveal that after ten years as an executioner Henry Pierrepoint was sacked in 1910 when Albert was five. He had arrived at Chelmsford prison on 13 July 1910 with his assistant John Ellis to prepare for a hanging the following day. He was drunk, he shouted at Ellis, hit him, and when restrained by warders went on shouting until the prison governor put them in separate rooms. In a letter, Ellis complained to the prison commission that it reflected badly on the profession of executioner when prisoners saw Pierrepoint drunk.

Then in another 'badly managed' hanging in Dublin Henry Pierrepoint assaulted two priests who were trying to console the condemned man. 'I gave them every indulgence I could until they became a pest to me, delaying me in my duty,' Henry wrote in his notes. He 'pushed them off' and pulled the lever. He was not awarded his £10 fee and soon after was 'removed from the Home Office list'.

He became an out-of-work drunk. Albert, the dutiful eldest son, left school at twelve to provide for his mother, two brothers and two sisters. He worked as a piecer in a textile mill near Oldham, leaning over the spinning-machine to repair broken threads. It was repetitive low-paid work. In 1922, four years later, his father died and Albert became the main breadwinner, depended on by his mother. He lived with her and supported her for twenty more years. He gave her his frugal earnings, dreamed of his true vocation and had no girlfriends:

> You just didn't fall hopelessly for a girl when you'd no money and no decent clothes on your back, when work was very hard to get and a fatherless family was depending on it. You developed your own sense of responsibility. You didn't become too involved with a girl too early, because your own maturity told you that all too easily it could only lead to two people becoming very miserable.

Albert said he pored over his father's papers and a thick, shiny diary 'black like a Family Bible' inscribed on the fly leaf EXECUTION BOOK in capitals. In hand-ruled columns Henry had recorded details of all the executions he carried out: the date and prison, particulars of each client – name, age, height, weight, the muscular condition of the neck (thick set, flabby, short) and the calculated length of the drop. The Book, as Albert called it, also recorded the birth of Henry's children, useful addresses of assistant executioners, notes of expenses for professional trips, and a section on veterinary medicines: horse remedies, and bran mash with saltpetre for cows with coughs. Albert, 'never a scholar' and not a reader of books, was fascinated by this diary. It became his manual and fuelled his career aspiration.

He was also much influenced by his father's notebooks of reminiscences. 'My father's memories became mine,' he wrote.

I remembered as if it had been part of my own life the man at Leeds gaol who as my father adjusted the rope round his neck complained, 'It's too tight' . . . I saw through my father's eyes 'the bravest man I ever hanged', the soldier who had come home from the South African war and found his wife unfaithful. He carried his little daughter in his arms up the stairs of his North London home and cut her throat . . . Then he went to the police and gave himself up. They asked why he had done it. 'So that she would not grow up like her mother,' he replied.

Such recollections inspired Albert. In the late 1920s he worked as a drayman, delivering goods for a wholesale grocer, but yearned to 'be something more of a person' and to earn an executioner's wage. He was enticed too by the perks that might come with the job.

My father, travelling to attend an execution in Swansea, contrived to go by rail from Manchester to Conway and the Menai Straits, then on south going anti-clockwise round almost the whole of the scenic Welsh coast.

Though Henry Pierrepoint had returned home from such expeditions skint and drunk, Albert, prompted by his uncle Tom, in 1931 applied to the Prison Commissioners for the post of assistant executioner. There were five such applicants a week. 'I am not afraid of anything,' Alexander Riley, a scaffolder from Manchester, wrote on his application: 'I'm a British subject and all my parents think I'm quite capable of carrying out any duties.' Harry Kirk was turned down on first application: 'he appears to have a somewhat morbid interest in the work aroused through having a friend who carried out many executions in Arabia', the Commissioners wrote. He was appointed when he reapplied.

Albert did not tell his mother about his application or successful appointment. He went on a six-day training course, was given 9s 2d for his board, and a third-class railway ticket home. He became an exemplary assistant with a reputation for efficiency and attention to detail. He learned to calculate the drop, adjust the ropes, fix the noose, open the trapdoors: 'cap, noose, pin, push, drop'. Often he worked with his admired uncle Tom. In the 1930s he assisted him at thirty-two executions.

Tom Pierrepoint prided himself on the speed with which he despatched his clients: his record from cell to gallows was sixty seconds. But in 1940, when he was seventy, complaints were made about his proficiency. And there were complaints that he smelled strongly of drink during two executions at Durham prison. In December Dr Landers, medical officer at Wandsworth, in a memo to the prison commissioners, said Pierrepoint was no longer fit for duty: 'he was uncertain and it was doubtful whether his sight was good'. 'Owing to wartime difficulties of replacement' he was kept on until in 1943 the medical officer of Liverpool prison complained he endangered the life of the assistant executioner whose job was to pinion the legs of the person being hanged.

> Mr Pierrepoint on this as on previous occasions appeared to allow only the barest margin of safety in assuring himself that the assistant was clear of the trapdoors before pulling the lever . . . He obviously regards speed as the hallmark of efficiency and there hardly seems time for him to ensure the assistant is clear of the trap . . . This zeal for speed may be related to a desire to show that his ability is unimpaired by advancing years.

Aware his uncle's supremacy must end and assured of his own skill, in 1940 Albert applied to become an official executioner. When the buff envelope marked OHMS arrived his mother told him, 'You'll have no luck at all as long as you live if you take that job. Your father never had any luck.' After that she never mentioned the subject again. 'It was a curious revival of the atmosphere that had existed when my father was alive.'

Albert described himself as an 'executioner with confidence'. Fabian became 'a very close friend'. Both were casuists, men of maxims, guided in their moral judgements by the prevailing laws of the land. Justice was what the law decreed. Albert Pierrepoint's adherence to the rules was not modified by reference to the complex circumstances of the troubled individuals to whom he meted out punishment of such an irreversible sort. Like Fabian, his prime consideration was to do his job well and according to the rule book, to be rewarded and win affirmation and acclaim.

In 1943, aged thirty-eight and assured of an income, Albert married Anne Fletcher, who ran a sweet shop two doors down from the grocer's where he had worked. The wedding was at St Wilfrid's church, Newton Heath, near Manchester and the reception was at the Mowbray Conservative Club. Like his father, Albert did not tell his wife about his profession and she asked no questions. 'In forty years I have never discussed my experiences with her. We have lived in mutual respect as well as love.'

I detest speaking about my craft in front of women and I have never done so. I have never discussed executions with my mother or my wife, and never yielded a word to casual women who have questioned me . . .

One of the men I had to execute soon after I started courting Anne was a dwarf. I didn't even tell her I was going on a job, let alone discuss the problems of the length of coil, the height of the noose and the drop to be calculated for the abnormal muscular formation of a dwarf.

Albert and Anne had no children but she was wifely and liked playing bingo. When work took Albert away, all he said as explanation was, 'I shan't be seeing you for a couple of days.'

The Lüneburg Court

At the end of the war the fall of the Third Reich resulted in a great deal of work for Albert Pierrepoint. Never had he been so busy. Most killing is authorised and paid for by the state and between December 1945 and October 1948 he hanged 226 Nazi war criminals. On a particularly hectic day, 14 November 1947, he despatched sixteen. He found the work tiring: 'these multiple executions were exhausting'. In Britain, over the same three-year-period he hanged twenty-seven men.

On 15 April 1945 the British Army liberated Belsen concentration camp. They found more than 10,000 unburied corpses and 60,000 sick and starving survivors. In September 1945 trials took place in the British zone of occupation at Lüneburg in Germany of forty-five men and women who had staffed the camps of Belsen and Auschwitz. They were accused of war crimes. At Nuremberg 264 miles away the trials were of Nazi leaders and architects of the Third Reich. At Lüneburg the accused were everyday Nazis who put policy into practice. People who were 'only doing their job'.

The Lüneburg trials, held in a British military court convened under Royal Warrant, lasted from 17 September to 17 November 1945. The alleged crimes were against Allied nationals. The accused were defended by British or Polish serving officers. There was no right of appeal and it was not the business of the court to judge crimes committed by one German against another or in countries outside the United Nations.

The defendants were charged with the murder and ill-treatment of millions of people, mainly Jews, who had been forced into these camps. Listed was a saga of starvation, gassing, beating, use of savage dogs, experiments performed on internees in the so-called interest of science, and calculated brutality and neglect so that uncounted people suffered and died.

In the courtroom the accused were arrayed with numbers round their necks. Witnesses, survivors, had their names and the surface of their personalities restored. The functionaries of genocide had degraded them and when they were starved, stinking and desperate it was convenient to treat them as dreck and say this is what Jews, gypsies, homosexuals and communists are like.

All those charged pleaded not guilty and said they were only doing their jobs. The court was told it must consider what was reasonable conduct in the circumstances in which the accused found themselves. Hitler was executive and legislator, Himmler head of the Gestapo, the SS and Minister of the Interior. The prosecution case was not to consider whether putting Allied nationals in these camps was wrong per se, rather that when they were there they should not have been ill-treated. It was not the task of the court to judge the policy of the extermination or persecution of Jews. The defendants were called on compulsorily by their government to undertake the execution of its policies, just as this court had been called on by its government under emergency powers granted by parliament.

In the context of such a dystopia the court struggled to define what was and what was not a war crime. A rule of thumb for indictment was 'Can this killing which would normally be murder, this injury which would normally be unlawful wounding, this taking of property which would normally be theft, be justified as an act of war? If not it will be a war crime.' The rule it seemed for these defendants was not, as with Sidney Sinclair, an equivalent to the M'Naghten Rule of being off their heads, or that war was in itself a crime, but rather that their actions needed to accord with a sanitised or civilised rule book of killing and inflicting pain. The trials would not have taken so long, or been so conceptually confusing, had they proceeded from the premise that state killing and all its apparatus was a crime: Krupp's, Vickers, Little Boy, Fat Man, soldiers, executioners, John Edgington & Co Ltd manufacturers of execution ropes, and the whole shebang.

The guidebook for indictment by the court was the *Manual of Military Law*. The accused, the court made clear, were not being tried in connection with all tasks performed, or the fact of running a concentration camp, but for carrying out their tasks in a brutal way. The *Manual of Military Law* stated:

> Members of the armed forces are bound to obey lawful orders only. They cannot escape liability if in obedience to a command they commit acts which both violate unchallenged rules of warfare and outrage the general sentiment of humanity.

The general sentiment of humanity was not outraged by war. It was hard to define the point of individual responsibility for brutality. Subordinates were not responsible for the orders of their superiors. Defence counsel, quoting the *Manual*, said the instigator of an offence should receive a more severe sentence than the person hired to commit it. Was this court going to mete out to these minor characters a punishment which could not be exceeded at Nuremberg?

They were functionaries within a regime not of their conceiving. Personal culpability existed only in so far as they were individually cruel and sadistic. As a modern peacetime analogy the factory farm functions on the premise that the countless animals processed in it have no ultimate right to life, freedom, choice or natural expression because a large number of human beings desire to eat them and a large number of businessmen desire to profit from them. The animals are processed, experimented on, distorted, killed and sold but a civilised society enforces a legal imperative for the factory farmworker and abattoir worker not to inflict gratuitous cruelty on the wretched creatures in their care.

Kramer

Josef Kramer, commandant of Belsen, was the most notorious of the forty-five accused. To the Lüneburg court he stressed that all policy decisions came from above, he was merely an administrator who carried out the routine of the camp. It was outside his power to decide who was put into the camp or sentenced to death in it: 'We were members of the Wehrmacht; as soon as war broke out we became members of the Wehrmacht and I am a member of the armed forces of Germany. The destruction of the Jewish race was an avowed war aim.'

From the scale of activity of 'members of the Wehrmacht' it was clear people could be found who were willing, for money and by command, to do any vicious act, inflict any torture, suspend all compassion or care, yet view themselves and be viewed as law-abiding and worthy citizens deserving of a uniform, badges of honour, payment by the state and social entitlement.

In court Kramer said he had wondered whether it was right, sending people to gas chambers, but he was working under difficulties. There was not enough food for people at Belsen, there were epidemics of typhus and spotted fever, he had asked for a brake on sending more internees yet still thousands more were sent.

For the prosecution Brigadier Glyn Hughes, deputy director of medical services with the 2nd Army, testified to what he found on entering Belsen in April 1945. Hughes went round the camp with Kramer who, he said, was indifferent to all he saw. He described piles of corpses, some in the same bunks as the living. Camp huts, designed for a maximum of a hundred people, in the most crowded housed a thousand. Floors were covered in excreta, there was nowhere for anyone to lie down, most internees had gastroenteritis, were too weak to leave the huts and the lavatories had long been out of use. He spoke of an 'unbelievable' lack of flesh on bones, gangrene on bodies, pleas for help, the stench, the terror toward SS guards. He said, 'I have been a doctor for thirty years and have seen all the horrors of war, but I have never seen anything to touch it.'

In the store rooms were medical supplies, 600 tons of potatoes, 120 tons of tinned meat, 30 tons of sugar, 20 tons of powdered milk, cocoa, grain and wheat. There was a fully staffed bakery capable of turning out 60,000 loaves a day.

The court was shown films of the scenes found and a map of Belsen before the camp was burnt down. Witnesses testified that Kramer made selections for the gas chamber and if his victims cried because they knew what awaited them he beat them. They testified to his shooting internees who tried to take discarded rotten potatoes, to how sick and starving prisoners were made to stand to attention for hours for roll-calls supervised by him and if they moved they were hit. They said there was no attempt to improve conditions, bring medical supplies, beds, provide a living diet or make provision for the sick. The prevailing attitude as spoken by Kramer was 'Let them die.'

Dr Ada Bimko, a Polish Jew, first encountered Kramer at

Auschwitz. She worked in the hospital and with other internees kept records of four million people destroyed in the crematoria. Experiments like artificial insemination were carried out in Block 10. Prisoners for the gas chamber were sent to Block 25 and waited days without food or drink before lorries arrived for them. Kramer kicked those too weak to work.

Abraham Glinowieski said when Kramer found he had bread and a pair of boots, he gave him twenty-five lashes. Another witness described how Kramer made a group of Russian girls kneel in the rain for twenty-four hours when they stole bread and how several of them died.

Weingartner

Before working at Belsen, Peter Weingartner was a Blockführer in the women's compound at Auschwitz. He was leader of a project where a thousand women were made to carry sand from the banks of the river Vistula and load it into lorries. He set dogs on them, denied them their bread ration, beat women who dug up some turnips until they bled, ordered two women found to possess wire cutters to be hanged.

At Belsen Weingartner again became a Blockführer. Abraham Glinowieski broke down in the witness box as he told how Weingartner caught his brother, took him into a room, bent him over a chair, put his knee on his neck then beat him with seventy-five strokes. Abraham Glinowieski took his brother to the hospital, where he died.

Bormann

Juana Bormann told the court she joined the SS in 1939 'to earn more money' and because she was lonely and friendless. In March 1942 she was promoted to Auschwitz, then two years later transferred to Belsen. She worked with Kramer and other staff, Irma Grese and Elisabeth Volkenrath, with whom she had been friendly at Auschwitz. Internees called Bormann the *Wiesel*. Two of her frequent punishments were collective deprivation of food and setting her large Alsatian dog on prisoners. A witness, Helena Kopper, showed the court scars on her arm from the dog's attack. Another witness testified to how she set the dog on a worker with a swollen leg who could not walk. She encouraged the dog to tear the woman's clothes, then go for her throat. The woman was taken away on a stretcher.

At Auschwitz Bormann, as overseer, made selections for the gas chamber and would say to the doctors, This one is weak, she can be taken away too. Questioned, Bormann denied all charges, said she boxed the ears of prisoners but nothing more and when on gas chamber parades only kept order and did not select one person rather than another.

Grese

Irma Grese was twenty-two at the time of the trial. Her father was a dairy worker, she was poorly educated and when she was fourteen her mother poisoned herself. Grese left home two years later. She had wanted to be a nurse but was conscripted into concentration camp service when she was eighteen. She worked at Ravensbrück and Auschwitz, then became a warden at Belsen.

Witnesses testified to her full-blown sadism: she wore heavy boots, carried a pistol, commanded Jewish girls to cross the wire perimeter fence then shot them (she despatched thirty in a day), made internees kneel for hours holding heavy stones above their heads, put on gloves before beating people with her fists, lashed naked women with a plaited whip, made Jewish women parade naked for the gas chamber selection, made internees fall down and get up for hours or crawl at increasing speed while she whipped them or set her dog on them. And so on.

Questioned, Grese was unremorseful, denied she ever had a dog, said the belt she was alleged to have beaten prisoners with was too flimsy for such a job, that she only carried a revolver because she was ordered to do so and only hit Jews when they tried to run away.

Volkenrath and Others

Witness testament to brutality and murder went on for fifty-four days. Those too ill or traumatised to attend court submitted sworn affidavits. Britain's government and the War Crimes Commission voiced frustration at the time taken over these trials. Germans were viewed with the same disdain as Truman had voiced toward the Japanese: 'savages, ruthless, merciless and fanatic'. The mood from Britain was for cursory and punitive justice. For Fleet Street it was too much gruesome news for readers over too long a time frame.

One after another, witnesses spoke of images riveted into their minds: of an elderly woman from Leipzig who asked to be excused parade because she felt ill but was then beaten until she died; of a woman pushed with a stick into a ditch and prodded down until she drowned; of a prisoner named Grunwald beaten to death for going to a lavatory at a prohibited time; a Greek Jewish woman shot in the head for stealing bread; blood pouring from the mouth and ears of a man beaten with a stick; a girl beaten with a whip because she asked for more soup; starving people having food taken from their mouths and then being beaten.

Elisabeth Volkenrath had worked as a hairdresser before conscription into the Nazi party. Josephine Singer described how an elderly Czech Jewish woman, whom Volkenrath threw down some steps, died from her injuries. Nettie Stoppelman gave witness to how Volkenrath took bread, water and cigarettes from starving internees. Helene Herkovitz described how she made her run behind a bicycle to SS headquarters then, with others, beat her with a rubber truncheon, put her in a cellar, gave her only bread and water every three days and on release made her work in the latrines, where she caught typhus.

Karl Francioh, in charge of kitchen number 3 in Belsen's women's camp, shot dead a pregnant young woman bending over to pick up potato peelings. When the British army was about to arrive he fired on women in his kitchen, killing fifty of them.

Ilse Forster, in charge of kitchen number 1 at Belsen, beat Sophia Litwinska, who had tried to take food, until her head was swollen and her arms and back blue and purple. For the same reason she beat to death a young girl of sixteen.

Stanislaus Starotska, leader on Block 7, beat internees who were out of line and pushed a woman on to the electrified perimeter fence and to her death.

Franz Stofel and Wilhelm Dorr, camp guards at Belsen, shot stragglers along the transport route. When a convoy of 610 prisoners was being moved there under their command, 590 arrived.

Dr Fritz Klein denied he selected internees for the Auschwitz gas chambers. 'My only part in the matter was to say this man is fit, this man is not fit.' He said if he had refused the job other doctors would have done it. He agreed Belsen was a torture camp. He said he wanted complaints sent to Berlin about this but 'One could not protest when in the Army.' The prosecution said he was a party to the whole. Defence argued that when a British soldier refused to obey an order he faced a court martial where he could contest its lawfulness or unlawfulness. Klein had no such protection. The accused now stood before lawyers. The court endeavoured to determine the relative responsibility or culpability of each and approach a semblance of justice by ordering punishment.

Harold Le Druillenec from Jersey testified how he and others dragged corpses to burial pits from sunrise to dusk and that anyone who faltered was hit. Other witnesses spoke of how guards shot internees for no reason, of experiments with lethal injection by Josef Mengele in the crematorium at Auschwitz, the wrenching of gold teeth from prisoners' mouths, the sterilisation of women, the loading of them on to lorries to be taken to gas chambers, abandoned unburied bodies, rampant typhus, crude medical facilities.

Judgement at Lüneburg

So it went on. Day after day. Incontrovertible witness to complicity in killing and cruelty, and at worst pleasure in it. What they shared, these ordinary people, who before employment by the Nazi party had worked as clerks, cleaners and land workers, who were most of them married with families, who in more ordinary times might have moved through life with unremarkable prejudice against foreigners, Jews, gypsies, homosexuals, but came, through collective circumstance, to serve in an industry of death, was the ability to close their ears and eyes to the sight and sound of suffering. In more ordinary times, had they not been offered or assigned the jobs they were, their lack of imagination, empathy or moral concern might have been normal. Out of sight is out of mind for most. News of war, famine, massacre, earthquake, bomb blast, drought affecting unknown people and creatures at a distant place on the planet is little obstacle to the enjoyment of morning coffee, toast and marmalade. Empathy is selective. Those same people in the Lüneburg court might have done much to help the people and creatures they loved.

At the end of the fifty-four days there was again semantic exchange between prosecution and defence on individual responsibility within the context of war and brutal command. The charges against the prisoners at Lüneburg were of individual acts of gratuitous cruelty within the context in which they were compelled to work. Defending counsel said the prosecution should show what the accused could have done and failed to do when faced with gas chambers at Auschwitz and starving prisoners at Belsen. It was not sufficient to say that the creation of the Belsen camp constituted a war crime and since these people were at Belsen they were war criminals. They reiterated that the accused were not on trial as the architects of genocide. Hitler's inner circle was in another court.

The camp was chaotic, disease was rife, the place was hopelessly overcrowded, there were few people in authority compared to the mass of prisoners. Account should be taken of the difficulties of the accused, there was disorder on a colossal scale and no clear guidelines as to how they should have behaved. They were harshly punished if they did not follow orders. Force was necessary to restrain internees when food was scarce. Roll-calls were the only way to distribute rations. Hitting prisoners was necessary to keep them in order. A distinction should be drawn between a cruel flogging and 'a quick cut with a stick because a prisoner had done something wrong'.

The prosecution argued that intentional injury was only legally justified if it served some military purpose. Despite the premise of Belsen, wardens might have behaved humanely. The determining criteria seemed to be if Starotska pushed women against the electrified wire of the camp's perimeter and killed them, that was indictable, though he was not answerable for the wiring or obliged to dismantle it. If the commandants of the gas chambers imposed their own system of selection and herded Jews in to be gassed rather than Poles, that was a capital crime in a way that an unpreferential manner of gassing people was not.

In the courtroom all the accused, reminded of it, appeared to understand the illegality of violence and murder. No M'Naghten Rule was needed to test their sanity. What they questioned was who was responsible for this dystopia. In their view it was not themselves. They were only doing their job.

On 16 November 1945 the court delivered its verdict: of the forty-five accused, thirty were convicted and fourteen acquitted. Nineteen of the convicted were given sentences ranging from one year to life. The remaining eleven, including Josef Kramer, Peter Weingartner, Fritz Klein, Karl Francioh, Juana Bormann, Elisabeth Volkenrath and Irma Grese, were sentenced to death. Britain's chief executioner was commissioned to despatch them.

On 10 December Field Marshal Montgomery, who oversaw the surrender of Lüneburg to the British, rejected appeals for clemency and announced the prisoners were to be hanged. The victorious nation desired, through the judgement of the courts, to define the gulf between civilisation and barbarism. Justice moved to the architect of the noose, drop and gallows, the payment of the hangman. It was over to the cold meat shed. Over to Albert Pierrepoint.

Ladies First

The condemned were held at Hamelin prison, a yellow stucco building with a sandy courtyard, close to the river Weser. Inside were cavernous corridors, a foetid smell and cells each with a tiny barred window set high in the wall.

Albert Pierrepoint was to hang them all on Thursday 13 December 1945. It was the largest mass hanging on a single day in the history of British executions and he was in sole charge of it. It was the most demanding day of his career. He had thirteen clients to kill – the eleven sentenced at Lüneburg and two others from Holland. At home he never did more than five or ten a year. His uncle Tom, his revered role model, in forty years only hanged 294 people.

He was given the honorary rank of lieutenant colonel and flown out from RAF Northolt to Bückeburg two days in advance. He wore his customary suit and tie. At Northolt airport he was pursued as a celebrity by photographers and reporters. He arrived in Germany in the evening, was met by a British officer, driven in freezing rain to Hamelin and billeted near the prison in an old hotel turned into an officers' mess. He did not get to bed until late.

Next morning he went early to the prison. He could speak no German and the officer at the gates spoke no English and would not let him in. Pierrepoint had to wait for the arrival of his assistant, Sergeant Major O'Neill, who was to act as interpreter but had not before witnessed an execution.

Pierrepoint needed to know the weight and height of each of his clients so as to calculate the correct drop. He personally had to weigh and measure them all, a task that at home was done by prison officials. He thought it an unacceptable breach of gallows etiquette: the condemned man or woman should not see his or her executioner face to face, distance should be kept, there was protocol to these matters, a civilised procedure. Back home they did things better.

He and O'Neill were forced to set up their measure and scales at the end of the corridor that ran alongside the cells. Prisoners could see this activity through the grate in their cell door. Pierrepoint thought that too quite wrong. Unkind. Each of the thirteen prisoners was then brought singly to him and asked his or her name, age and religion. O'Neill translated for

Pierrepoint, who weighed and measured them. While this was going on there was a scraping noise from the prison yard. Workmen were digging thirteen graves. Pierrepoint viewed this too as inconsiderate and complained to the governor. Nothing could be done. It was cold and the ground was stony and hard.

The gallows had been erected by the Royal Engineers according to British Home Office specifications. Pierrepoint tested it with a number of sacks of equivalent weight and found it satisfactory. He made his calculations, had his lunch, then:

> With the bundled records under my arm I went back to my room and spent the next two hours working out the length of drop that would be required for each of the condemned persons. It was not a simple task for I had to allow for the adjustment of the drop after each execution, and this controlled to some extent the order in which I took the prisoners. I was very anxious not to confuse any of the drops. It would have been easy, in this unprecedented multiple execution, to have called for the condemned in the wrong order. But however complicated the operation I had come to the decision that I must take the women first. The condemned cells were so close to the scaffold that the prisoners could not but hear the repeated sounds of the drop. I did not wish to subject the women for too long to this. I determined to carry out the execution of the women singly at the start and follow with double executions for the men.

Unlike his German clients he had not forgotten his English manners. It was ladies first in the matter of passing through doors. Gentlemen guided and eased their passage. It was a busy preparatory day. As they went back to the mess O'Neill said, 'Albert, I have read about executions, but I never thought there was so much work to do.' 'Yes,' Albert said, 'it is not as easy as you read.'

At six next morning a batman woke Pierrepoint, who was met at the prison by O'Neill and two mandatory witnesses: Brigadier Paton-Walsh a former deputy governor of Wandsworth, and Miss Wilson deputy governor of Strangeways prison in Manchester, who had to be present because women were being hanged.

In the execution chamber at 9am the officers stood to attention. 'Paton-Walsh stood with his wrist watch raised. He gave me the signal. I walked into the corridor, "Irma Grese" I called.' The German guards then closed the wickets on the twelve other doors. Irma Grese's cell was too small for Pierrepoint to go inside, so he pinioned her arms in the corridor. 'She seemed as bonny a girl as one could ever wish to meet,' he said. He made a chalk mark on the trap where she was to stand, tied her legs together and put the obligatory white cap over her head. She said 'Schnell' which O'Neill translated as 'Be quick', and Pierrepoint pulled the lever.

Ten minutes later he did Elisabeth Volkenrath, then half an hour after her Juana Bormann, who was fifty-two, no more than 5 feet tall, weighed 101 pounds and, Pierrepoint said, was trembling. She said to him in German, 'I have my feelings too.' At 10.38 Albert and his helpers 'paused for a cup of tea', then adjusted the scaffold for double executions for the men. Before lunch at 1.00 he did two double hangings: Josef Kramer and Dr Fritz Klein, followed by Karl Francioh and Peter Weingartner. In the afternoon he hanged the remaining four and by 4.30 they were all dead. Through a miscalculation they were a coffin short, so the thirteenth corpse was wrapped in hessian, a procedural oversight that marred a well-organised day.

In the evening Pierrepoint was given an engraved clock at a mess party in his honour. He viewed it as a treasured possession and kept it on a mantlepiece at his home.

Pierrepoint was fastidious about working in what he considered a principled way: respect shown to the condemned man and especially woman, careful calculation of the drop, the swift and accurate breaking of the neck. Had he been a concentration camp commandant he would have fulfilled his commission within the remit of his manual. He bridged the moral distance between himself and his victims with ease. His was, like theirs, paid employment and he would not have done it for free, but he worked according to the rule book and considered himself the servant of higher minds than his own.

The following day he was flown home. It had been a difficult and tiring two days but this was only the first of many such visits to Hamelin.

Albert Pierrepoint did not want to be a hangman for ever. Though he kept the day job, in 1946, with an eye to retirement, he took over the lease on a pub near Manchester called Help the Poor Struggler. He described himself as a social character who enjoyed meeting people, which was why being a publican appealed to him. His fame made Help the Poor Struggler popular. The Manchester CID drank there. Though he refused to talk of his profession as executioner to the ordinary drinker, in his pub's singing room he was acclaimed for his conjuring tricks and rendition of 'Danny Boy'. His wife Anne 'proved herself an excellent hostess'.

The Penalty of Death

On Saturday 1 March 1947 newspapers in Britain reported that sentence of death had been passed on Sidney Sinclair. Few gave his name as Harold Hagger. There were reminders of the circumstances of the crime: the victim was strangled with the man's vest she wore as a scarf, she lived the life of a recluse in a hut she had had built near Wrotham Hill, she was a pensioned telephone operator.

More prominent coverage was accorded to other news. The winter had been outstanding for the strength and frequency of snowfalls, frost, east winds and lack of sun. Ernest Bevin, the Foreign Secretary, announced agreement with France to curb post-war German reconstruction from becoming a threat to peace, Argentina renewed its claim to the Falklands, electricity, which had been in short supply, was restored to most industries in London and the south-east, but not to domestic consumers or dog racing, and gardeners were advised to sow their peas, beans, rhubarb and radishes.

Without the judgements at Lüneburg and Nuremberg, Sidney Sinclair would most likely not have been sentenced to death. A 1938 Criminal Justice Bill that proposed to abolish the death penalty, keep young offenders out of prison and rehabilitate or detain recidivists was abandoned at the outbreak of war. It advocated an end to corporal punishment, 'hard labour' and 'penal servitude'. Abolitionists had worked diligently for such reforms and thought the post-war election of a Labour government with a huge majority would bring success to their efforts. It was a government with a mission and mandate for social welfare and it was anticipated it would implement the Criminal Justice Bill of 1938.

But public opinion was against abolition. The scale of horror revealed over a span of two years at Nuremberg and Lüneburg was thought to justify extreme retribution. The prevailing thinking was that hanging was too good for those who had inflicted such remorseless pain and suffering on others. There was a fear that evil might not be specific to Japs and Huns. Cruelty, lovelessness, indifference to suffering, greed, hatred and brutality might be universal. Murder and crimes of violence were more frequent in Britain than before the war. People talked about the erosion of traditional moral standards. The press was full of stories of the senseless violence of juvenile gangs. Old Testament ideas of justice held sway: an eye for an eye. The principle of 'a life for a life' was rooted in people's minds, the sense that killing could only be curbed by counter-killing. There was no mood for the tolerance world of pacificism, understanding, truth and reconciliation.

'We have just concluded a great world war, in which we took millions of human lives quite deliberately in order to protect things which we thought more valuable,' Quintin Hogg, Conservative MP for Oxford, said in a House of Commons debate on capital punishment.

We have just been hanging our defeated enemies after the trials at Nuremberg. They were prosecuted not as an act of war but as an act of what was claimed to be justice . . . If we were going to say that it was at all times and in all circumstances wrong to take human life, whatever evil doing the malefactor may have committed, then the time to say so was before Nuremberg and not immediately after.

The government delayed introducing the 1938 bill and omitted the abolition clause from it. The argument was that the public was not ready for it. Britain had won the war. The enemy was vanquished. The House of Lords and many judges wanted to retain the death penalty. Police and prison officers believed criminals would be more likely to use lethal weapons if the penalty for murder was imprisonment rather than death. They argued that those serving life sentences might kill prison officers if they thought they would keep their own lives.

James Chuter Ede, the Home Secretary, was an abolitionist before and after his stint at the Home Office. But opinion polls indicated there were two retentionists for every one abolitionist. Politicians must please voters, and the bulk of the working class, who were mainly Labour voters, favoured hanging. Chuter Ede was moderate, cautious, practical, not an innovator and liked to steer clear of controversy. In June 1946 he turned down an appeal for Radclyffe Hall's lesbian novel *The Well of Loneliness*, banned as obscene in 1928, to be republished. 'The 1928 proceedings provide a fixed point in regard to one aspect of sexual morality in a field where it is peculiarly difficult to establish any satisfactory standards,' he said.

As for the morality of killing, the abolition of capital punishment proposed in the 1938 Criminal Justice Bill would have to wait twenty-six years. Instead, a Royal Commission on Capital Punishment, which took five years to report and was 500 pages long and worldwide in scope, was presented to Parliament in September 1953. It suggested limiting the death penalty rather than abolishing it.

Countdown to Execution

The prerogative of mercy was in the Home Secretary's hands. Melford Stevenson petitioned Chuter Ede for Sidney Sinclair's sentence to be commuted, on medical grounds, to 'penal servitude for life'.

Dr Landers, Wandsworth's medical officer, knew an appeal for clemency would lead to another scrutiny of Sinclair's mental state. He kept a daily handwritten diary of his behaviour and state of mind, caged and sentenced as he now was. Landers went through the motions of a revision of evidence but he too seemed to regard the sentence as a fixed point. He told prison warders to keep constant watch on Sinclair and report oddities of behaviour to him. He went over all existing biographical detail: childhood, schooling, prison and army records, marriages and assaults. He paid special attention to Harold Hagger's leap to freedom from the Carlisle to Wigton train.

On 2 March 1947 he recorded that the prison guards reported Sidney was 'playing cards and quite cheerful' and had gone to bed at 10.30pm and slept soundly after a dose of the barbiturate Luminal. There was nothing unusual to note.

Two days later Wandsworth's prisoner governor, Major L.C. Ball, told head office that, subject to reprieve, 18 March was fixed as the date for Sidney Sinclair's execution. The Prison Commissioners sent him instructions about the etiquette for execution day: the deed was to take place at 9am; the prison clock chime should be disconnected for that hour; executioners should be lodged in the prison so as not to be seen entering it or crossing the yard; prisoners who usually worked near the execution shed should be distracted with additional exercise in a yard remote from it; the governor should ensure usual prison routine was followed at the time of execution and that prisoners were dispersed throughout the prison at their respective tasks: 'Their minds will be occupied and any noise caused by the trap doors should pass unnoticed.' Early-morning exercise should proceed as usual and if there were, in the judgement of the medical officer, young prisoners likely to be adversely affected by an execution they should be transferred.

Thus the compassion or concern of the keepers of the gallows. Execution, like butchery, was best conducted out of sight. Witnessing infliction of suffering was unacceptable. The practice of public hanging was thought medieval and barbaric. Concealment was the civilised approach. Death in general and execution in particular was an unsettling subject. If what was going on at 9am in the cold meat shed was too apparent, prisoners might cause trouble. They could live alongside a murderer like Sidney Sinclair, a muddled no-good man, but killers hired by the state, who referred to the manual — observing them at work might disturb the smooth running of the prison camp.

Thursday 6 March was a day of chaos on the roads and disruption on the railways with snowdrifts ten feet deep in Wales and the Midlands. There were riots in Lahore and martial law in Palestine, and on the Hainault estate in Essex an application to erect 302 prefabricated houses was approved. Sidney's Luminal was stopped because it made him groggy in the day, and the governor of Wandsworth sent Dr Landers, the medical officer, a note saying subject to appeal or reprieve the High Sheriff of Kent had fixed the date of 18 March for 'the execution of the above named condemned prisoner'.

On 8 March *The Times* reported 'there is no sign of winter's grip on Britain relaxing', milk deliveries were cut and coal pits blocked by snow and, in a letter to Daisy, Sidney wrote, 'I wish my head would keep alright, but I never complain to make myself a nuisance to people here.' Dr Landers interviewed him again after that letter. Sidney made a last-ditch attempt to appear M'Naghten mad: the headaches were in the front of his head, they were nearly always there since the train accident, but sometimes they got worse:

> My eyes fade suddenly and I can hardly see. It lasts for ten minutes. I can tell when it's coming because I start blinking. Twice I've been unconscious. I don't know what I do in an attack.

He showed Landers two scars on his forehead from when he fell on the pavement and cut his forehead in Bolton in 1928. 'They weren't anything to do with the train.' He retold his alarming accidents when he pinned a man against a garden wall with his lorry and knocked another off his bicycle. Landers asked if he wore glasses. Perhaps, like Thomas Pierrepoint, it was doubtful whether his sight was good. Sidney said he didn't and never had, though he couldn't read small print. He hadn't been to a doctor about his headaches, though sometimes when driving he went to a chemist to get a dose of medicine for them. Landers remarked that he appeared to sleep well. Sidney said that wasn't true. He'd drop off for a few hours, wake up, then drop off again.

Landers asked if there was any family history of insanity or epilepsy: there was not. Sidney was healthy as a boy, attended school until he was fourteen, married when he was twenty-six but had no children by that or his second marriage. He told of how he went to the London Hospital about his infertility in 1929 and they said because of his accident 'the seed was not strong enough'.

Landers asked him to go over the events of that October day. Sidney had no difficulty now in reiterating his version. Nothing would make him admit what really happened: his guilt, the woman's innocence, his lewdness, her celibacy. He would go to the gallows unable to tell the truth about himself, how unacceptable he was to himself let alone to anyone else. His delivery made this doctor too doubt the veracity of his account.

I was stopped by this woman and I gave her a lift. She asked me to pull into a fork along the road because she wanted to talk to me. I pulled in and switched off my headlights. She told me I couldn't interfere with her because she'd got her rags on, but that if I gave her some money she'd play about with me.

Next I saw was she'd got my wallet in her hand and was putting it down her breast. I hit her on the side of her face, the right side, and she started kicking and screaming. I grabbed at the scarf round her neck and it came away. I put it over her head to stop her screaming. I held the ends of the scarf in my two hands. I don't remember pulling it. I remember putting it round her neck to stop her screaming. The next I remember is holding it in my two hands and it was round her neck. I saw she was dead. I looked at the clock in the lorry cabin and reckoned I had been holding the scarf for twenty minutes. I'd picked her up at 5.20 am.

I know the time because I looked at the clock and thought it very early for a woman to be out. When I looked at the clock again it had just gone a quarter to six.

After it I forgot it then the wife read it in the paper next day. I said to her 'I was on that road that day.' I nearly told her, but I didn't. She said, 'You needn't bother to go tell the police.'

I went on driving for a week after it then I went to the doctor to get a certificate to say I was unfit to drive.

From the amendments in this version it seemed that strangulation might not have been the fifteen- to twenty-second process described by Keith Simpson if twenty minutes later the vest was still in Sidney's hands and still round the murdered woman's neck. Landers asked him if he was quick-tempered. Sidney told him about going up to Daisy with his hands stretched out and the gurgling noise in his throat, but he said he didn't hit people. The last time was a policeman a long time ago. He told him how in Pentonville he smashed up his cell and cut his own neck with a piece of glass. Dr Landers looked but could see no scar. Harold said the cut wasn't deep enough.

Landers asked if he tried to have sexual intercourse with Dagmar Petrzywalski. Sidney told him she talked about it and would have done it if he'd wanted to, though he hadn't suggested it and had no desire for it, but it was money she was after. Landers asked him how often he had sex with his wife. About once a month, Sidney replied. Had he ever had symptoms of gonorrhoea or syphilis? He said he had not.

'Nothing unusual to report,' Dr Landers wrote on 9 March in his daily bulletin about the condemned man. Sidney was eating and sleeping well and in two weeks had put on half a stone in weight.

Next day Sidney told the officer shaving him, for he was not allowed to shave himself, that he felt dizzy. The complaint was relayed to Dr Landers though the prison officer said Sinclair did not appear dizzy.

For the umpteenth time Sidney was weighed and measured: his pupils reacted to light, his knees jerked under a reflex hammer, he smoked his ration of cigarettes. He was taken to the Maudsley Hospital for another EEG. This again was said to show mild abnormality and again there was no explanation of what the abnormality signified. There was no evidence of epilepsy, no 'indication of traumatic dysfunction', no signs of organic disease or symptoms of depression. Dr Landers sent a note to the governor saying there had been no incidents of medical note concerning Sidney Sinclair since his arrival. His general health was good. A report on him and a summary of his case was sent to the under secretary of state.

Hope of Reprieve

On 12 March the trial of Rudolf Höss, architect and SS Kommandant of Auschwitz, opened in Warsaw, Britain's royal family toured South Africa in perfect sunshine, Britain's women were called on to return to work because of 'the shortage of man power' and the governor of Wandsworth prison was told that the secretary of state had decided to 'direct a medical enquiry under section 2 subsection 4 of the Criminal Lunatics Act of 1884 into the mental condition of Sidney Sinclair who is now lying under sentence of death in His Majesty's Prison at Wandsworth'.

Dr William Norwood East, a former senior medical officer at Brixton, and Dr J.S. Hopwood, medical superintendent of Broadmoor Criminal Lunatic Asylum, were asked to conduct this enquiry. Dr Norwood East was seventy-five and had strong views that society should be protected, and excessive claims not made by psychiatrists when dealing with criminal cases. Dr Hopwood was sixty-one, had trained as a pathologist and worked at Broadmoor for twenty-four years. He said, 'Only about half the patients in Broadmoor are dangerous, the problem is knowing which half.' He founded a patients' magazine and the Broadhumoorists, a dramatic club in which each autumn patients put on a three-act play, but essentially the hospital was custodial, patients' behaviour was unpredictable, there were few tranquillising drugs and the war years had been particularly stressful.

In the condemned suite of cells at Wandsworth prison all the attention that Harold Hagger never received as a child, and more, was now directed at him. He continued to eat his privileged food, put on weight, smoke his cigarettes and play cards with the guards. He appeared conspicuous for his equable temperament.

On 13 March floods followed the thaw of snow, the Thames burst its banks and in Basutoland King George VI and Queen Elizabeth sat in chairs on the grass for a fireworks display in their honour. 'Again and again the rising and falling lights lit up the Queen and were reflected from her tiara and every time this happened waves of cheering went rolling round the crowded acres,' *The Times* special correspondent reported. One firework, a 'falling star', landed on the hat of a member of the royal entourage. At Wandsworth prison the governor Mr Ball, the deputy governor Mr Truswell, the chaplain the Reverend Shaw, Dr Landers and eight other officers as well as doctors from Brixton and Maidstone were all interviewed by Dr Norwood East and Dr Hopwood, who were compiling their report for the Crown. The consensus was that Sidney Sinclair was 'a little below average intelligence but far from being feeble-minded', he was not psychopathic, had no extreme mood swings, had shown no signs of 'hysteria or other psychoneurosis', he did not seem mentally unstable, there was nothing to suggest he was epileptic and as for his alleged blackouts, nothing had been observed by doctors and prison officers except that he lay on his bed for a short time because he complained of a headache and feeling giddy. He did not lose consciousness or have a fit. He was not morose, irritable or restless. Sidney Sinclair was normal, quiet, respectful and well behaved.

Dr Taylor from Brixton prison repeated that he thought Sidney impulsive and easily provoked, his original wife said he used to strike her and he had been convicted on three occasions for assaulting police officers, but Taylor did not think his impulsiveness and temper an excuse for the crime. He had drunk no alcohol for three or four days before it, when interviewed he was calm and showed no evidence of stress, and his memory, attention, perception and reasoning were all sound. Only the Wandsworth prison chaplain thought there was something unusual about Sidney Sinclair but he could not say what it was.

On Friday 14 March the under secretary of state sent a letter from Whitehall to the Commissioner of Police at New Scotland Yard saying that following the medical enquiry as to Sidney Sinclair's mental condition he could find no sufficient ground to justify advising His Majesty to interfere with the due course of the law.

It was all up for Harold Hagger. There was no way out now. No counter-appeal, no chance of counter-intervention. To call him neurotic and unstable did not quite define him. It was more that there was something missing from his make-up: love perhaps, a moral base, empathy for his victims, concern for others, respect for himself. At no point in his life did he assume authority or control. Such paid work as he found meant the carrying out of orders. He only lived in a home provided for him: army barracks, a prison cell, a woman's cottage. He wanted to be liked and to be obliging in the pubs, to win at cards, to buy his round. He was careful with his clothes and thought he could charm the girls, but his sexuality, fuelled by compulsion, anger and anxiety, seemed to impart no joy, even when restrained from violence. He could not unaided change. His criminal character entrenched at an early age. There was predictability to his thieving and his lies but he did not, like his executioners, plan to kill, the ultimate crime. He had not thought to find a lone woman on that deserted road, on that dark and rainy morning. When it came to his own killing he faced it if not with courage then with a kind of resignation.

On 15 March there was a strike of 700 catering staff at the Savoy hotel, Ivor Novello's musical romance *Perchance to Dream* was in its third year at the Hippodrome and Sidney was told by Wandsworth's deputy governor of the rejection of his appeal and that he was to be hanged three days later on Tuesday 18 March. The coroner at Wandsworth requested the attendance of Chief Inspector Fabian at the inquest which would follow and was planned for 10.45am He said he would phone Fabian at 10.30 the morning before. After such arrangements were made most of those who had worked on the case had Sunday off.

The day before he was to die Sidney played cards from 11.15am to 1.20pm with the prison officer on duty, there was a national shortage of potatoes, the government announced its intention to produce 5,300 million bricks in the coming year, the Ballets Russes returned to London for the first time since 1939 and Daisy, who had broken down with the strain and humiliation of her pregnancy, the awfulness of Sidney's crime, worries about money and how she would manage, and the horror of waiting for the man she thought of as her husband to be hanged, was admitted to hospital in Cambridge.

Execution Day: Tuesday 18 March 1947

Albert Pierrepoint only had two commissions at Wandsworth prison in 1947: Sidney Sinclair and David Williams, who was twenty six and had murdered his wife. He had three at Pentonville, one at Strangeways, one at Bristol, one at Mountjoy and another seventy-two at Hamelin, but Wandsworth was his preferred gallows.

He and his assistant Harry Critchell arrived at the prison at 4pm on Monday 17 March. Pierrepoint thought Critchell efficient and liked working with him. He was glad not to have Harry Kirk, who was not, in his view, executioner material. They hung a bag of sand equivalent to Sidney Sinclair's weight on the gallows and left it hanging overnight to stretch the rope.

The execution ropes, made by John Edgington & Co Ltd, whose contract with the government lasted eighty years, had leather sewn into the noose end to strengthen them.

The prison governor visited Sidney that evening. It was the custom for the governor to convey respects to the condemned prisoner. Next morning the chaplain called on Sidney at eight and told him if he had faith, though worms would destroy his body, his eyes would see God who was the resurrection and the life. All concerned attended to the discipline of agenda, tradition, protocol, precise timing and the remit of their jobs. At 8.40 Fabian arrived and waited outside Sinclair's cell with Pierrepoint, Critchell, Dr Landers, two prison officers and the chaplain. On a signal from Fabian, Pierrepoint and Critchell went into the cell. Pierrepoint pinioned Sidney Sinclair's hands behind his back, then he was taken to the drop, flanked by two prison officers. Fabian, the governor, medical officer and chaplain went into the execution chamber by another door. The chaplain again exhorted the Lord not to punish Harold or Sidney for ever but to have mercy on him and receive his soul.

Pierrepoint positioned Sidney on the drop on a marked spot so that his feet were directly across the division of the trapdoor and put a white cap over his head and the noose around his neck while Critchell pinioned his legs. The chaplain gave a final exhortation to God to hear Sidney's prayers and pardon him his sins, then Pierrepoint pulled the lever.

Dr Landers went to the pit 'to see that life is extinct'. A prison officer then locked the pit and Sidney was left to hang for an hour. Sir Bernard Spilsbury, Keith Simpson's rival, did the post-mortem and reported dislocation and wide separation between the fourth and fifth cervical vertebrae, the spinal cord torn across at the upper end and haemorrhage round the base of the brain. Sidney Sinclair's neck was broken as was Dagmar Petrzy-walski's. The inquest at 11am, held by Mr Harvey Wyatt, was attended by Fabian, who had identified the body, and the prison doctor. The verdict was returned that Sidney Sinclair whose real name was Harold Hagger met his death at Wandsworth prison on 18 March 1947 and 'death was due to injuries to the brain and spinal cord consequent upon judicial hanging.'

It was all over by lunchtime. While prisoners were eating, Sinclair was buried in an unmarked spot in the communal graveyard and the chaplain further exhorted the Lord to play His part. It was hard to find room for Sidney in the prison grounds. Bodies were already buried three deep. He had no grave or marker, no tile on the prison with details of his name or names, dates of birth and death. His death certificate was issued by the General Register Office Wandsworth. Copies of the report of the execution were sent to all involved. The governor returned unused forms to the Prison Commissioners.

Daisy, on the day of the hanging, was moved to a private room in the Cambridge hospital because she could not stop crying. Ellen visited her and found it heartbreaking that she cared so for this man, no matter what he had done.

8

AND AFTER

Next day the governor of Wandsworth completed the relevant forms and sent them to head office to be filed away:

Record of an execution
Particulars of the condemned prisoner:
Name Sidney Sinclair
Register Number 10170
Sex Male
Age 45 years
Height 5'6¾"
Build Proportionate
Weight in clothing 175 lbs
Character of the prisoner's neck Normal
The length of the drop 6 feet 5 inches
The length of the drop as measured after the execution from the level of the floor of the scaffold to the heels of the suspended culprit 6 feet 6½ inches
Cause of death Dislocation and wide separation between 4th and 5th vertebrae
Amount of destruction to the soft and bony structures of the neck None

Name and address in full of the Executioner Mr Albert
  Pierrepoint, 303 Manchester Road, Hollinwood, near
  Manchester

Name and address of the 1st Assistant Executioner Mr Harry
  B. Critchell, 18 Moriton Place, Pimlico, London SW1

*Did they, in the opinion of the governor and medical officer, perform
  their duty satisfactorily?* Yes

Was their general demeanour satisfactory? Yes

Were they respectable? Yes

*Did they show physical and mental capacity and suitability for the
  post?* Yes

*Was there any ground for supposing they would bring discredit on
  their office by lecturing or granting interviews in regard to the
  execution?* No

*Were they likely to create public scandal before or after the
  execution?* No

All rules had been obeyed, all had gone well.

Harold Hagger's legitimate wife Sophia wrote that day to
Fabian:

> Could you advise me please Sir, I would very much like
> to get married again in the near future to a good man,
> as I am now the widow of Harold Hagger otherwise
> known as Sidney Sinclair. I would very much like the
> nesesary documents to prove that I can remarry again
> Thank you very much indeed for everything.
>
> Your obedient servant
> Sophia Hagger

Fabian told her she would need a copy of Harold's death certificate and could get this from the registrar of births and deaths at Wandsworth. Two years later on 5 February 1949 she married her 'good man', Francesco Ferrigni. He was fifty-nine, sixteen years older than Sophia. Her son Ronald, who kept the name Hagger, was a witness at their wedding. Ronald worked as a lorry driver and the following year when he was twenty-four married Rose Allen, a bookkeeper, at St Stephen's Church, Islington. He cited his deceased father as Harold Hagger, a labourer. Rose's father Albert, a street trader, gave her away. In time the couple had three daughters.

The day after Sidney Sinclair was hanged newspapers made only passing reference to his execution. 'Killer of Miss Peters had two names', the *Mirror* reported. Fabian told journalists Harold Hagger was well known to the police and had many convictions. But the news was of other things: the people of Shetland had presented a length of handwoven tweed and articles of hosiery to Princess Elizabeth on her twenty-first birthday, Oxford and Cambridge were practising for the boat race, Miss Florence Andrews of Maidenhead had celebrated her hundredth birthday, Benjamin Britten's opera *Peter Grimes*, banned by the Nazis, was given its first performance in Hamburg, the government welcomed President Truman's proposals for economic aid to Greece, and the cost of a 1.5 litre Jaguar saloon had gone up to £864 including purchase tax. Power cuts and increased costs of materials were given as the reasons for the rise in the car's price.

For Daisy there was much to sort out. Two women from the village helped when she miscarried at home. No doctor was involved. Abortion was illegal. It was a criminal offence to abort a foetus of whatever age unless the mother's life was at risk. The 1861 Offences Against the Person Act made abortion punishable by imprisonment from three years to life. In most villages and towns there were women who intervened for compassionate reasons, often dangerously. The law was not changed until 1967.

Daisy then had to revert to her former name. Sinclair was an invention of Harold Hagger and according to the law she was still Mrs Linsdell. She was entitled to a meagre widow's pension for she had a dependent child. There were many bureaucratic obstacles: hers was a singular case. Announcements had to be placed in local and national papers saying the marriage to Sidney Sinclair was bigamous. Fortunately, rental of the Little Abington cottage was in her name and she was liked in the village. There was much talk of Sidney's wrongdoing and ignominious death, but it became one more of the stories of village life of which there were many. Daisy stayed on in her thatched cottage for some decades, then moved into a newly built council bungalow with the luxuries of piped water and a gas fire.

Dagmar had died intestate. The net value of her estate was £420 15s 3d. The money went to her mother, who sold her bungalow Houston and Dagmar's hut The Vic within a year. The buyer was a chicken farmer who knocked both buildings down and put up hen coops. Mame Petrzywalski went to live with her son Ralph in Woking. Ten years later, in January 1956 when she was ninety, she too died intestate. The small amount of money she left, £204 6s 9d, was divided between Ralph and her grandson Jules.

Jules left the army and started up a typewriter repair shop in

Ruislip. In 1950 he fell off the roof of his house while replacing some slates and fractured his leg in several places. In hospital he was nursed with particular care by Anne Fennell, the ward sister. When his first wife Phyllis heard Jules and Anne were going to marry, she wanted him back. Jules had two daughters by this second marriage. A cold and unforthcoming father, he changed his name by deed poll to Peters, forbade his children to use the name Petrzywalski and told them little of the dramas of his and their family's past.

Annie Hagger was spared the pain of hearing that one of her sons was a murderer and had been hanged. Barry Simpson, son of Harold's sister Ethel known as Nance, was told the news in Holloway by a dwarf on a bicycle. 'Your uncle's been topped,' the man said to him. 'It's in the papers.' Barry passed the information to his aunts and uncles who were adamant their mother must not find out. Harold had been tried and convicted under the name of Sidney Sinclair, Annie Hagger could not read and anyway had closed her ears so that such ignominious news could never reach her.

Fabian was well pleased with the outcome of the case. Harold Hagger or Sidney Sinclair would not offend again. Justice had been seen to be done. A woman murdered, the murderer hanged. A life for a life. The law enforcers working on the case were relieved that 'enquiries into the prisoner's mental state failed to reveal any reason to interfere with the course of law'. Basher Hagger was a bad man, of that there was no doubt: immoral, impulsive, undisciplined. Unrestrained he would have offended again with theft, abuse, violence or even murder. He was, as Robert Fabian at their first meeting saw, an old lag. His family disowned him and felt he tarnished their name. His bigamous wife spoke up for him in so far as she had a voice: said, in the hope his life might be spared, that he was a good husband. Society viewed him as the lowest of the low, rejected him and broke his neck at an appointed time according to its construct of culpability, punishment, justice. Notification of the hanging was sent to the officer in charge of army records in Edinburgh, so he could update his bedraggled records on 'Private 28467 Harold Hagger, otherwise Sidney Sinclair'.

The Commissioner of Police personally commended Fabian for his first-class work. Fabian for his part praised 'the whole-hearted and untiring efforts of every officer of the Kent County Constabulary engaged on this enquiry'. He made special mention of Detective Inspector Jenner and recommended Detective Sergeant Rawlings for 'commendation or reward': 'his ability contributed in no small measure to the successful conclusion of the case'.

Fabian became a celebrity when his memoir *Fabian of the Yard* was turned into a television series. The BBC transmitted thirty-six episodes between 1954 and 1956. Fabian was played by Bruce Seton, who had starred in *The Cruel Sea* and *Seven Days to Noon*. Each episode ended with Seton sitting at his desk and dissolving into the real-life Fabian who told viewers what had happened to the real criminal in the real case they had been watching. Tragedy, crime, violence, the law, fiction and entertainment merged.

Keith Simpson, the Home Office pathologist, also turned grief and horror into entertainment, not least because of his bright and larky prose style. His *Forty Years of Murder*, published in 1978, became a bestseller and was reprinted eighteen times.

In 1945 King George VI had said it was time to 'make the

world such a world as you desire for your children'. The abolition of capital punishment was not a post-war manifesto pledge from a Labour government concerned with social justice. It was treated as a point of view, as personal as the belief that war was a misguided way to resolve conflict or prison no way to reform offenders. The House of Lords, the Establishment, the Public, kept to the biblical axioms of deterrence and due proportion between crime and punishment. The gallows were not dismantled until 1964.

Albert Pierrepoint went on hanging people until 1955: sixty-four more in 1947, fifty-six of them at Hamelin; sixty-two in 1948, fifty-five at Hamelin, the others at Cardiff, Perth and Pentonville; twenty-four in 1949, eleven of them at Hamelin; nineteen in 1950, fifteen in 1951, twenty-three in 1952, thirteen in 1953, thirteen in 1954 and six in 1955 including Ruth Ellis for shooting her lover. But peacetime hanging was not particularly profitable for him. He was freelance and six jobs at £15 a go did not compare with his wartime commissions.

He gave notice in January 1956. He had travelled to Manchester on 2 January to prepare to execute Thomas Bancroft, who had hit a child and the child had died. It would have been Pierrepoint's 436th execution, but after he had done his sack calculations and late that day, Bancroft was reprieved. Snow prevented Pierrepoint from returning home. At his own expense he had hired bar staff to cover for him at his pub. He was paid only travelling expenses to the prison and not the execution fee. He complained to the prison commissioners that he had given his time and was out of pocket. They said payment was at the discretion of the Sheriff of Lancashire and he should address his complaint to him. In February the Sheriff sent him an additional £4 but not the full fee of £15. Pierrepoint resigned. 'I regard this kind of meaness as surprising in view of my experience and long service,' he wrote in his resignation letter. 'I request the removal of my name from the list of executioners forthwith.'

Celebrity memoir proved a profitable secondary career for him as for Fabian. He sold his story to the *Sunday Chronicle*. The prison commissioners reminded him about his obligation under the Official Secrets Acts of 1911 and 1920. Pierrepoint replied:

> Substantially I shall not go beyond what has already been published including the evidence given before the Royal Commission on Capital Punishment . . . Naturally I have had experiences which would cause considerable controversy but these are locked in my heart and I am never going to divulge them.
>
> I am afraid that I must keep my decision to ask for my name to be removed from the list of executioners although I am aware that the other persons on the list may not be capable of carrying out an execution to the satisfaction of all concerned.

Threats of litigation against him petered out. In a ghost-written autobiography, published a decade after capital punishment was abolished and eighteen years after his own retirement, he voiced opposition to hanging: 'executions solve nothing and are only an antiquated relic of a primitive desire for revenge which takes the easy way and hands over the responsibility for revenge to other people,' he wrote. None the less, he said, for he had hanged 435 people, he still believed he 'was sent on earth to do this work and that the same power told me when I should leave it.' He dedicated the book 'with grateful thanks for her loyalty and discretion, to Anne, my wife, who in forty years never asked a question'. He continued to work as a publican and lived with her in Ivanhoe, a bungalow outside Southport. He liked gardening. As old age encroached he developed dementia. His leg irons, ropes, a mask of his face, his manacles and diaries were sold at Christie's auction rooms in St James's Piccadilly for £19,800 two months before he died of Alzheimer's disease in 1992 at the Melvin Nursing Home in Southport.

ACKNOWLEDGEMENTS

I was a child of the forties, born in the Crown and Anchor Edmonton at the beginning of the Blitz on London – on the billiard table, or so my mother told me. Her sister Sadie was married to the publican. My father nicknamed me Doodlebug, which got shortened to Doodie. The pub was two or three miles from where the villain of this story grew up in the early 1900s.

I have inchoate memories of ration books, blacked-out windows, air-raid sirens, bombs, Spam and dried bananas. I thought the point of the war was to get into the shelter ahead of the shadowy people hurrying towards us in the night, whom I supposed to be The Germans. I benefited from postwar socialism. My school fees and fares, textbooks, public library card, spectacles, the braces on my teeth, concentrated orange juice and cod liver oil were paid for by the welfare state. The Labour landslide victory of May 1945 brought in a government that valued the needs and contribution of people above unbridled self-interest and vast profits to the bosses. Three books that give background perspective to the period and to events at Wrotham Hill are Juliet Gardiner, *Wartime Britain 1939–45*, Peter Hennessy *Never Again, Britain 1945–51* and David Kynaston's *Austerity Britain 1945–51*.

I chose murder as the motor of my narrative. I researched

who was hanged in Britain soon after the war then dithered between Harold Hagger and Margaret Allen, who dressed as a man, worked as a bus conductor and in 1948 for no clear reason hammered her elderly neighbour Nancy Ellen Chadwick to death.

I settled for Harold. Home Office papers about his criminal career, the police investigation of the murder, his arrest, trial, medical records and execution were my main research source. There are three large files of some 300 pages of these papers: documents, correspondence, photographs and reports, in no particular order, in the National Archives at Kew. They are referenced as MEPO 3/2743, MEPO 6 and PCOM 9/740.

I am indebted to Martin Hagger for help with my searches and researches. Harold Hagger was his grandfather's cousin. Martin, a keen genealogist, has compiled an extensive website of the Hagger family tree: http://homepage.ntlworld.com/ martin.hagger1. He provided me with, or pointed me toward, numerous transcripts of General Record Office birth, marriage and death certificates; census returns; wills from http://hmcourts-service.gov.uk/cms/1226.htm; naturalisation certificates from the Probate Registry in High Holborn and maps from old-maps.co.uk. He drove me to the graveyard at West Kingsdown where Dagmar Petrzywalski and her father are buried and to the Kent Record Office where I found accounts of the murder in back copies of the *Kent Observer*.

On 19 June 2010 at the annual Therfield village fête he introduced me, in the Fox and Duck, to other Haggers. They were and are a close-knit clan, loyal to their Therfield roots. Harold was thrown out by his parents with all mention of him forbidden. They said he tainted the family name. His more distant relatives take a philosophical view. Barry Simpson, his nephew, brought up by Harold's mother Annie – Barry's grand-mother – gave me his memories of their life in north London. Doreen Oakman, who is related to both of Harold's parents, for Haggers and Bullards often intermarried, and Audrey Green who has Hagger ancestors, gave me a picture of Therfield village life before and during the war.

On the Petrzywalski side, my thanks to Shirley Mallon. Dagmar was her great-aunt and Dagmar's nephew Jules, her father. Shirley too has researched her family's history. She gave me background information about the Petrzywalskis including copies of her father's prisoner-of-war papers obtained from the International Red Cross.

In August 2010, on a day trip we called ghoulish tours, Shirley, Martin and I recreated the journey Harold Hagger made on that October day in 1946 when he murdered Dagmar Petrzywalski. Martin feared he bore some sort of collective family responsi-bility for Harold's foul deed and wrongly half-expected Shirley to feel animosity towards him.

My special thanks to Terry Lane. Her grandmother Daisy was unaware that Sidney Sinclair, the soldier she thought she married in 1940, was Harold Hagger, a criminal with a string of convictions who already had a wife. Terry gave me some account of the chaos and pain Harold Hagger brought to the lives of her grandmother, mother and aunt.

I am grateful to Hilda Thorn, who still lives in Hever Avenue in West Kingsdown. Her family, the Taylors, were neighbours of the Petrzywalskis. Hilda shared memories of helping her father build their bungalow as a child, the development of the Hever Estate, wartime conditions in Kingsdown and the shock to local people of Dagmar Petrzywalski's murder. My thanks to Zena Bamping, who researched and wrote *West Kingsdown*, a history of the village, for putting me in touch with Hilda.

Thanks too to Nolita Challis, daughter of John Dickerson of the family firm of haulage contractors who employed Sidney Sinclair as a driver. Nollie has archived the firm's papers back to the 1930s. She helped me with a history of the company and even traced a photograph of the lorry in which Dagmar Petrzy-walski met her death.

Other useful local sources were *Kelly's Directory of Kent*; an East Malling blog http://www.eastmallingmemories.co.uk/4436.html; Michael J. Fuller, *The Watermills of the East Malling and Water-ingbury Streams*; Roy Ingleton, *Policing Kent 1800–2000*; the Kent Police Museum at Chatham; Clive Thomas's booklet 'Law and Disorder in Wrotham over the Centuries' published by the Wrotham Historical Society; and 'Murder Most Foul', no. 45 from the True Crime Library. I used Colindale Newspaper Library for press coverage of many events and *The Times* Room at the London Library for period detail.

The web has become an essential research source. All the Law Reports of the trials of war criminals at the British Military Court in Lüneburg from 17 September to 17 November 1945 are online. And even idle googling yields unexpected information. Typing Norman Hay-Bolton, the name of the doctor who certified Dagmar dead, revealed an article, 'The Japanese Community in Pre-War Britain' by Keiko Itoh, that gave intriguing facts about Dr Hay-Bolton's past. And Martin's search for Dr O'Kelly, Dagmar's London landlord, found 'Co. Kildare Online Electronic History Journal' which lists Irish people killed by WW2 bombing, including 'Dr

Edward J. O'Kelly, Maynooth, killed in an air-raid at his residence, 30 Oakley Square, London, in April 1941'. How else would I have known Dagmar's precise address when she was made homeless in the Blitz?

As it developed, this book became a sort of fugue about killing, with many of its characters involved in the industry of death. For Robert Fabian, the detective who headed the murder investigation, I referred to his autobiography *Fabian of the Yard* and *London After Dark*. For Keith Simpson, the eminent pathologist who gave vital information to Fabian derived from Dagmar's autopsy, I drew from his autobiography *Forty Years of Murder*, his textbook *Forensic Medicine* published in 1947 and the memoir of his private secretary Molly Lefebure, *Evidence for the Crown*. For Albert Pierrepoint, Britain's chief hangman, I used his autobiography *Executioner Pierrepoint*; Leonora Klein, *A Very English Hangman*; Steve Fielding, *Pierrepoint: A Family of Executioners*; the Report by the Royal Commission on Capital Punishment compiled between 1949–53; and *Execution Suite: a history of the gallows at Wandsworth Prison 1878–1993*.

My thanks and gratitude for their encouragement to: Georgina Capel my agent and Jon Riley editor-in-chief at Quercus. Thanks too to Serena Dilnot who copy-edited the manuscript and to Philippa Brewster who commented on an early draft and to David Smith who found a few howlers on the proofs. Josh Ireland, my editor at Quercus, made many an improving point, steered the book through production, dealt with my endless queries and researched several photographs. Leo Nickolls designed the jacket. Bill Donohoe drew the maps. This is the fourth book of mine indexed by Douglas Matthews. I always hope he will agree to do the index. By coincidence during his

National Service he was stationed at Wrotham Hill during the early part of 1946.

Photo credits: the photo of the Dickerson lorries, plate section page 4 top, was supplied by kind permission of Mrs Betty Dickerson. My thanks, too, to Shirley Mallon for the Petrzywalski family group, plate section page 5; to Barry Simpson and his daughter Michelle Roberts for the snapshot of Annie Hagger, plate section page 6, and on the same page, to Terry Lane for the photo of her grandmother, Daisy. Copyright on other photos is as follows: Ian Tyas/Getty Images p247; Mirrorpix p217 and plate section p1, p7 top right and bottom and p8; Press Association p1 and p179 and plate section p3 top, p4 bottom and p7 top left; Public Record Office pgs 49, 87 and 111 and plate section p2 top and bottom.

And as a last word, and without a shred of evidence, I believe Hedy was found by a friendly thatcher, walking Webster his spaniel down Forge Lane in the early morning, two weeks after the murder. Though Hedy never entirely overcame her reservations about human beings, she bonded quickly with Webster and learned to respond to her new name, Bella. She lived relatively happily ever after.

INDEX